WOMEN CRIMINALS
AND
THEIR LIFE-STYLE

WOMEN CRIMINALS
AND
THEIR LIFE-STYLE

Mridula Maniyar

Kaveri Books
New Delhi - 110 002

Women Criminals and Their Life-Style

by **Mridula Maniyar**

First Published in 2004
Edition 2026

ISBN-10: 81-7479-063-2
ISBN-13: 978-81-7479-063-7

Published by
Kaveri Books
4832/24, Ansari Road
New Delhi-110002 (India)
Tel: 011-4707 2321
E-mail : info@kaveribooks.com
kaveribooks@gmail.com
Website: www.kaveribooks.com

PRINTED IN INDIA

Dedicated

To

My Beloved Late Parents

PREFACE

Women who form one – half of our population have always played a specific and crucial role in history and society. Today, modernization and social change have influenced all spheres of life. Criminal tendency among women has increased considerably due to change in the social structure and organization of the family. The changing social norms and values as well as the impact of other cultural patterns culminating in the complexity of life are largely responsible for this change. Due to the liberation movements, more women are now entering into the arena of employment and competition and have become more prone to criminality.

Thus, there is a great need to study women criminals because the place and role of women in the Indian setting has undergone changes during the last two decades, leading to a greater participation in the criminal activities by women. Since the research on women criminals is still meagre and rudimentary, because of its fragmentary nature, scope and coverage, the present study identifies, examines and explains women's criminality in the socio-cultural, economic and psychological context. Thus, an effort has been made to understand the life style of women criminals.

I wish to express my deep sense of gratitude to Dr. Aruna Khasgiwala, my guide, for encouraging me to initiate the present research work and subsequently for giving able guidance and valuable suggestions leading to the final form of the study.

I am extremely thankful to Dr. M. D. Vyas, Professor, Faculty of Social Work, for giving necessary encouragement from time to time for completing the research work and for giving valuable suggestions at various stages.

I also wish to express my feelings of gratitude to the librarians of Tata Institute of Social Sciences, Delhi School of Social Work, Smt. Hansa Mehta Library, Faculty of Social Work Library and Documentation Centre of Delhi for extending their help.

I owe much to the Inspector General of Prisons, Government of Gujarat for providing me the facilities for data collection in connection with this research work.

I am much obliged to the Superintendents of the Jails, Jailors and other staff members for their help and co-operation rendered during my data collection. I also would like to extend my thanks to the I.G. of Police, Head Quarters, Government of Gujarat for providing me with the State level data required for my research.

I wish to express my deep sense of gratitude to all the respondents from both the Central Jails of Baroda and Ahmedabad.

I am extremely thankful to my family members for their inspiration and support throughout the time I worked on my study.

Last but not least, my sincere thanks are also to Mr. G. R. Narula and Ghanshyam for the decent typing of the entire research work.

Mridula Maniyar

CONTENTS

LIST OF TABLES

Table No.	Title

List of Figures

List of Graphs

1

INTRODUCTION

"Women on the whole have better, softer
qualities than men. And on the whole, they
don't go as devilish as men. But when a
woman becomes devilish she beats all records.
No man can equal her."

Morarji Desai (1977)

The concept of crime is elusive, complex and multi-dimensional. Although the transgression of values and violation of norms may be done by anyone irrespective of the sex or age differences, yet it appears that the world of crime is a man's world. Crime is increasing at a rapid rate and most of the researchers on crime have confined themselves to males, because crime has been considered a male-behaviour. In India statistical reports on crime have always revealed men involved in greater offences than women, who are considered to be more religious-minded than their male counter parts and less prone to unethical and immoral activities.

Women who form one half of our population have always played a specific and crucial role in history and society. Women enjoyed considerable freedom and privileges in the spheres of family, religion and public life in the vedic age. However, gradually over a period of years, the entire social structure has undergone a revolution of morals and ideals. Rapid urbanization and industrialization, new socio-economic stresses and strains, break-up of the age-old institution of joint family, late marriages, free mixing of men and women, growth of films on crime and sex and widespread circulation of pornographic literature had profound effects on women generally. When all these factors coincide, the strains prove too great for some women especially those with inherently unbalanced personalities to divert them from a law abiding life to one of crime. The changing social norms and values as well as the impact of other cultural patterns culminating in the complexity of life are largely responsible for this change.

In a different background of the problem, Caldwell (1956) observed that homes that contribute to crime and delinquency may be classified into six major types :

a) The broken home.
b) The functionally inadequate home.
c) The home with a physically or psychologically abnormal parent.
d) The socially, morally or culturally abnormal home.
e) The criminal home.
f) The economically insecure home.

Elliot and Merrill (1961) found as an usual phenomenon that, most delinquent girls and women brought to the courts come from under privileged and rather sordid home backgrounds. Most criminal girls and women are driven by frustration and conflicting desires and by their low standard under which they have been reared.

Another very important and influential institutional aspect of human behaviour is the role of economic phenomena on individuals. Women are now entering into the arena of employment, and competition have also become more prone to criminality. Women were primarily apprehended for offences such as shoplifting, domestic theft, violation of excise and prohibition laws, prostitution and infanticide, but women are now occupying positions of high status and are taking part in "white collar crimes" like cheating, criminal breach of trust, smuggling, etc. Women have appeared as aiders or abettors of crime in many cases, directly or indirectly. Women are also involved in kidnapping, abduction and trafficking in women and girls. *Women like men suffer from jealousy*, enmity, hatred, etc., which lead them to criminality. Today women are involved in all sorts of crimes with the aid of the latest techniques. Most criminologists admit that lower class women are more subjected to police action than members of the middle or upper class. The Police are likely to suspect a lower class female than an upper class woman and also the lower class person has less chances to avoid the courts and legal steps than does the upper class person. According to Reckless (1967), the crime rate among lower class persons is higher because they are exposed to more demoralising and disorganizing conditions of living and also they are exposed to unemployment, over crowding, bad housing, death, accidents, disease, illiteracy and other cultural handicaps.

The multiple causes for female criminality include :

- Economic causes - financial difficulties, destitution.
- The domestic causes for committing crimes are ill treatment by the family members, neglect by the members of the family and an unfaithful husband.
- Social causes are bad influence, husband instigation and psychological reasons or desire to satisfy certain psychological urges.

  The social factors seem to be more important in female criminality. Thus, it can be seen that economic, social and psychological factors are responsible for making women criminals.

SECTION – I

Nature of Female Crime

Of the total crimes committed in India, about 5 per cent are committed by females. While between 1971 and 1980, the average of female crime was 29,300, between 1981 and 1990, it was 64,680. In 1993, of 16.29 lakh crimes under the Indian Penal Code committed in the country, 95,533 crimes (i.e 3.8 %) were committed by females, while of 38.03 lakh crimes committed under the Local and Special Laws, 2.16 lakh (i.e 5.7 %) were committed by females. In 1997, out of 25,75,827 total cognizable crimes committed in the country under IPC, 1,31,683 crimes (5.1%) were committed by females, while 48,01,700 crimes committed under the Local and Special Laws, 1,85,462 (3.9%) were committed by females (Crime in India, 1993 and 1997).

Table 1.1

Women Arrested under IPC Crimes During 1997 – Crimes Headwise

Sl. No.	Crime Head	Female	Percentage to Total
1.	Murder	3,473	4.4
2.	Attempt to Commit Murder	1,954	2.7
3.	Not Amounting to Murder	237	2.9
4.	Rape	317	1.6
5.	Kidnapping & Abduction	1,500	5.4
	(i) of Women & Girls	1,273	7.1
	(ii) of others	227	2.3
6.	Dacoity	102	0.4
7.	Preparation & Assembly for dacoity	6	0.1
8.	Robbery	132	0.5
9.	Burglary	1,141	1.7
10.	Theft	4,193	2.5
11.	Riots	24,696	5.4
12.	Criminal Breach of Trust	321	2.3
13.	Cheating	958	3.3
14.	Counterfeiting	17	1.8
15.	Arson	235	1.5
16.	Hurt	23,541	5.5
17.	Dowry deaths	3,690	23.9
18.	Molestation	327	0.9
19.	Sexual Harassment	53	0.8
20.	Cruelty by Husband or Relatives	17,429	21.4
21.	Other IPC Crimes	47,361	4.8
	Total Cognizable Crimes under IPC	1,31,683	5.1

Source : Crime in India - 1997

It can be seen that there has been an increase in female criminality from 1971 onwards. From 1.7 per cent in 1971, female crimes under the Indian Penal Code increased to 1.9 per cent in 1978, 3.1 per cent in 1990, 3.5 per cent in 1992, 3.8 per cent in 1993 and 5.1 per cent in 1997. But this increase is not so high when compared to the increase in male criminality. While the incidence of crime under the Indian Penal Code among males increased by 56 per cent during the period from 1968 to 1978 and by 61.4 per cent during the period from 1983 to 1993, the IPC crime among females increased by 48.5 per cent from 1983 to 1993. Further, the Prison Statistics published by the National Crime Records Bureau shows that female crime is increasing fast in the recent trend.

There are more female crimes in America, England, France, Canada, Japan, Thailand, etc., in comparison to India. For example, against 8 female crimes per one lakh of population, there are 1,154 crimes in America, 561 in West Germany, 316 in Thailand, 138 in France and 133 in Japan. Sociologically, however, female crime in India may be considered a crucial problem because of its impact on the upbringing of children and the overall fabric of society (Ahuja, 1996).

According to Hoffman – Bustamente (1973), the difference in the rate of male and female crime is basically the result of the difference in their respective roles. The basic role of wage-earning by men is performed outside the home for which they have to compete with others. In the process of competition, sometimes when they are not able to achieve their goal through legitimate means, they use illegitimate means. On the other hand, the basic role of a householder is performed by women within the four walls of the home for which they have not to compete with anybody and are not forced to use anti-social means for achieving their goal. Moreover, compared to men, women are more God-fearing, moral and tolerant. They are also subject to greater social restrictions. The police and the courts also take a more sympathetic attitude towards female offenders. In short, the important factors of difference in the rate of male and female crime may be described as under :

- Differential sex role expectations.
- Sex differences in socialization patterns and application of social control.
- Differential opportunities to engage in crime.
- Differential access to criminal subcultures and careers.
- Sex differences built into crime categories.

Types of Offences

Crimes are generally categorized as traditional and modern. The traditional crimes committed by women can be of two types-either petty or heinous. Homicide, infanticide, attempted suicide and murder fall among the heinous crimes and theft, shoplifting, cheating, hurt, quarrels, public nuisance, etc., are among the petty offences. The modern crimes are more often the organized type like the white-collar crimes, political crimes, communal and conventional types.

Murder has become more frequent among women criminals than among their counterparts. It is reported that women commit homicides and suicides in moments of emotions and jealousy, and the weapon they generally use is poison. Infanticides are mostly committed by unmarried mothers, poverty-stricken or mentally weak women by suffocation or strangulation.

Prostitution is considered as an offence. Women Prostitutes are habitual criminals and they commit other crimes like black-mailing, pick-pocketing, etc., with the usual sex offence. In the past economic insecurity was the problem of the women entering the trade. Today women enter this profession in order to fulfil their desire for a luxurious living.

In the past individual offences were common compared to the organized crimes of the present day. Various types of business crimes, dacoity, robbery, burglary, etc., are organized crimes in which our country is witnessing the active involvement of women.

In contrast to the conventional offenders who commit crimes for monetary gains or due to jealousy, political offenders commit crimes for their direct or indirect political ends by engaging in activities like protest, marches, mass picketing, etc. Political offenders are caught for disorderly conduct, breach of the peace, trespassing or loitering. In this era women's involvement in this category of offences cannot be ignored. Terrorism, naxalism, etc., are conventional crimes among political offences and women also take participation in these types of offences. Women are occasionally found active in communal riots, arson, etc.

The prevalence of white collar criminals among the professionally qualified women can be found now-a-days. Women's involvement in the white collar crime is found in the medical field, medicine and drug field, in the legal profession, in misleading advertisements, etc. Many business crimes are committed recently by the highly educated women in the upper socio-economic classes.

Social Work Profession

Social work is an emerging, fast developing profession. Its focus is on the interactions between individuals and systems in the social situation (Yelaja 1979).

Individuals are dependent on systems for help in obtaining material or emotional resources and services and opportunities they require to actualize their aspirations and to help them cope with their life tasks. The principles of social work are applicable in correctional settings. Different methods of social work, like casework and groupwork, are applicable to correctional institutions, probation and parole. The social work principles, based upon an understanding of the dynamics of the helping process, hold great promise for useful service in correctional settings.

Correctional Social Work

According to Studt (1959), "Correction is a social process by which modern society deals with officially identified lawbreakers". Thus correction is a part of social control. The correctional agency tries to rehabilitate or neutralize the delinquent or criminal behaviour of adolescents and adults through corrections.

With the increasing knowledge (which has become available in the 20th century) about the dynamics of human behaviour and how it is modified, it has become possible to give attention to the rehabilitation of the offender. Hence, correction as a social work process has been understood as the administration of penalty in such a way that the offender is "corrected". It means the criminal's present behaviour is controlled and his general life adjustment modified (Sikka, 1980). So the correctional task requires both control over the behaviour of the delinquent or criminal during the period of his penalty and services designed to help him achieve a socially acceptable mode of participation in the community.

According Younghusband (1978), the goal of social work in correction is the reformation and rehabilitation of the offender. The Social worker helps the offender to change his offending behaviour, so that he can relate constructively to others and become socially acceptable. This is done through working with the individual to help him to change through the better understanding of himself and by tapping his own strengths and resources and through the modification of his environment to bring about a more healthy social climate in which he has to live. The worker encourages the offender to talk about his problems, to feel about them and to come to an insightful understanding of himself, accompanied by his socially constructive behaviour.

According to Boehm (1959) the tasks of the social worker in corrections include four particular aspects :

(1) Investigation and surveillance for the purpose of securing information about the client's failure or success in meeting the obligations of his legal status.

(2) The use of controls to modify client behaviour.

(3) Acting as a legal authority in the client's life with responsibility for value change.

(4) Correctional decision making.

The social workers' most important task in correction is to change the values and behaviour of the offenders so that they become similar in action with the values of the particular community. Therefore, the social worker's aim is to help the offender, and not to punish him. The goal is to utilize the knowledge and skills of the profession in a corrective manner, to rehabilitate the offender, to help him to help himself, so that he can return to, and become a part of, his society and to lead a constructive life. Keeping in mind the importance of social work intervention in correctional settings, the present researcher made an attempt to study the life style of the women criminals in Gujarat.

Devasia et al. (1989) explained that the understanding of the etiology of crime is as old as the economical, biological and psychological approaches. Macro and micro level studies have repeatedly attributed to social, cultural, economic and psychological variables in etiology of female criminality. A female criminal can be better understood in the context of her social roles as determined by her biological differences, her personality make-up and her professional position, all of which are inter-related.

In India, only a few studies worth or name have been conducted on prison life of women criminals in relation to their socio-cultural background and prison life, how far the socio-cultural background influences a person to commit crime and the impact it has on prison life. Although the nature and pattern of pressures operating on these women in connection with their offences have been studied further probe may throw light on the various social pressures forcing women into criminality. It has been found by most of the studies (like Ahuja, 1969, 1970; Sanyal, 1974; Rani, 1983) that a large number of crimes committed by these women are found to be due to their maladjustments in the families. It also needs to be analyzed as to how the adjustment process gets affected to cause criminality. The analysis of the relationship pattern between different members of the family also becomes important to study.

Thus, there is a great need to study women criminals because the place and role of woman in the Indian society has undergone considerable changes during the last two decades leading to a greater participation in the criminal activities by them. Since the research on women criminals is fragmentary in nature, scope and coverage, and is still in its initial stages, the present study identifies, examines and explains women's criminality in the socio-cultural, economic and psychological context.

The strategy to deal with the problem of crime and the individual criminal has undergone radical changes. Earlier, no attention was paid to the human aspect of the criminal. Today, society goes beyond retribution and deterrence and includes the reformation and rehabilitation of offenders as objectives of punishment. The objective of the modern criminal justice system is prevention of crime and treatment of offenders, which can be achieved only by the re-socialization of the offender and by the restoring of the woman criminal to her original society as a normal law-abiding human being. The re-socialization of the offender will be possible only if scientific methods for the modification of deviant human behaviour are adopted. Professionally trained social workers can play a significant role by taking up this amazing task of the behavioural modification of the women criminals. Correctional work is concerned with the re-shaping or re-moulding of human behaviour. Correctional social workers can seek to understand the behaviour of the offenders, help them in achieving a more effective intellectual, social, or emotional functioning and promote more successful societal adjustment of offenders. The sole aim of prison reforms is to see that criminals, men or women, come out of prisons as better persons, physically, morally and psychologically.

So, various types of social work interventions, like curative, preventive, developmental, reformative, corrective and rehabilitative processes hold great promise for service in proper correctional settings.

Sex Differences in Crime

Sex ratios of crime have suggested that there are sex differences among the patterns and types of crimes committed by males and females (Steffensmeier, 1980). Statistical studies have indicated that delinquency and crime are found to be very closely associated with the male sex. According to Sutherland and Cressey (1966), "The male sex has a great access of crimes in all nations, all communities, all age groups and all periods of history for which organized statistics are available."

Parsons (1954) offered that the principal task of women is to nurture and socialize children in the domestic sphere while men are expected to provide financial support for the entire family, performing work outside the home. Men dominate the occupational system which is the arena of the most important competitive process in which the individual must achieve his status. Women, located in the family, are dependent for their position and income on the occupational status of one member, the husband and father. Cohen (1955) contends that the sub-culture of delinquency was uniquely masculine in character. Females were unable to 'prove' themselves by acts such as theft or vandalism, as they represented the very antithesis of their sex-role expectations. The mentally healthy woman was perceived to be one who is not crime-prone because she does not possess the necessary masculine traits thereby implicating that women who get involved in crime exhibit masculine characteristics.

Unlike the numerous theories explaining male criminality researchers interested in the female offender do not find such a gamut of theories. These texts have merely referred to the female offender in a footnote or in the appendix or a few short paragraphs or pages, devoted to a brief summary of Lombroso and the "female emancipation" theories.

The subject of crime among women does not appear to be only an event of this century as traditionally women were arrested for committing offences. In India, though the traditional social patterns have been exercising considerable influence on women, yet they were arrested for offences such as abortion, witchcraft, etc., and harsh penalties were imposed on those committing these heinous crimes.

According to Saxena (1994), scholars have generally viewed deviance amongst women broadly from two perspectives. One group perceives women who commit crimes as poor creatures, who are victims of male oppression and society's indifference and disinterest. The other group perceives women offenders as being more cunning than men, as having learnt how to commit crimes that are more difficult to detect and as enjoying the chivalry of male, law enforcement officials to avoid arrest, conviction and imprisonment.

These two basic themes have persisted in the literature and, on the basis of available literature, information can be gathered relating to the beliefs, notions, myths, etc., regarding criminality amongst women. Femininity is usually described as emotional, gullible, submissive, passive, illogical, sneaky, unambitious, dependent, gentle and child-like. According to Grosser (1951), it is this inability of females to express themselves through their criminality that accounts for the varying sex ratio in crime statistics.

Haskell and Yablonsky (1974) have asserted that, "Since men are expected to be aggressive, males are more likely to be delinquent than females, who are expected to adopt a more passive role." Some have argued that girls commit less delinquency than boys because the traditional feminine roles ensure that they are more closely controlled by their parents and others (Moss,1972 ; Hoffman-Bustamante, 1973 ; Shover et al. 1980). Considering these, women offenders are assumed to have different motives for crimes than men (Klein, 1973). Images of criminals are also linked with carrying out of serious crimes with the help of use of weapons, physical force and violence capabilities traditionally defined as masculine (Hoffman-Bustamante, 1973; Norland and Shover, 1977).

In general, these stereo types of the adult male and female roles in a society and the consequent expected behaviour of male and female have actually been used as the explanation for the differential rates of male and female criminality in the past (Omodei, 1981). The analysis of female criminality in regard to this belief has its theoretical basis in the works of Lombroso and his associates, 1899 ; Thomas, 1907/1923; Gluecks, 1934; Freud, 1933 and Pollak - 1950.

Due to these existing beliefs and stereotypes expressing female criminality almost entirely to physiological or psychological causes (Klein, 1973), the criminal behaviour of women has been regarded as a neglected area. Unlike her male counterpart, the female offender is rarely considered in her social context, her criminality was considered a less significant social problem, and as such there has been very little written about the female offender in sociological literature (Mukherjee and Scutt, 1981).

The *'Journal of Social Defence'* editorial (1975) reported that initially crime amongst males was the sole concern, but over the period, due to the change in the social structure, the criminal tendencies amongst women have also become a source of concern to the society. Currently, the rapid increase in recorded female criminality and delinquency has drawn attention to the radically changing role of women in contemporary society. It has also caused a spirited controversy as to whether the increase in crime is related to the changing role of the female. During the past few decades there are signs of an increasing interest in the area of female criminality. The coverage of women in mass media is increasingly informing the public about the diverse ramifications and dimensions of women offenders. It may be difficult to assess the nature and pattern of female criminality in the absence of meaningful statistics over a period of time due to the problems with crime statistics which are often referred to as "dark figures". There is a difference between the actual crime committed and the reported crime which is called the hidden criminality.

Weis (1976) takes strong exception to the view that increased female criminality is a consequence of women's liberation. He claims that such a relationship is "tenuous" at best and suggests that, rather than "liberation" being the cause of increasing female criminality, it is more likely a result of what he terms "sex-role determined opportunity". Females, according to Weis, commit female-oriented crimes and the rapid growth of this type of criminality reflects the growth of opportunity to commit female-oriented crimes. Feminists objected to both the assumption that females were achieving any kind of parity with men in economic and social spheres and the stereotyping implicit in the premise that female criminals were somehow "liberated" when their behaviour patterns showed more similarity to male patterns (Pollock - Byrne, 1990).

Saxena (1994), explained that women are beginning to emulate their patterns in both forms and dimensions of criminality. As women's role changes and becomes more open to opportunities associated with the male role, their activities will also be transformed in kind and degree, including the frequency and variety of their criminal activities.

The last half - century has opened up many pursuits, which provided the women new opportunities for crimes. The growth of interest in female law-breaking has been stimulated by the women's movement, the push for sexual equality and related trends. Simon (1975) and Adler (1975) have explained the recent increase in the incidence of female crime in terms of the breakdown of prevailing patterns of sexual inequality. According to Simon, development like women's progress toward achieving social equality with man, have stimulated not only the portrayal of new "violent" women by the media, but also a flurry of speculation among criminologists. It has been observed that, since past two decades there is an increased popularity in explaining the extent and nature of female criminal activity. However there is no evidence at all of a vast uncharted sea of female crime, or that women are more likely to become criminal the more they are emancipated or empowered. Indeed, the most detailed and vivid recent studies of women offenders in Britain (Carlen, 1983, 1985, 1988) strongly suggest the opposite, that women's offence is strongly associated with poverty and the stresses it brings, with neglect and deprivation and often with exploitation and abuse by men. However, because of their comparatively small number, which makes levels of statistical significance more difficult to obtain, there continues to be a paucity of research on the women offenders as compared to the amount of research done on the male offenders.

It has been concluded (Crime Prevention and Criminal Justice, Newsletter, 1984, U. Nations) that the evolution of the nature and extent of violent crime is related to the social and economic conditions of society and the changes taking place in its moral value system at a given point in time. According to Ghose (1986), in the Indian context, to understand the relationship between women and criminal behaviour, there is a need to examine the women's unique economic and social position in our society. Indian girls are taught to regard their self-prestige and the prestige of the families. Since childhood they are made to be dependent formally on their parents and is expected to go through the roles of a disciplined daughter, a submissive daughter-in-law, a sacrificing mother and a dominating mother-in-law. They are required to restore extreme courage and fearlessness in them to commit daring offences, which will severely be condemned by family members, relatives, friends and society. She is respected, admired and is considered that she should be duly protected. Therefore when any woman destroys this image by committing a heinous offence, the whole society receives a severe blow. Consequently, for the female criminal it becomes extremely difficult to regain her former status and re-adjust herself easily in her family environment. Thus, the value of dependence and security in Indian women prove to be the main factors in hindering them from taking any initiative or expression on any emotion unless driven by mal-adjustment.

The economic position of women depends on their location in the institution of personal survival, life support and emotional protection known as the family. Although women have been taking part in the economic life, the notion continues to exist that women's sphere of action is limited by the horizons of the small family world. Her major concerns are to look into the physical and emotional well-being of other family members.

According to Rao (1981), due to the changes in the social and economic position of women, sexual emancipation, changes in sex role patterns and alterations in economic opportunities for women have led to increased criminology on their part, largely due to the availability of increased crime opportunities. This has led to develop an interesting debate on the relationship between female criminality and women's liberation movement. The nature of familial and social controls over women, for instance, domestic roles, lack of access to education, inadequate working conditions, low religious and cultural status, appears to have pushed them into the "deprived" class. The crimes committed by men still far outnumber the crimes committed by women, but some researchers note that the female crime rate in some categories is increasing faster than that of men. Adler (1975), Austin (1982) and Price (1977) suggest that this increased rate can be attributed to the changes in the gender roles promoted by the women's movement and the consequent increased opportunities for women to engage in crime.

The "liberation" or "emancipation" theories contend that the movement has made women more aggressive, competitive and like men. In addition, the outgoing pace of industrialization and urbanization appears to be facilitating the process of modernization in our society. It appears that these conditions have led to the emergence of new concepts and patterns of life (Saxena, 1944).

The historical development of research approaches toward the etiology of female crimes and the characteristics of female offenders is traced through the correctional literature of the last century. The changes of theories and focus of research are related to the changes in the general attitudes toward women over this period. The current status of the literature indicates that the female offenders are changing along with the role of women in society. The criminological knowledge of the female offender is incomplete in many areas and increasingly obsolete. Those studies based on male populations are of untested validity for women. The vast bulk of criminological research has concerned itself with male offenders and male correctional institutions or treatment programs with male participants.

Although the literature on female offenders has been comparatively limited, studies have been done and, in fact, the development of the study of female offenders reflects the larger development of the criminal behaviour in general. That is, the study of female criminality, when traced historically, can be seen to mirror the phases through which the general study of criminology has passed.

A look at these phases reveals that the study, crime and criminals, including females, has gone through at least five major stages of development, each characterized by a particular type of focus (Rasche, 1974).

These stages are also discussed in the writings of Brodsky (1975) and Srivastava (1989). In this chapter, an attempt has been made to discuss the traditional and modern perspectives of women criminality.

Stages in the Criminological Study of Female Offenders

The first stage, which was called the pre-scientific stage, continued up to the start of the twentieth century. The few things written about female criminality in this stage concentrated on environmental causes, that did not seriously consider women as criminals and thereby worthy of any specific study or research. The later criminologists regarded this stage as the beginning of the theorizing attempt. They could not discover much material that could make any significant contribution to criminological theory on female criminality. The pre-scientific stage of criminology resulted in the development and growth of the penitentiary system in the early nineteenth century America. The penitentiary was the product of the development of a casual theory of crime which pin-pointed a corrupt environment and negligent upbringing as the causes of criminal behaviour.

The second stage of criminological research involved the search for constitutional causes, which reflected a beginning interest in the criminal as an individual and was greatly influenced by the views of Lombroso and Ferero. This stage was composed of studies that looked at the physiological and psychological factors related to female criminality. Lombrosso was not alone in his search for physiologically constitutional characteristics of female criminals. Most notably Matthews in 1923, Burt in 1925 and Seagrave in 1926-all studied female offenders from the point of view of physical size and development, sexual development, illness and disease, but few really outstanding casual relationships were ever uncovered (Smith, 1962).

Meanwhile, other constitutionally oriented researchers were studying the mental attributes of female offenders in an effort to connect delinquency with mental abnormality or disease. Weidensall (1916), found that the criminal woman tended to be slow to comprehend instructions and thus tended to act "blindly without comprehension", instead of stopping to think matters through. The fact that a large proportion of the female criminals confined in institutions were mentally deficient was supported by Spaulding in 1923 and Gluecks in 1939. Fernald in 1920 found two influences which seemed to be related to female delinquency :

(1) Poor economic background and lack of education or training.

(2) A somewhat inferior mentality.

Fernald clearly asserted a multi-casual approach to crime and, by the 1930s, the study of female criminals had firmly entered its third stage.

The third stage which occurred in the 1930s, combined constitutional causes with environmental factors. One of the most overly-discussed environmental factors in non-scientific circles was that of sexual emancipation. In 1931, Cecil Bishop felt that the emancipation movement had resulted in :

- More women becoming "criminally-minded".
- A "better class woman" turning criminal more often.
- Women being involved in sexual misdemeanors at a younger age than ever before.

This voluntary involvement in criminal behaviour was especially aggravating. Bishop believed, at a time when women seemed more pressed by economic or family conditions to turn to crime or become victims of white slavers and others who forced them into criminal behaviour. Bishop's treatise was essentially non-scientific, but it reflects well the temper of the times regarding female criminality. Another most interesting of the studies to come from this period was that of the Dutch lawyer, Euginia Lekkerkerker, who visited the United States in the late 1920s to study female reformatories. Although sophisticated, extensive and insightful, Lekkerkerker's work received less attention compared to a study by Sheldon and Eleanore Glueck (1934). The Gluecks clearly advanced the multi-causal and empirical approaches in criminology. Studying almost 500 convicted women, following them up for years after their release, the Gluecks came to the conclusion that mental inferiority, economic hardship, lack of education and familial instability-all played a part in setting the stage for a woman to behave criminally.

Having established the approach to crime causation as multi-causal, criminological researchers began inspecting more closely the various aspects or factors of female criminality and thus during the 1940s the study of women's criminality entered its fourth stage, which might be called the numbers and offenses stage (Statistical Stage), with a good deal of attention given to the number of offences committed by women. In this stage, studies were devoted to reporting and analyzing the types of crimes committed by women, as well as to attempts to explain why significantly fewer women were criminally adjudicated. The numbers-and-types stage ultimately culminated in 1950 with the publication of "The Criminality Of Women" by Pollak, one of the most significant works on female criminality to date.

It was unavoidable that the new insight into the relationship between the women's social position and her criminality should lead researchers in the 1960s to question the social system of females in reformatories and prisons. The progression to this study marks the entry into the fifth stage of the study of female criminality, which is called the women's prison stage which existed until recently.

The explanation of female criminality is divided by Srivastava (1989) and Saxena (1994) into two broad categories:

- Classical Theories.
- Contemporary Theories.

Nagla (1982) traces the trend of theories dealing with women's criminality in their historical perspective in general and the traditional theory in particular. Furthermore, he analyzed the issue by emphasizing the roles of women and the changing form of criminality. Classical literature on women and crime, dating back to the late nineteenth and early twentieth century, some of the most significant and distinctive studies have been done by pioneers like Lombroso and Ferero (1989), Thomas (1923), Freud (1933), Davis (1961) and Pollak (1950, 1959) who emphasized the constitutional factors as related to female's criminality. Other influential writers in search for physiological and constitutional characteristics of female criminals were Mabel Fernald (1920) and Spaulding

(1923). The contemporary theory revolves round such writings of Merton (1949), Durkheim (1951), Pollak (1981) and the Radical theory of Quinney (1977), etc. The contemporary theorists reject the earlier theories rooted in the physiological and psychological explanations of crime causation. In recent years it is the socio-economic and environmental factors which have been given importance in explaining women's criminality. They are mainly, the strain theory, the learning theory, the masculinity theory, the control theory, the labeling theory, the role theory, etc.

Style of Life

The distinctive aspects of a style of life are cultural, but some are due to the situation in which the members typically find themselves. According to the well known sociologist Johnson (1966), the term " Style Of Life" must be understood in a comprehensive sense. He further said that the style of life might be more or less distinctive with respect to all the following points :

- Prenatal care
- Amount and kind of facial and body decoration.
- Characteristic standards of personal grooming.
- Posture, gestures and general physical bearing.
- Speech patterns.
- Kinds and quality of clothing.
- Type of residence and its location in the community.
- Items of house furnishing and their style.
- Type of occupation for men and women.
- Amount and kind of education and the schools at which it is obtained.
- Patterns of family life, including husband-wife relations and the training of children.
- Religious beliefs, membership, amount and kind of participation.
- Taste in reading, radio programs and other modes of communication.

- Recreational patterns.
- Participation in formal organizations, contribution of money and services to civic enterprises.
- Political affiliation and opinions.
- Standards of sexual morality and interpersonal conduct in general and funeral customs.

The sweep of this incomplete list shows that the term "Style Of Life" is not inappropriate. The style of life also includes social class and sub-culture. Prison culture can be of a particular sub-culture. The conception of distinct groups is accompanied by the conception of sub-cultures.

The life style is the overall pattern of living, whereby an individual attempts to meet his or her biological, social and emotional needs. A life style provides the context in which the individual confronts the crisis of intimacy versus isolation described by Eric Erikson (Newman and Newman, 1975).

The personality theory of Adler (1929, 1931) describes the "Style Of Life" as the system principle by which the individual personality functions. It is the whole that commands the parts and explains the uniqueness of the person. He further explains that every person has the same goal of attaining superiority. But there are innumerable ways of striving for this goal. Every one has a style of life, but no two people develop the same style. One person tries to become superior through developing the intellect, while another bends all of his or her efforts to achieving muscular perfection. The intellectual has one style of life, the athlete another. Everything is done with an eye to the ultimate goal of achieving superiority. All of a person's behaviour springs from his or her style of life. The person perceives, learns and retains what fits the style of life and ignores everything else.

The style of life is formed very early in childhood, by the age of four or five and from then on experiences are assimilated and utilized according to this unique style of life. His attitudes, feelings, become fixed and mechanized at an early age and it is practically impossible for the style of life to change thereafter. The person may acquire new ways of expressing his unique style of life, but these are merely concrete and particular instances of the same basic style that was found at an early age.

Adler says that the style of life is largely determined by the specific inferiorities, either fancied or real, that the person has. The style of life is a compensation for a particular inferiority. Adler, instead of seeing persons as specially to be understood through their intra-psychic conflicts, asserts that the individual who is an irreducible whole could be known through his social goals and his relationships to other people, especially with his family. These taken together distinguish his particular "Style Of Life" and this, rather than sexuality, betrays his basic motivation.

Theorists who approach the problems of therapy from this direction have summarized that the roots of a person's difficulties lie in his basic misconceptions about the nature of things; he mistakes ideas he acquired at some former period of his life. He is likely to be quite unaware of these cognitive structures. The conclusions to which they lead him are axioms, taken for granted. Adler discusses the effects of this phenomenon, under the term, life style.

The present research is concerned with the life style of women criminals, which has been studied under different dimensions, namely, the socio-cultural, economic and psychological dimensions. To understand the concept of the life style, an effort has been made to cover socialization processes, interpersonal relations, the presence / absence of parents, relations with siblings, husband-wife relationships, daughter-in-law / mother-in-law relationships, etc. Life is such a process, which essentially maintains a functional continuity between the present and the past. In the present study retrospection on the part of the respondents of the home climate and other processes during their life, that is, prior to their marriage was taken into consideration. An attempt has also been made to analyze how the conflicting situations and maladjustment in the lives of these women after marriage had motivated them to the take to various forms of criminal behaviour.

After introducing the research problems, it would be quite meaningful to give the details of various criminological theories frameworks, perspectives and approaches, which play an important role in guiding various researches.

SECTION - 2

Theorising About Female Crime

Various theories about crime have been propounded from time to time but only a few among them have dealt with female criminality. The theories of female criminality have ranged from biological to psychological, from economic to social. Crime causation theories have a direct influence on the correctional treatment of female criminals. The historical neglect of the female criminal meant a neglect of causation theory. This is perhaps due to the fact that female criminals constituted a small percentage of the total crime or an insignificant subset of male research populations, or they were generally viewed as an "embarrassment than a threat to society" (Mannheim, 1965).

Here, the present researcher shall explain the growth of the theories and conceptual frameworks for studying women criminality.

Early Theories - Global Context

Cesare Lombroso (1903)

Cesare Lombroso, a nineteenth century (1836-1909) physician-scientist and professor of psychiatry and anthropology at the University of Turin, is primarily important in the historical context. His theories are no longer taken seriously because they cannot be supported scientifically; but he should be respected for making pioneering though primitive efforts, to understand the criminal man and woman.

The core of Lombroso's belief was that crime is an atavism (a throwback to a more primitive level of humanity's evolutionary development). According to this theory, crime can be inherited and the criminal usually has certain anomalies (physical differences from the norm) that will identify that person as a criminal. Among the anomalies characterizing male criminals, according to Lombroso, were a sloping forehead, receding chin, excessive body hair, insensitivity to pain, a protruding supra-orbital ridge (the ridge above the eyes) and lobeless ears. However, Lombroso said, women do not have these anomalies as often as male criminals. In fact, they were not physically very different from "moral" women, except for prostitutes who did show more physical abnormalities than the non-prostitute female criminal. Lombroso sought physiological characteristics and followed a school of thought (Positive School Of Criminology), which involved taking elaborate cranial measurements. However, after a lot of painstaking and detailed work, Lombroso was forced to conclude that the concept of the "born criminal" which he developed by studying male offenders was rare among women. But he went on to try to explain this finding by asserting that women were innately inferior to men morally. Thus, most women were "occasional offenders", whose latent criminal tendencies would surface when normal constraints were missing. However, when a woman did fall into the category of a "born criminal", Lombroso asserted that she was "more terrible than the male", because of her innate depravity, her insensitivity to pain "which breeds lack of compassion" and her childish qualities, that is, jealousy, cruelty, revengefulness and moral deficiency. The normal female could be transformed into a "born criminal", whose propensities for evil were "more intense and more perverse" than those of the male born criminals. Lombroso stated that the born female criminal was rare, but he was savage in his description of her and used an Italian proverb to make his point : **"Rarely is a woman wicked, but when she is, she surpasses the man".** This belief was not unique with Lombroso. He was supported by others like Corrado Celto who quoted : **"No possible**

punishments can deter women from heaping up crime upon crime. Their perversity of mind is more fertile in new crimes than the imagination of a judge in new punishments." While Euripides is summoned to declare, **"The violence of the ocean waves or of devouring flames is terrible. Terrible is poverty, but woman is more terrible than all else".** Lombrosso listed the following factors to demonstrate his view of how the female criminal differed from her male counterpart :

(1) The female's psychology is more dependent upon her biological constitutions than is the male's.

(2) Women are organically conservative.

(3) A less active cerebral cortex (part of the brain associated with thought processes) makes the female more likely to become prostitutes than to turn to other types of crime.

(4) Women are influenced by selectivity, that is, men seek handsome women for mating and biological rejection is therefore a factor in the development of female criminality.

(5) Women are more often led into crime by heightened suggestibility and temptation and are therefore less morally deficient than men criminals.

(6) The role of women places them in the home, where they are unlikely to become criminal.

Lombroso was close to some truths about the female criminal in his findings, but the differing psychology and the role of the woman are factors influencing her criminal behaviour, which are not biological traits. Only psychology and sociology can offer meaningful explanations of these aspects of behaviour.

***Kingsley Davis* (1937)**

Kingsley Davis presented a functionalist explanation of one specific type of crime by women called prostitution as an illegitimate extension of the female sex role. He argued that prostitution arises in circumstances where demands for sexual novelty cannot be supplied within the marriage and/or where some men are cut off from access to being sex partners because they are unmarried, ugly or deformed in some respects.

Commercial prostitution arises as a black market in sex. The problem with this theory, according to Klein and Simon, is that it lends support to the sexist thesis that the only proper role for women is that of child bearer and housewife, because, according to Davis, the deviant women merely adjust to their feminine role in an illegitimate fashion. Davis saw women, who chose prostitution as maladjusted and neurotic. Unlike Lombroso and Freud, Davis did not suggest that women behave like "rebels" or "men", but referred to the psychological masculinization of female behaviour.

***Sigmund Freud* (1931, 1933)**

Freud offered a physiological explanation of female criminality, holding that the law-breaking of females represents a perversion of, or rebellion against, the biologically natural female role. Freud interpreted crime among women, career aspirations on their part and kindred activities as evidences of a "masculinity complex". He maintained that all females experience some degree of "penis envy" and jealousy of males, but "normal" women ultimately manage to accept and internalize societal definitions of femininity centered about a single-minded interest in motherhood. The "Normal" woman also come to exhibit "normal" feminine traits of passivity, masochism and narcissism. In all of this, Freud engaged in the implicit condemnation of all departures from cultural stereotypes of the proper role of women, holding that it was "natural" for females to behave according to these narrow expectations.

The Freudian theory claims that women who are not passive, who are not content with their roles as mothers and wives, are maladjusted. The source of their maladjustment is penis envy. The evidence for the existence of the masculinity complex is manifest by the woman's pursuit of masculine goals: success and recognition in the occupational sphere, power and money. The devious ways of compensating for the lack of a penis are attending universities, pursuing an autonomous or independent course of life, or joining feminist movements. Freud labeled the women who engaged in such behaviour "immature, incomplete, or cases of arrested development".

The critics of Freudian interpretations of female crime have scored them on two related counts. First, these arguments are defective as explanations of the genesis of female criminality, for they contain erroneous assumptions about the biological characteristics of women and they also fail to take cognizance of the social-structural factors in criminal etiology. Klein and others charge that these views are sexist in character, for they support and reinforce those social arrangements which relegate women to child-bearing and domestic worker roles.

Freud along with Dollard (1939) also gave the theory on Frustration-Aggression which explains that frustration produces aggression and aggression results from frustration. However, the manner in which it is expressed and the object at which it is directed, will depend on controls-both internal and external-to personality-operating at the time of crime.

W.I. Thomas (1923, 1937, 1967)

Thomas offered an explanation for delinquency on the part of young females which characterize them as engaging in departures from lines of conduct that are biologically and psychologically "normal" for women. He felt that women criminals are not sex role abnormals. They engage in role expressive and role supportive criminal behaviour, such as sexual conduct, shop lifting and other types of delinquent behaviour, which are extensions of their female role. Thomas described the female as a passive opposite to the active male. All humans sought excitement and response, but women sought excitement and response through sexual means - that is, prostitution. Thomas, like other researchers who looked at female criminals, defined women's criminality solely in terms of sexuality.

Thomas also gave the Theory Of Four Wishes, that is, response, recognition, security and new experience, which would help in understanding the nature of crime.

***Otto Pollak* (1950)**

Pollak, a modern American sociologist, challenged the basic assumptions concerning the extent and quality of women's involvement in criminal behaviour. He argued that women have been commended and praised for their drastic under representation in criminal activities but, in fact, they do not deserve such praise. According to Pollak, women's participation in crime has not been significantly lower than that of men's; rather :

- The types of crimes women commit are less likely to be detected.
- Even when detected, they are less likely to be reported, for example, shoplifting, domestic theft and theft by prostitutes.
- Even when crimes are reported, women still have a much better chance than do men of avoiding arrest or conviction because of the lenient double standard employed by law enforcement officials which is favourable to women.

Keeping the "masked" character of female crime, Pollak advanced the theory of "hidden" female criminality to account for their substantially lower official statistics which, according to him, is a function of women's roles in society, the psychological components of femaleness and certain physical factors. He claimed that women engage in hidden crimes like abortions, murder by poisoning, offences against children, etc., because of their greater skill at deceit and cunning behaviour acquired through sexual socialization. Besides, the surreptitious and cunning nature of women acquired through differential socialization process, Pollak also suggested that the biological factors including lesser physical strength, as well as the psychological concomitants of menstruation, pregnancy, menopause, etc., enter the etiology of female crime.

The shared proposition of all these four scholars is that female crime is the result of the physiological or psychological characteristics of individuals. They have not given any importance to the socio-cultural factors, but have viewed the biological characteristics as pathological distortions or departures from the normal inherent nature of women. The assumptions in all these explanations about the biological and psychological traits of the "normal" and criminal women are questionable. Rita James Simon (1975) has also contended that all the above explanations are incorrect because they contain erroneous presuppositions about the normal traits of women. Females were considered as biologically predisposed toward passivity and other "ladylike" characteristics, such that aggressiveness was viewed as a violation of their true nature. Yet, all these works, in some form or the other, exert an influence on the contemporary understanding of female crime.

Contemporary Theories

Giseila Konopka (1966)

Konopka's study on "The Adolescent Girls In Conflict", is that the girls are driven to delinquency by an emotional problem, that is, loneliness and dependency. Thus she emphasizes on the female emotions as the cause for delinquency in girls. Konopka's assertion about female personalism, emotionalism and above all sexuality is familiar with the characteristics already described by Thomas. She states that "thwarted ambition" has a strong impact on the way girls behave, but for the girl, unlike the boy, it is not related to economics, but it is directly related to being a woman, that is, a "normal" well-adjusted girl by definition cannot become delinquent. Smart (1976) criticizes Konopka for ignoring the social and economic factors and stresses more on the individual problems as characteristics of delinquency.

John Cowie, Valerie Cowie & Slater Eliot (1968)

Cowie et al. have discussed the biological basis of the masculinization of female behaviour. They like Lombroso and Ferreor's approach, proposed that criminality is a sign of pathology and female delinquents show masculine traits. The main perspective was that the biological difference between the sexes is a significant cause in determining the difference in the nature of the crimes committed by men and women. Bearing strong resemblance to the works of Lombroso and Ferreor, Cowie et al. thus saw female criminality in terms of the biological constitution of the female sex, such as excessive weight or other physical problems.

***Clyde Vedder & Dora Somerville* (1970)**

The views of Vedder and Somerville regarding female delinquency are similiar to those of Konopka and Freud. They view delinquency as blocked access or maladjustment to the normal feminine role. Ignoring the social and economic factors, they attributed the high rates of delinquency to the lack of sexual opportunities for women. Like Konopka to a great extent and like Thomas to some extent, Vedder and Somerville maintain that female delinquents are those who extend femininity in illegitimate fashion.

Thus it shows that the contemporary works are on the etiology of female crime which stresses the patterns of differential sexual socialization, differential sex role expectations, etc. Emphasizing the sociological factors of crime causation, contemporary writers criticize the earlier theories for offering physiological and psychological explanations as causal factors.

The scholarly studies of the early 1970s mark the impact of feminism on criminology. There is an explicit awareness of the role of social structure in the female patterns of crime, and social influences were seen as dominant rather than the biological ones. The sexist images of women and stereotypical notions about their deceptiveness, greed and untrustworthiness were discredited. It was firmly believed that women are neither purer nor more manipulative than men, but they are very simple creatures of their social system.

In the 1970s several reviews of the early theories criticize the misconceptions and stereotypes. Smart (1977), Crites (1976) and Klein (1973) were among those who criticize the early theories. Their reviews point out the flaws in attributing the socialized differences to the biological factors, identify the methodological inconsistencies and criticize the formal treatment of women by the criminal justice system as discriminatory.

Freda Adler (1975)

Adler has explained the recent increase in the incidence of female crime in terms of the breakdown of prevailing patterns of "sexual inequality". According to Adler, a growing trend towards female assertiveness, manifested in the contemporary women's movement in the United States as well as in other ways, has led to consequences in the area of criminality. She has held that along with the masculinization of female crime, there has been an increase in the frequency and nature of female crime. She recognizes equality between the sexes, the emancipation of women and the women's liberation movement linked to changes in the rate and pattern of female criminality. Women's socio-economic emancipation had an important impact in the area of female criminality. She feels that women are moving out of traditional crimes such as prostitution and shoplifting into grand larceny, embezzlement, robbery and crimes of violence, such that their participation in these offences has increased much more markedly than has men's in recent years. Adler has studied prostitution, drug addiction and juvenile delinquency among females. She has attributed these crimes to the liberation movement of women and women's assertiveness. She contends that educated girls and women are more willing than ever to challenge traditional restrictions and social roles. The easing of restraints on women is further likely to increase female crime. Thus, Adler argues, that the female offender is in fact a product of a "raised consciousness" founded on feminist ideology.

Rita James Simon (1975)

Simon has also explained the recent increase in the incidence of female crime in terms of the breakdown of prevailing patterns of sexual inequality. According to Simon, increased labour-force participation of women and other developments in the direction of sexual equality have expanded the crime opportunities and pressures towards law-breaking among women. Simon has analysed the various dimensions of female criminality like the extent and types of the crimes committed and their treatment by the court and prison officials. She however has not studied the issue of the etiology of female crime. According to her, the increase in female crime is due to the expanding occupational opportunities for women.

Although unwilling to deny the possibility "that the women's movement will significantly alter the behaviour, the perceptions, the beliefs and the life styles of the women already involved in criminal careers", Simon feels that this new-found freedom might alleviate frustration and could lead in turn to a reduction in violent crime by women, which is contrary, to Adler. As Adler implies, there is a rather direct link between the emancipation of women and their increased criminality. Other writers like Crites (1976), Klein and Kress (1976), also express female criminal behaviour as an illegitimate expression of the legitimate female sex role expectations and lack of opportunities.

Haskell and Yablonsky (1978)

They have advanced some reasons for the lower female arrest rate and for the apparently lower female participation in crime :

- Female roles are more closely defined.
- Females are more closely supervised.
- Females receive greater protection.
- Females have opportunity for household employment.
- Male roles are more active
- Men are likely to be chivalrous.
- The public perceives men and women differently.
- The police react differently to men and women.

Mawby (1980)

Mawby has given five explanations which relate female offending to the social roles of females in society :

(1) Expectation of appropriate behaviour.
(2) Social Control.
(3) Opportunity.
(4) Career Models
(5) Attitudes.

The fine issues are, however, somewhat speculative.

As in the recent years more importance is given to the socio-economic and environmental factors, the researcher will highlight these factors to explain women criminality. A review of the major theories in criminology, such as those of the Chicago School, differential association, strain theory and subcultural deviance, will show that they either do not help explain or are inconsistent with female criminality (Leonard, 1982; Morris, 1987; Naffine, 1987).

Most of these traditional theories not only did not attempt to explain this differential but totally ignored female criminals. Often only males were used in samples and the language describing causation referred only to male development, male values and male motivations. Feminist criminologists have provided excellent and comprehensive critiques of these theories (Leonard,1982 ; Morris,1987 ; Heidensohn, 1985).

However, some of these general theories are explained here :

Strain Theory

The essence of the strain theory is that criminality is caused by pressure or tension. The source of this tension is stimulated aspirations to achieve certain goals blocked with obstacles to their legitimate achievement. Frustrated individuals turn to crime either to release this tension or to achieve their goals via illegitimate avenues.

The originator of the strain theory is the American Sociologist Robert Merton (1949), who borrowed ideas from the French sociologist Emile Durkheim (1951). Durkheim in fact had restructured the term from the Greek word meaning "without law". Although under the sway of Durkheim's thinking, Merton used the word "anomie" in a quite different sense. To Merton, anomie was not a state of normlessness, which precipitated anti-social behaviour, but the condition experienced by individuals taught to want the goals of their culture but denied access to them.

It was another American social scientist who took up Merton's idea of "strain" explicitly to explain the different patterns of male and female crime, in particular the crimes of youth. Albert Cohen (1955) interpreted strain as the main catalyst to the formation of delinquent gangs by male working-class American youth. Although Cohen unintentionally extends his theory by proposing that when their aspirations for status are frustrated in the middle class milieu, lower-class boys tend to set up a delinquent sub-culture, whereas Cloward and Ohlin (1960) intentionally extend Merton's theory by suggesting that whether or not the potentially delinquent lower-class youth will actually become delinquent, depends on the factor of differential illegitimate opportunity.

Ruth Morris (1964/1983) accepted the ideas of Cohen and Cloward and Ohlin in the mid-1960s when she shifted the focus of strain theory to delinquent girls. Morris hypothesized that "obstacles to economic power status are more likely to lead to delinquency in boys, while obstacles to maintaining positive affective relationships are more likely to lead to delinquency in girls".

The anomie theory has been criticized for lacking empirical support, for ignoring value pluralism and for slighting the fun of delinquency. But the theory has been praised for replacing the psychological with the sociological approach to deviance and for offering a valid premise concerning the aspiration-opportunity gap.

Learning Theory

The idea that criminality is a learned behaviour goes back to 1939 when Edwin Sutherland introduced the theory of Differential Association Theory in Principles of Criminology.

The theory states that a person will become criminal if he or she associates more with criminal than with anti-criminal people and ideas. The application of his theory to women is particularly helpful in emphasizing that criminal behaviour is learned in interaction with other persons in a process of communication and is not psychologically or biologically determined.

Thus, Sutherland (1960) has emphasized the sociological factors which cause the female criminality, explaining the individual's crime in terms of her past experiences rather than situations. Over a number of revisions of his text in collaboration with Donald Cressey, Sutherland crystallized his theory of differential association in 1966.

The first explicit application of the differential association theory to females was by Ruth Morris in her effort to explain female conformity. She hypothesized that there is a relative absence of a deviant sub-culture for female delinquents and absence of sub-cultural as well as cultural support for female delinquency (Morris, 1964).

Glasser (1956) extends the "differential association" theory by suggesting that "differential identification" is the determining factor for turning the differential association into criminal action, while Burgess and Akers (1966) identify that determining factor as "differential reinforcement".

Sutherland's theory has been criticized for its failure to explain the behaviour of lone criminals, for offering an empirically vague concept and a tautological explanation and for wrongly assuming the learning of special skills as necessary for committing crime and delinquency. But the theory has inspired substantial empirical research. It has also pointed out that Glasser's theory has received some but not conclusive empirical support, while the Burgess - Akers theory can explain repeated but not initial deviance.

Control Theory

Control theory reasons that what causes conformity is control and therefore the lack of control causes deviance. There is a group of control theorists of three sociologists, Walter Reckless, Ivan Nye and Travish Hirschi. Reckless (1973) refers to the casual factor of conformity as containment, Nye (1958) social control and Hirschi (1969) bond to society.

This theory has been well supported by empirical data, but it is applicable to unsophisticated delinquent behaviour only. This theory seems unable to explain more sophisticated adult deviant behaviour, aside from presenting an over-simplified view of social control. The control theory differs from both the anomie and differential association theorists who approach the problem of explaining deviant behaviour by asking :- "What causes deviance"? But the control theorists approach the problem in a round about way and ask :- "What causes conformity"? They will automatically find out what causes deviance. As causes for deviance is simply because of absence of what causes conformity. Although the control theory differs from the anomie theory, Hirschi prefaces his theory with an excerpt from Durkheim's Suicide. Considered as a whole, the literature applying the control theory to woman is inconclusive. Ever since Hindelang (1973) discovered that the presence or absence of social bonds bore a weaker relation to female delinquency than to male delinquency. However, the control theory would predict that girls who are most like boys (masculine girls) would offend as much as boys because of a similarity of strength of social bonds, which should be weaker than those of more feminine, more conforming girls (Naffine, 1987).

Labelling Theory

The Labelling theory can be traced back from Husserl (1859 - 1938) and his philosophy of phenomenology, within criminological circles. The idea that external social stigmata or "labels" make "the criminal", is usually attributed to the American social scientist, Howard Becker. According to the labelling theory, superordinate people apply the deviant label to subordinate people, being labelled deviant produces unfavourable consequences for the individual so labelled and labelling as deviant, generates favourable consequences for the individuals, groups or communities that do the labelling. But the labelling theory has been criticized by some sociologists for being unable to tell us the causes of deviant behaviour and for over-simplifying and exaggerating the influence of labelling on the development of a deviant career.

When the labelling theory was applied to women, two approaches were applied by criminologists. One was to employ the sort of close observation used by Becker on his male musicians to develop accounts of the interior lives of women. The other was to adopt Becker's attitude to women, to depict them as clinging to conventional society-inert, colourless and unattractive. In 1977, Harria theorized the greater conformity of females in terms of their manipulation by powerful men who convince them that crime is a wholly inappropriate activity for women. Although not explicit in her debt to labelling theory, Fox (1977), presents another interpretation of female conformity by employing the idea that women are controlled by social constructs of appropriate feminine behaviour.

Role Theory

The Role Theory only explains the differential rates of male and female criminality. The Role Theorists highlight the way in which opportunity structures predispose males rather than females to crime. Some of the criminologists have used the Role Theory in explaining female crime in terms of sex roles, other than biological or psychological variables.

Frances Heidensohn (1968) was the first criminologist to voice clearly the need for a theory of female criminality which was sensitive to the impact of the female sex role on the behaviour of women.

According to Marie Andree Bertrand (1969), sex-typed behaviour does not come "naturally"; rather, culture manipulates its members to produce sex-typed behaviour. Moreover he implies that society has a vested interest in precipitating and maintaining such sex differentiated behaviour and society does not want women trained or practised in such matters. Thus for the first time female criminality was depicted as a rational response to social experience and a beginning of a critical analysis of the relationship between sex roles and the behaviour of women.

Both Heidensohn and Bertrand pointed out that, owing to close supervision and social restrictions on women, socialization, development of consciousness and self-perception vary considerably between boys and girls. Girls are usually trained to be passive, domesticated and non-violent and are not allowed to learn how to fight or use weapons. Contrary to this, boys are aggressive, ambitious and outward-going. Girls thus shrink from violence and do not possess the necessary technical ability or strength to engage in crimes of violence, armed robberies, gang fights, etc. At worst, they engage in petty or domestic offences. Heidensohn thus paved the way for a radical revision of theory on the female offender. Heidensohn's call for a more sophisticated "role theory" came at a time, when the women's movement was gathering momentum. The Role Theory emerged at a time when both sociology and criminology were concerned with the individual's adjustment to society's needs, while the women's movement, from which the Role Theory was later to take its direction, developed with the understanding that social roles, rather than individuals, should be fluid.

Dale Hoffman-Bustamante (1973) provided a more sophisticated theory of female criminality that takes into account socialization factors and opportunity theory. According to her theory, five major factors affect the differential involvement of females in crime :

(1) Differential role expectations for men and women.

(2) Sex differences in socialization patterns and application of social control.

(3) Structurally determined differences in opportunity to commit particular offences.

(4) Differential access or pressure toward criminally oriented sub-cultures and careers.

(5) Sex differences built into crime categories.

Her explanation points to the different childhood experiences of boys and girls. Whereas males are allowed a great deal of free time and are exposed during their wanderings to various opportunities for delinquency, females tend to have greater responsibilities at home. They are more controlled by social rules to be "ladylike" and reserved.

Other theorists of the 1950s like Talcott Parsons (1949), Grosser (1951) and Cohen (1955) also opined the role theories and analyzed the female offender in terms of her social situation. Theories were by and large dependent on the simple division of sex differences. Talcott Parsons held that the low incidence of female crime was due to the ready availability of a female adult (since mother normally stayed at home) upon whom the female child modeled her behaviour. The male child, however, frustrated by the lack of a role model (father at work) and as a protest against the femininity of the mother, engaged in delinquent behaviour. Grosser presented a more detailed exposition on the Role Theory. He maintained that, while juvenile delinquency is role "expressive" (of masculinity) or "supportive" for males, it is inconsistent with the stereotyped notions of femininity. It is this inability of females to "express" themselves through their criminality that accounted for the high disparity in the sex ratio in crime statistics. Cohen contended that the subculture of delinquency which presented a solution to the status problems of adolescents was uniquely male in character. Females were unable to "prove" themselves by acts such as theft or vandalism as they represented the very antithesis of their sex role expectations.

Carol Smart (1976) and Jocelynne Scutt (1976) attempted in 1976 to update the Role Theory by incorporating within the role of school, peer group and occupational group, besides family, as socializing agents. But both of them had strong reservations about the value of the Role Theory as an explanation for female criminality. The major criticism of the Role Theory came from Smart, who in her critical assessment contended that, the "Role Theory fails to examine the social origins of sex roles and to deal with the inferior status of women in historical and cultural terms. Her work was exceptional in the field of women and crime since it introduced a new direction in the criminology and sociology of deviance by investigating female crime from a committed feminist position. Exploring classical and contemporary studies she found and criticized that in both the studies, sexist assumptions about female criminality were frequently described. Critically examining the works of Lombroso and Pollak, who dealt particularly with female crime, Smart contended that it is necessary to explore the ways in which women are sexually exploited. She connected such exploitation with their economic and political dependency.

Scutt focused on Parson's interpretation of the role theory, where boys unable to envisage their father's role, but encouraged to be "manly" and aggressive cannot cope with the role and rebel against this role by engaging in criminal behaviour. Scutt also identifies a third area where females are subject to sex role socialization, that is, their peer culture. He asserts that the female adolescent's peer group may be a complicating factor in her socialization, that is, peers do not always encourage the type of behaviour which is considered sex appropriate by the family. For example, the peer culture may incorporate sexual "promiscuity" - behaviour which is strictly forbidden by the family.

Both Smart and Scutt attempted to update and diversify the role theory by incorporating within this approach a number of social factors other than the family, occupational opportunity structure, education and peer culture.

Crites (1976) advanced a new approach within criminology to the subject of women and crime, which is quite similar to that of Smart. In her work, she indicated the increasing interest in women and crime and did not accept the stereotypical views about women. She also rejected the contentions that women are rapidly becoming involved in violent and aggressive offences, or that the women's movement is contributing to increase in crime.

Klein and Kress (1976) dealt specifically with the issue of women and crime. Their work provides an insight and focuses on the crimes women commit. They criticize the existing studies for failing to consider the economic and political position of women and their sexist expression which may play as a factor in crime. They contend that, in order to understand female crime, the economic system along with the historical and present role of women in society, must be examined thoroughly. Klein and Kress proposed that women are as restricted in their criminal roles as they are in legitimate ones. They further noted that the women's movement is not crimiogenic. Women occupy and perform roles in the straight and criminal worlds, which are defined by their sex-determined lack of opportunity. Thus, female criminal behaviour is an illegitimate expression of legitimate female sex role expectations and opportunities.

Bowker (1978) dealt extensively with statistics on women and crime and provided a new literature by discussing the criminal justice system in terms of male domination. While discussing the male and female patterns of crime, he concluded that, by rejecting early explanation and to explain the quantitative differences in male and female crime, both criminological theory and sex-role theory will have to be explored. He also maintained that, "development, situational and macrostructural variables, namely social, education equality, economic equality and socio-economic status" are involved in the causes of female crime and the roles women play within crime.

Balkan and Berger (1979) wrote an article on female delinquency and the women's movement. They related female crime to sex role expectations and socio-economic conditions. They contended that female property offences reflect roles in the market place, the increased opportunities, the current economic crisis and increased economic goals among women. They further argued that the rising juvenile violence among female is due to the economic climate and not to the women's liberation movement.

Hill Reuben (1949) has referred to the crisis for the family created by the committing of crime by a woman and consequently her imprisonment. This crisis requires a new type of adjustment on the part of all the members of the family. Hill defines crisis as a situation which blocks the usual patterns of action and calls for new ones. This crisis situation and the adjustment to it affect :

- The individual
- The pair (husband-wife)
- The children
- Other family members (if any)
- The family's relationship with its kinship, groups, neighbours, etc.

Somebody has to take the roles of the mother, householder, cook, etc., which were being performed by the imprisoned woman. On the part of the husband, some sexual adjustment is required. Hill discusses the process of family adjustment in terms of "role-conception", that is, socially prescribed roles each member plays in a family life. He says, "good adjustment to separation (due to imprisonment) involves closing of ranks, shifting of responsibilities and activities of the wife to other members, continuing the necessary family routines, maintaining husband-wife and mother-child relationships by correspondence and visits and utilizing the resources of friends, relatives and neighbours.

Radical Theory

Radical theorists have used the Marxist theory to explain criminality, but again the principles and applications of this theory have largely ignored women. This neglect is all the more strange when one assumes that Marxist theorists would accept the fact of women's oppression and male domination in society (Morris,1987; Heidensohn,1985).

According to Mann (1984), Marxist feminists have used the theory and its analysis of capitalism to explain how women enter into crime and also how they are treated by the system. Capitalism and paternalism are combined in this analysis, both contributing to the woman's powerlessness. This use of Marxist analysis, however, was not offered by the male theorists, who devoted little attention to the economic subjugation of women.

From time to time different theories tried to explain the cause of crime. However, no single theory explains all crimes and delinquency. The behaviour and personality pattern of the criminals indulging in different types of crimes are quite different from each other; thus it becomes difficult to apply one theory in explaining the causes of becoming a criminal of other type. However, the understanding of criminal behaviour would require examining the individual and the situation because basically the criminal behaviour depends upon how the individual perceives and interprets a situation (Bartol, 1980).

According to Reckless (1961), although crime as a behaviour problem or a social problem is complex and not easily understood, the criminality of woman is even more complicated and less understood. Leonard (1982) commented that theoretical criminology is unable to explain adequately the phenomenon of women and crime, since it is sexist and focuses on the activities, interests and values of man, while ignoring a comparable analysis of women. Leonard like others noted that women have not been committing more violent crimes, but rather more petty property crimes like shoplifting, fraud or forgery, (Warren,1979; Steffensmeier,1980; Challinger,1982; Box and Halle,1983).

Other contemporary researchers have also drawn similar conclusions (Krohn et al. 1983; Visher,1983). Heidensohn (1985) concluded that understanding the association between women and crime is not through feminist criminology but through "using insights into the role, position and social control of women which can be derived from other sources of women's oppression". Similar to her work, Carlen (1985) established that the feminist criminology have not been very successful due to two reasons. Firstly, many feminist writers have viewed crime as essentially a male activity and secondly attempts to identify a global theory of crime, which would explain the behaviour of both men and women in crime or a special theory of woman's crime are theoretically unsound. Morris (1987) argued that stereotypical images of women have had a profound influence on the discussion of women's crime. These are used to explain both the lack of criminal behaviour and the nature and extent of their criminality; they are also used to account for both victims in the criminal justice system. Critically examining the manner in which these attitudes and conceptions of women's social roles affect their position within the criminal justice system, the author highlighted the special problems women experience there. Naffine's study (1987) is a feminist re-examination of the existing research producing a different interpretation of women, which recognizes her reason, purpose and her essential humanity. It examines critically the range of modern criminological theories in women from the late 1960s to mid 1980s. The main conclusions of the study draws the importance of the programme to create a new feminist criminology which recognizes the female offender as a reasoning purposeful subject.

Perhaps because of the absence of women in these major theories of crime, criminologists concerned with female criminality continue to develop new theories to explain female crime rates. Very few criminologists concentrated directly on female criminals during the long gap between Pollak and current theorists. During the 1950s and 1960s, explanations continued to concentrate on the background of the female criminal and her particularly "feminine" traits.

In India very few studies have been conducted and thus have very scarce relevant literature. The attitudes towards women in the literature of early and contemporary studies were closely linked with basic assumption about the determinants of human behaviour. Rao (1981) has pointed out that the lack of sociological attention to the problems presented by female offenders in India is perhaps due to the observation that a smaller number of women come into contact with the law enforcing agents than do men. Singh (1980) pointed that the phenomenon of female crime gets complicated since female offences are considered more serious as compared to male offences and this difference is believed largely due to the sociological position which the women occupy in Indian society. The other reason why female criminals in India are under-represented and why there are few studies on them, both at juvenile and adults level, is considered due to cultural feature of crime in India, "women in an agrarian society are in a protected status with a little exposure to crime-provoking situations" (Sandhu, 1983).

Theories Related to Indian Context

The available theories in regard to women as offenders and victims of crime are both quantitatively poor and qualitatively deficient and hence competent studies on women and crime are still lacking. The lack of a purposeful and perspective analysis of the issues concerning women and their criminality in India can be realised by the constraints of empirical research in this area since women are less frequently remembered both as offenders and victims of crime (Shukla and Saxena, 1984).

In India, it was after Ram Ahuja undertook research in 1967-68 and published a book in 1969, 'Female Offenders In India', presenting a new theoretical paradigm on the causation of female crime, that newer studies gradually came to be undertaken in this field. Looking at the Indian scene, it can be seen that not many sociologists have been attracted towards criminological studies. According to Nagla (1982), exclusive sociological studies had given the descriptive account of statistical figures without discussing the nature and pattern of crime. Sharma (1965) studied female offenders in Uttar Pradesh and highlighted the social and psychological factors in female crime. In 1985, she also worked on murders committed by women. Rao (1967) and Ahuja (1969,1970, 1996) made attempts to study female criminality from the sociological point of view. Sohoni (1974), Bhanot and Mishra

(1978) and Singh (1981) furnished a statistical account of the nature, extent and pattern of female criminality. But little attention was paid to the psychological aspects and factors contributing to criminality of women (Mohan,1971; Singh,1973; Nirmal,1977; Yadav,1979; Mohan and Singh,1980; Sanyal,1975; Sharma,1987). From these research studies it can be seen that female offenders got the attention of scholars only since the late sixties and early seventies.

Shariff and Sekar (1982) studied the female inmates of Remand Home in Bangalore and pointed out defective family environment (pathological family patterns), faulty discipline by parents, broken homes, parental rejection, etc., as the causes of deviant behaviour. Mishra and Gautam (1982) too in their study have pointed out that female criminality is largely due to broken homes and the crisis of changing social values. Sanyal and Agarwal (1982) studied female convicts and found that criminals had a feeling of insecurity and a feeling of low self-esteem.

Ahuja's study (1969, 1970, 1996) conducted in Rajasthan, Madhya Pradesh and Punjab analysed the nature and magnitude of crime among women and explored the causes of the crime and developed the "Social Bond Theory" to explain the etiology of female criminality. He holds that woman's criminality can be theorized in terms of "contradictory or ill-defined roles in the family". Role Collision (in which husband and wife, or daughter-in-law and parents-in-law, etc., have roles which are in conflict in some respect), role incompatibility (in which the woman plays the roles which have contradictory expectations) and role confusion (in which there is lack of agreement among family members about the expectations of a given role) - all these create a situation for a woman which compels her to indulge in deviant acts. The causal factor for female crime is "family maladjustment" and the pattern of family relationships. By analysing the structural problems of family organization and through studying the types of functional problems in women's families of procreation, the crimes committed by women are examined in terms of "maladjustment in interpersonal relationship within the family".

Figure 1.1

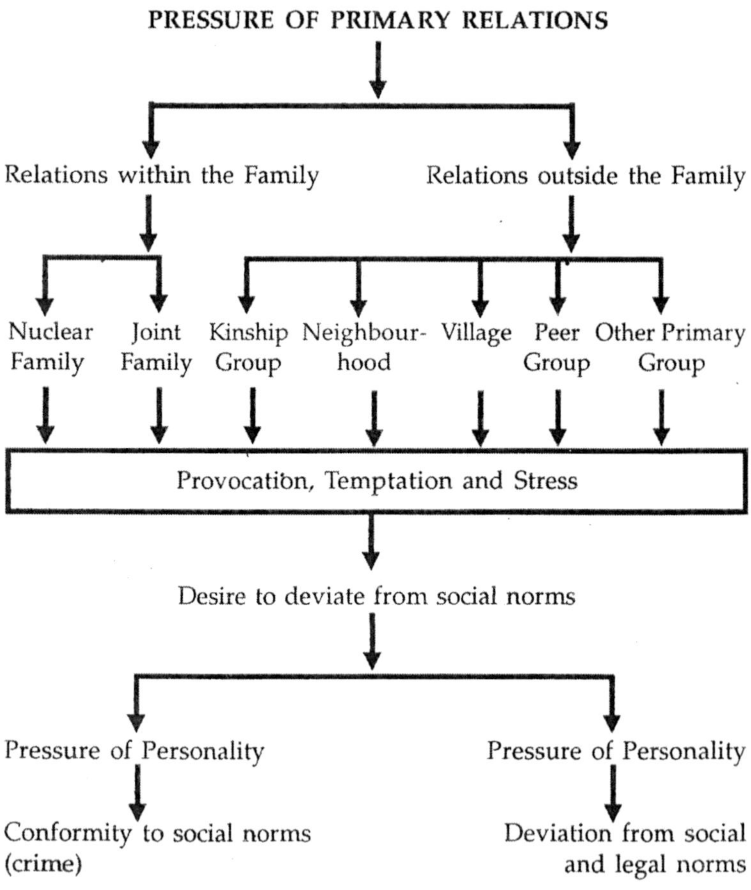

The above diagram shows that factors endogenous or exogenous to family create provocation, temptation, strains and stresses in a woman's life. These provocations or stresses produce a desire or a need to deviate from social and/or legal norms. The personality structure or the socio-psychological characteristics like temperament, attitudes, frustrations, deprivations or dominant underlying needs prevent some women from this deviation but fail to do so in other cases. Thus both personality system and the pressure of environment in which a woman functions contribute to a woman's criminality.

This theoretical model focuses on "strength of character", "role conflict" (role collision, role incompatibility, role confusion), "opportunity" and "totality of situation" in the family. The totality of situation includes the varied situations in the family taken together. Suppose a woman fails to get her husband's love and affection (Situation S_1) and in-laws' care and support (Situation S_2) and has illicit relations with a person (Situation S_3), it will be the totality of the three situations together ($S_1 + S_2 + S_3$) that will lead her to criminality (example, husband's murder). Further, her personality characteristics will determine whether she will really commit murder (one type of behaviour) or suicide (other type of behaviour) or elope (third type of behaviour) or continue to live in the family (fourth type of behaviour).

Thus, woman's "crime" (husband's murder will be the outcome of interaction between her personality system and the totality of the situations in her family. It (crime) will develop in (interaction) process over time through a series of stages. In this process (spread over time), "criminal behaviour" will emerge not because of the past alone but because of the current situation and triggering or precipitating circumstances too. In simplified form, this conjunctive theoretical model in women's criminality accounts for the differences in women's families and other institutional structures as well as in their personalities.

According to Paramguru (1984), women like men, are also motivated by the same fears, inhibitions, jealousies which wrap the human mind. Poverty, marital maladjustment, illiteracy, broken families, emotional tensions, imbalances in sex matters, social disorganizations commonly lead women to crime. Adwani (1978) stressed that in the case of female criminals, the etiology of crime is mainly due to the immaturity to perform the marital roles and the inability to shoulder divergent role expectations which consequently lead them to be maltreated by their husbands and in-laws. These situations ultimately create serious problems of adjustment, motivate them toward various types of criminal behaviour. The husband's bad habits of drinking. gambling, drug addiction, husband's nature being argumentative, suspicious, bad tempered, aggressive, greedy, his illicit affairs with other women, low income and excessive expenditure, a forced marriage, etc., are the major areas of conflicts faced by women murderers in Tamil Nadu (Prasad, 1982).

Rani (1983), in her analysis of "homicides by females" concludes that domestic factors including the deprivation of love and care of their parents or husbands and in-laws or a combination of both, victim's provocation and lover's friend's instigation contribute substantially to homicides by females. Thus unhealthy marital and family relations lead to family maladjustment and becomes a primary significance in the causations of crime by women.

Focusing on female murderers in the Central Jail, Jabalpur, Trivedi and Krishna (1983) found, among specific reasons, marital maladjustment and domestic quarrel, as the main motives behind homicides. Devasia and Devasia (1984) found in their study that family plays an important factor in female homicide where disruption in marital relationships often leads to the killing of the husband by a married woman and vice versa. In a recent study by Sharma (1985), sudden provocation, clash involving two families, land disputes and intra-familial conflicts have been found to be the chief motives for mass murder by women.

Some of the researchers found frustration as a chief motivating factor in the creation of aggressive behaviour in murderers. It is observed in backward and low socio-economic status groups, marital violence is more prevalent, since the people of this class face more deprivations throughout their life and hence are more frustrating. In these lower class groups, often women become the victims of aggressive behaviour resulting from frustrating situations. They are frequently abused, beaten up and thrown out of their houses. After such beatings, when the woman loses patience and tolerance, she resorts to violence which may be directed towards herself resulting in suicide or towards the cause of frustrations, resulting in homicide (Mohammed, 1984).

Most of the studies (Ahuja,1969, 1970; Sanyal,1974; Rani,1983) found that the large number of crimes committed by these women are due to their maladjustments in the families of procreation. Thus it needs to analyse how the adjustment process gets affected to cause criminality and the relationship pattern between different members of the family. There is also a need to probe on various social pressures and forces operating on women and contributing to crime.

To understand the etiology of crime, various approaches like biological, psychological, economical and sociological approaches have been made. Macro and micro level studies have attributed to social, cultural, economic and psychological variables to understand the etiology of female criminality. During the last two decades, due to a greater participation in the criminal activities by women, there is a greater need to study women criminals as the place and role of woman in the Indian society has also undergone changes. Since the research on women offènders because of its fragmentary nature, scope and coverage, is still lacking in academic expression, the present study identifies, examines and explains women's criminality in the socio-cultural, economic and psychological context to understand the life-style of women criminals.

2

Research Methodology

The historical development of research approaches toward the etiology of female crimes and the characteristics of female offenders is traced through the correctional literature of the last century. Until recently, the issue of female deviance was neglected by the mass media and serious academic study. The system of criminal justice, predominantly a male one, gave more emphasis to male deviance. But the increasing crime rate among women in recent years has drawn the attention of sociologists, criminologists and others.

The vast bulk of criminological research has concerned itself with male offenders and male correctional institutions or treatment programmes with male participants. These studies based on male populations are of untested validity for women. The Bedford Hills Reformatory for women in New York engaged its own psychologist in 1910 and opened a Laboratory of Social Hygiene for the purpose of research in 1912. A Massachusetts reformatory for women established a research department at about the same time. But most of these early pioneering efforts at research were short-lived due to insufficient financial support and official apathy. Research after that took its samples from male institutions, and female populations were neglected.

Background of the Problem

The correctional field has ignored women in prison. The needs of the small number of female inmates are low on the correctional priority scale. Information on women's prisons and the women incarcerated within them has not been available until recently.

Thus, this study attempts to study the life style of women criminals. Women criminals form a special group of criminals, whose population in prison is increasing year by year. In India statistical reports on crime have always revealed men involved in greater offences than women, who are considered to be more religious minded and less prone to unethical and immoral activities than their male counterparts. Today, however, with the upsurge of women offenders in the country the former notion is proved wrong. Women like men suffer from jealousy, enmity and hatred, which motivate them for criminality. In short, the present study is concerned with an examination of the socio-cultural, economic and psychological dynamics of female criminality.

Even after the fiftieth year of national independence, women coming in conflict with law, as compared to their male counterparts, continue to suffer a severe handicap in their passage through the criminal justice system. Due to their marginalization in the sharing of socio-cultural and economic opportunities for growth and development, they are rendered vulnerable to various kinds of abuse and exploitation and finally enter into a criminogenic life style. Once a woman is accused of or held guilty of committing an offence, the societal reaction is generally much sharper than that against the male in a similar situation. Thus, an attempt has also been made to study the correctional environment and the adjustment of women criminals in the prison system.

Criminality among women has important consequences on the social structure and thus they cannot be neglected. Crimes and the resulting imprisonment deprive not only the offender herself but also those related to her husband, children and in-laws. When an inmate enters the prison, she undergoes a transition from liberty to rigidly restricted movement and confinement. Social interaction with the outside non-criminal community is limited. This results in complete segregation which may tend to degenerate human values. The inmates tend to relate themselves to the inmate community and in the process internalize the culture of the prisons.

In recent years, several studies have been done in India and abroad on these deprived groups of anti-social personalities. However, no studies on the life style of women criminals have been done in India. Thus, keeping this in mind, the main thrust here is on studying the life style of the women criminals, who are convicted under different terms, those who are detained under PASA and those who are in custody as undertrials in the Central Jails of Baroda and Ahmedabad. The relationship with various socio-economic background variables and other important variables like motive, the nature and place of crime, the reasons for arrest and temperaments, moral values, life styles traits, family environment, institutional environment, guilt feelings and various causes for crime have been studied.

Significance of the Study

During last few decades much attention has been devoted to women criminals and the pattern of life led by them before and during imprisonment. In India a few studies have been conducted, but they are mostly of the sociological type. Probably, the present study may be the first attempt to study the life style of women criminals done on the prison population, particularly on the female criminals of this country from a social work perspective. As a social worker, a need was felt for exploration and assessment for holistic social work intervention. The experience as a practitioner and social work educator for more than twelve years made the researcher interested to study the women prisoners. The knowledge, skills and attitudes help the professional social worker to deal more effectively with the offender, that is, for the reformation and rehabilitation of the offender. In correctional settings the social worker provides a safe emotional climate in which offenders can express and verbalize them. The social worker also assists the offender in modifying his or her environment. With his knowledge of community resources, the social worker is also able to help the offender and his family to tap the different kinds of financial and social resources to meet their needs. The social worker also provides the needed information to the offenders in correctional settings. Another important function of the correctional social worker is reorganizing the behaviour patterns of the offender.

Thus, social work has an important role to play in the control, correction and prevention of crime. It attempts to help the individual, his family and the community to face and solve crime through utilization of the individual, family and community resources. Case work, group work and community organization are the basic processes utilised by the social worker in correctional settings. The social worker helps particularly with police departments, courts, probation, institutions, parole and prevention. Therefore, professional social work in correctional settings is a comprehensive constructive social attitude - therapeutic in some instances, restraining in some other instances and preventive in its total social impact.

The present study may prove significant from this view-point as it has attempted to study in a scientific manner the family environment, correctional institutional environment, life style, temperament of the criminals, guilt feelings, moral values and causes of crime.

This research work studies the relationship between various social, cultural factors and criminal behaviour associated with criminality, analyses the nature and pattern of women's crime and identifies various causes in social and environmental surroundings and various situations to which criminal behaviour responds. The whole gamut of criminal process beginning with arrests, passing through conviction and incarceration and ending in release and re-adjustment with the society involves a number of deprivations. The present study examines some of the deprivations and problems faced by women who were imprisoned and their perceptions in regard to imprisonment. The study also involves the basic assumption that every prisoner in prison will be influenced by the social and physical surroundings of the jail and that influence will be mediated through her expressed attitudes, behaviour and perceptions. The present study therefore examines the women criminal's attitude towards prison system, prison staff and prison culture, which is a sub-culture in the prison, as the conception of distinct groups is accompanied by the conception of sub-cultures and having a specific life style to live with.

Objectives

- To analyse the personal and social antecedents of women criminals in terms of their age, marital status, rural - urban, education, occupation, income, marital history, family life, etc.
- To examine the nature and pattern of crime and the causes of criminality amongst women.
- To study the moral values and feeling of guilt amongst women criminals.
- To examine the temperaments of women criminals.
- To study the relationship between family environment and criminal tendency amongst women.
- To analyse the attitudes of women criminals towards their stay in prison and to assess the perception of women criminals towards correctional institutional environment.
- To study the life style of women criminals.

Research Design

The present research is a field study of exploratory type, attempting to explore the life style of women, who are convicted or detained or in custody in the two Central Jails of Baroda and Ahmedabad in Gujarat. The research has also made an attempt to study the relationships of various important variables in detail. A comprehensive and bi-variete assessment of women having a common background, that is prison culture, helped in designing interventive strategies for reformatory and correctional goals.

Universe and Sample

Keeping in view the objectives of the study, research attention has been focused on the two Central Prisons only. As Central Prisons have a sizable population of both long- and short-termers, therefore, the Central Prison was considered an appropriate locale to undertake the study. The sub-jails and district jails are usually small jails, located at the intermediate towns which provide an alternative arrangement for keeping the under-trials, before they are convicted and shifted to Central Jails. On the other hand, the population of the Central Prisons consist of almost all types and varieties with different terms of imprisonment. After consultation with the prison officials, it was found that in Gujarat convicted women criminals are imprisoned only in Baroda Central Jail. At the time of data collection, Ahmedabad Central Jail had only few undertrials and detained (PASA) criminals. Since it was important to study a reasonable number of prisoners, the researcher had to include undertrials and detained (PASA) criminals along with the convicted women criminals. While a sample has its conveniences, one has to be careful that a good sample must be adequate in size in order to be reliable (Young, 1977). At the same time, the sample must be representative of the universe for which one must have a reasonably good knowledge of the universe. In the present study, in both the jails the size of the convicted inmates was not large enough to permit any kind of sub-sampling. Moreover, there was a lot of heterogeneity of the kind of crimes that these criminals had committed and, therefore, it was difficult to give adequate presentation to all the various kinds of criminals either in drawing a simple random or a stratified random sample. Thus it was decided that rather than a sample, the entire Universe should be studied. Consequently, the present study has been conducted on the total population of women criminals, who were imprisoned, detained or kept under custody in the two Central Prisons of the State of Gujarat, which constituted the total Universe as well as the sample of the study.

The incorporated table represents the prisonwise distribution of the number of women criminals concerned.

Sr. No.	Prisons	Number of prisoners
1.	Baroda Central Jail	87
2.	Sabarmati Central Jail	15
		N = 102

Methods of Data Collection

Interviewing was the major method used for collecting the Data. The main tool for interviewing was a well structured schedule for women prisoners, observation guide and several standardized scales, which were administered to the respondents.

Thus the source of data collection were the women offenders who were interviewed thrice for completing all the aspects of the interview schedule. The investigator's remarks about each inmate, specific observations and Jail records were secondary sources of collecting information regarding each respondent.

Experiences of Data Collection

The establishment of rapport was the most essential part of data collection. In the beginning, the researcher discussed the areas of the study with the Inspector General of Police of Gujarat State and sought permission. After the permission was given, the researcher had a detailed discussion with the Superintendent, Deputy Superintendent and Lady Jailor. This helped in gaining co-operation from the prison staff. Initially the prisoners were reserved and cautious to give any reply, but the prison staff helped in removing the doubts of the inmates. The efforts of the researcher and the supporting words from the staff helped in establishing the rapport with the inmates. Thus the inmates became quite free and frank in giving responses to the researcher.

The researcher explained to the inmates that she was a university student and for the purpose of making a scientific study on the life of women prisoners, she would be taking their interviews. The lady Jailor and the researcher stressed on the fact that she was a student and had nothing to do with the administrative organisation. The inmates were also explained about the nature, purpose and aims of the study. Their co-operation was urged and was assured of the confidentiality of the study. In order to create interest among the inmates and to motivate them to give relevant answers, the researcher herself showed curiosity and interest in the respondents.

The researcher had also submitted a bio-data with her photograph and a copy of the permission letter to both the Central Jails of Baroda and Ahmedabad.

Pre-Testing

After the schedule was prepared, these were administered to a pre-test group of inmates. This was done in order to know the defects of the research design and make suitable modifications. Thus, after the pre-testing, a final version of the schedule was prepared and used for data collection.

Reference Period

With the permission of the Inspector General of Police (Prison) of Gujarat, the interviews were conducted during the period from November 1996 to April 1997.

Hypothesis

The hypotheses of this study are :

- Women criminals mostly come from illiterate, lower socio-economic background.
- Women criminals come from unhappy, broken homes.

- Motive behind women criminality is to overcome socio-economic condition.
- Pressure of environment is the principle cause of women criminality.
- Women criminals have low moral values.
- The inmates suffer from a feeling of guilt.
- The inmates' attitude towards authorities is hostile.
- Style of Life is conducive towards women criminality.
- The inmates have a negative attitude towards institutional program.
- The inmates with a longer stay are more adaptive towards institutional program than inmates with a shorter stay.

RESEARCH TOOLS

Research Tools are of prime importance for the adequacy and authenticity of data. A very thorough and extensive work has been done on the literature available and consultation from experts on exhaustive tools containing various scales on varied areas of women criminality was prepared and pretested. Before all the tools were finalised, their psychometric properties, limitations and strengths have been examined by experts, both in content of the problem under study and research methodology. These tools are presented below :

Interview Schedule

For the collection of information from the women prisoners, a schedule was prepared consisting of the following dimensions related to crime.

- Personal background of the female offenders-the respondents.
- Details of family background which included type and size of family, education, occupation and income of parents and husbands, childhood experiences and her later initiation into criminal behaviour, relationship before and after crime, nature of home conditions, etc.
- Details of marital life, which included social interaction

pattern in marital life, relationship between husband and wife and in-laws, respondents' experiences of marital life.

- Details regarding patterns of criminal behaviour of women criminals, nature of crime and motives behind crime commission, history of punishment, nature of punishment and status as a prisoner.
- Respondents' perceptions in regard to the experiences of imprisonment on them and their adjustment in the prison, their attitudes towards co-inmates, jail officer, guarding staff and Superintendent, use of leisure time and suggestion for reformation.
- Details regarding the etiology of the criminal behaviour of individual women criminals, based on sociological and psychological theories.
- Schedule prepared to determine the guilt feeling of the inmates.

Scales

Correctional Institutions Environment Scale

Designed by Dr. Rudolf H. Moos the scale is composed of nine subscales that measure the social climate of juvenile and adult correctional programs. The nine CIES subscales assess three underlying domains or sets of dimensions: Relationship dimensions, Personal Growth or Goal Orientation dimensions and System Maintenance dimensions. This scale has test-retest reliability of .94. This scale consists of nine subscales namely: Involvement, Support, Expressiveness, Autonomy, Practical Orientation, Personal Problem Orientation, Order and Organisation, Clarity and Staff Control, that is, three subscales in each dimension.

The Involvement, Support and Expressiveness sub-scales measure Relationship dimensions. These dimensions assess the extent to which residents become involved in the unit, how much residents support each other and are supported by staff and the amount of spontaneity in these relationships. The next three subscales, Autonomy, Practical Orientation and Personal Problem Orientation, assess Personal Growth or Goal Orientation dimensions. Each of these sub-scales taps an aspect of the unit's treatment orientation. Autonomy assesses the extent to which residents are encouraged to be independent and responsible for their own decisions. Practical Orientation and Personal Problem Orientation reflect two major treatment orientations currently used in correctional institutions. For example, some units emphasize academic and vocational training programs and practical preparation for the resident's release. Other units value personal problem orientation and seek to increase the resident's self-understanding. The last three sub-scales, Order and Organisation, Clarity and Staff Control measure, System Maintenance dimensions. These dimensions are all related to keeping the correctional unit or institution functioning in a well-organised, clear and coherent manner.

Family Environment Scale

It is one of ten Social Climate Scales designed by Dr. Rudolf H. Moos and Bernice S. Moos. The FES comprises ten sub-scales that measure the social environmental characteristics of all types of families. The ten FES Sub-scales assess three underlying domains or sets of dimensions: The Relationship dimensions (Cohesion, Expressiveness and Conflict), the Personal Growth dimensions (Independence, Achievement Orientation, Intellectual-Cultural Orientation and Active-Recreational Orientation and Moral Religious Orientation) and the System Maintenance dimensions (Organisation and Control). The test-retest reliabilities are all in an acceptable range, varying from a low of .68 for Independence to a high of .86 for Cohesion. Both CIES and FES Scales were translated into Gujrati from English. Then the reliability coefficients were tested by the test-retest method by administering the scale on 20 families with two weeks interval, which was 0.8.

Temperament Traits

Temperament refers to those dispositions that are closely linked to biological or physiological determinants and which consequently show relatively little modifiability with development. The role of heredity is naturally somewhat greater here than in the case of some other aspects of personality. For Allport (1937), temperament is a special subsection within the broader domain of personality. His definition follows as :

Temperament refers to the characteristic phenomena of an individual's emotional nature, including his susceptibility to emotional stimulation, his customary strength and speed of response, the quality of his prevailing mood and all peculiarities of fluctuation and intensity in mood, these phenomena being regarded as dependent upon constitutional make-up and therefore largely hereditary in origin.

In order to understand the important stable traits which describe how normal, well adjusted people differ from each other nine temperamental traits were used in this schedule for personality measurement. Some of the temperamental traits have been borrowed from Thurstone Temperament Schedule. It is designed to assess the traits which are relatively permanent for each person. In a relatively short questionnaire nine areas of temperament are appraised. They are Active, Impulsive, Dominant, Emotional, Sociable, Reflective, Nervous, Introvert/ Extrovert and Aggression. A five point rating scale is administered to assess the temperament of the inmates.

Life Style Traits

The concept of lifestyles tries to see a whole range of behaviour patterns, related to demands made by the social, political, economic and cultural situations. Thus, it creates a close link between the living conditions of an individual, his or her activities and socially formed strategies for coping with life. This scale has eight areas to understand the life style of women criminals. Life Style was assessed by Thorne's (1975) "The Life Style Analysis Scale"' Eight Traits were selected from Thorne's Life Style Scale to test the Life Style behaviour of women criminals. Researcher prepared the statements for each area based on the suitability of assessing the life style of women criminals. These are Individualistic, Exploitive, Explosive, Resistive, Domineering, Conforming, Escapist and Evasive. A five point rating scale is administered to assess this scale.

Moral Values

This scale was prepared by the researcher on a three point rating scale, having twelve statements for assessing the moral values of the inmates.

Data Analysis Plan

The entire data were precoded and statistically analysed with the help of a computer except two sets of schedule. Scales were scored as per the score key and presented in Tabular forms. Two sets of schedule were computed manually by the researcher and tables were prepared. Simple Frequency and Bi-variate tables with percentage analysis were prepared. The following statistical analyses were done :

- Percentage analysis.
- Mean, Standard deviation and chi-square.
- T - Test.
- ANOVA and LSD.

Operationalization of Concepts

Woman Criminal

A woman who has been found guilty of criminal behaviour, sentenced to imprisonment and convicted under Indian Penal Code. Women above sixteen years of age, confined in the prisons have been treated as women criminals.

Convicted Prisoner

'Convicted' is an accused who is adjudged guilty and sentenced by a Court of law.

Undertrial Prisoner

'Undertrial' is an accused who is detained in Jail during the pending of trial against him by the order of a Court or in the cases where bail is not granted.

Detenu

'Detenus' are the offenders detained in prison, under any law providing for preventive detention.

Guilt Feelings

In its normal expression, a feeling of remorse in proportion to actual violations of responsibility or ethical codes. Pathological guilt is a highly exaggerated reaction to real or fancied transgressions. In psychoanalysis, this type of guilt feeling is defined as a conflict between the ego and its moral authority, the super - ego. In most instances, guilt involves the loss of self esteem and a need to make amends.

Moral

Characterizing a person or group, whose conduct is ethical or proper.

Temperament

Temperament is one's reactive make-up, the spontaneous side of one's personality. It is a combination of characteristic dispositions arising from the emotions, appetites and moods.

Temperament Components

- ***Active***

  A person, who usually works and moves rapidly. He is restless when he has to be quiet. He likes to be "on the go" and tends to be in a hurry. He usually speaks, walks, writes, drives, works and eats fast even when they do not demand speed.

- ***Impulsive***

  A happy-go-lucky, dare devil, carefree, acting on the spur-of-the moment type of person. The person makes decisions quickly, enjoys competition and changes easily from one task to another.

- ***Dominant***

  These persons think of themselves as leaders, capable of taking initiative and responsibility. They are domineering and likes to take charge of a situation.

- ***Emotional***

  The experience of subjective feelings, which have a positive or negative value for the individual. Most current theories regard emotions as a combination of physiological response with a cognitive evaluation of the situation.

- ***Sociable***

  These persons enjoy the company of others, make friends easily and are sympathetic, co-operative and agreeable with others.

- ***Reflective***

  He is meditative and reflective in thinking. Self-examination is his character. He is quite, works alone and enjoys work that requires accuracy.

- ***Nervous***

  A state of restless tension and emotionality with a tendency to tremble and feel apprehensive.

- ***Introvert/ Extrovert***

  Characteristics of individual psychological differences, whose extreme poles correspond to a personality's dominant orientation either towards the world of external objects or towards one's own subjective world.

- ***Aggression***

  Injurious and destructive behaviour. Aggression might be viewed as a motivational state, a personality characteristic, a response to frustration, an inherent drive or the fulfilling of a socially learned role requirement.

Life Style

The general behaviour pattern of an individual as expressed by his motives, his manner of coping, attitudes and other factors. In many cases the life style characteristics of a person are so well defined that his reaction to certain situations are fairly predictable.

Life Style Traits

- ***Individualistic***

  Refers to a type of person, who neither co-operates nor competes with others.

- ***Exploitive***

  Refers to a character pattern marked by the use of stealth, deceit, power or violence to obtain what one wants.

- ***Explosive***

  A personality with a pattern of frequent outbursts of uncontrolled anger and hostility, out of proportion to any provocation.

- ***Resistive***

  A person who opposes strongly and refrains from accepting something.

- ***Domineering***

  A person having a commanding influence over others and making others obey him.

- ***Conforming***

  A person's tendency to change his behaviour under the influence of other people so that it would correspond to the opinion of one's associates, a striving to adapt it to their demands.

- ***Escapist***

  Any behaviour directed towards escape of the subject from a painful or otherwise unpleasant situation.

- ***Evasive***

  A person who tries to evade from answering or excusing. Not frank in his communication.

Family Environment

In this, three underlying domains or sets of dimensions were assessed like Relationship Dimensions, Personal Growth Dimensions and System Maintenance Dimensions.

1. Relationship Dimensions

- ***Cohesion***

  The degree of commitment, help and support family members provide for one another.

- ***Expressiveness***

  The extent to which family members are encouraged to act openly and to express their feelings directly.

- ***Conflict***

  The amount of openly expressed anger, aggression and conflict among family members.

2. Personal Growth Dimensions

- ***Independence***

  The extent to which family members are assertive, are self-sufficient and make their own decision.

- ***Achievement orientation***

  The extent to which the activities (such as, school and work) are cast into an achievement-oriented or competitive framework.

- ***Intellectual-Cultural Orientation***

  The degree of interest in political, social, intellectual and cultural activities.

- ***Active-Recreational orientation***

  The extent of participation in social and recreational activities.

- ***Moral Religious Emphasis***

  The degree of emphasis on ethical and religious issues and values.

3. System Maintenance Dimensions

- ***Organization***

  The degree of importance of clear organization and structure in planning family activities and responsibilities.

- ***Control***

  The extent to which set rules and procedures are used to run family life.

Correctional Institutions Environment

In CIE also three underlying domains or sets of dimensions were assessed like, Relationship dimensions, Personal Growth Dimensions and System Maintenance Dimensions.

1. Relationship Dimensions

- ***Involvement***

  How active residents are in the day-to-day functioning of the program.

- ***Support***

  The extent to which residents are encouraged to help and support other residents, how supportive the staff is toward residents.

- ***Expressiveness***

  How much the program encourages the open expression of feelings by residents and staff.

2. Personal Growth Dimensions

- ***Autonomy***

  The extent to which residents are encouraged to take initiative in planning activities and to take leadership in the unit.

- ***Practical Orientation***

  The degree to which residents learn practical skills and are prepared for release from the program.

- ***Personal Problem Orientation***

  The extent to which residents are encouraged to understand their personal problems and feelings.

3. System Maintenance Dimensions

- ***Order and Organization***

  How important order and organization are in the program.

- ***Clarity***

  The extent to which residents know what to expect in the day-to-day routine of the program and the explicitness of program rules and procedures.

- ***Staff Control***

  The degree to which the staff use measures to keep residents under necessary controls.

Significant Features of the Study

- This study is exploratory and descriptive and it highlights certain unexplored areas of women criminals of India.
- These undiscovered areas will help in designing intervention both for developmental and correctional goals.

- The most prominent feature is that two inventories which are clinically and cross culturally standardized were administered on Indian prison population which brought out significant results and confirms its reliability and relevance in the Indian context.
- Sample was drawn from three categories of women criminals. Each one of them had some circumstances and motivating factors under which the crime was committed.
- These findings may facilitate in understanding the life style of women criminals, especially the psycho-social, economic and socio-cultural dynamics of female crime.

Limitations of the study

- As the study has been conducted in Gujarat, thus the situation or motive for crime may not be the same in other States of the country.
- Time period was limited and thus data was collected within limited time and period.
- A little over 50% of women criminals are convicted criminals, but in order to reach a fair looking sample, Detunus and Undertrials were also included.
- There are only two Central Jails in Gujarat. Out of these two, only Baroda Jail has the facilities to keep convicted women criminals. Other jails in the State including Ahmedabad keep only Detunus or Undertrial women criminals. Thus, researcher could not get a bigger sample of convicted woman criminals for study.
- As a judicial enquiry was going on in one of the Central Jails, the researcher had to wait for a long period for getting permission for collecting data. After a long process and with certain conditions the researcher was allowed to go inside the women cell and collect data. The interviews were taken in the presence of a lady Jailor or a lady Havildar, which might have hindered in getting the right response.

Presentation of Report

The report will be presented as per the following design:

- **Chapter I - Introduction**

  This chapter deals with introduction on women criminality and sex differences in crime, historical overview of women criminals and women criminals in India. It also presents an evaluation of the various conceptual frameworks and theories on women criminals. It gives the significance of the study and its relevance in social work education and practice.

- **Chapter II - Research Methodology**

  This chapter gives a detailed account of Research design, objectives, hypothesis, sampling and tools of data collection. It also talks about the "Research Process", which the researcher has undergone.

- **Chapter III - Review of Literature**

  This chapter presents an extensive review of the studies conducted on women criminality both in India and abroad.

- **Chapter IV - Research Setting**

  It is based on the research setting and emphasizes the historical background of the Indian prison system, the prison set-up, procedural aspect, living conditions, work programme for women prisoners in Central Jails of Baroda and Ahmedabad. It will also highlight the recommendations of the National Commission for Women and National Expert Committee on women prisoners.

- **Chapter V - Profile of Women Criminals**

  The chapter highlights the socio-cultural and economic background of the women criminals. It discusses the realities of the offender's social life, social background and personal qualities such as age, caste, education, religion, occupation, family life, marital status, personal abuses encountered, causes of crime and nature, pattern and motive of crime.

- **Chapter VI - Data Analysis**

  This is based on the interpretation of data, which has sections as given in the following :

- Socio-economic background.
- Patterns of crime.
- History of imprisonment.
- Guilt feelings.
- Moral values.
- Temperament.
- Life style of women criminals.
- Family environment.
- Correctional institutions environment.

- **Chapter VII - Case Studies**

  This chapter deals with the case studies, which had been undertaken during the course of data collection.

- **Chapter VIII - Discussion and Suggestions**

  This chapter discusses at length the findings of the study and, based on this, suggestions are given. Based on the relevant conclusions, an interventive Plan for Action has also been given in this chapter.

3

REVIEW OF LITERATURE

Sociologists, psychologists and criminologists have concentrated their professional research studies on the male criminal for many years. The reasons may be because female criminals are simply less numerous than their male counterparts. Women's crime is assumed to be less serious than criminality among men and the preponderance of male theorists in the field. Since most social scientists are male, it is not surprising that they have usually studied other males. Moreover, what little work has been done suffers from bias and stereotypes about women. The studies came a long way from unscientific studies to scientific studies and were presented through thesis, anti-thesis and synthesis.

Within the past decade professional interest in female criminality has greatly increased along with interest in the general topic of women. However, there has been a small group of writings specifically concerned with women and crime in India. They are mainly, Ahuja (1969, 1970, 1996), Bhanot and Mishra (1978), Sharma (1965), Shastri (1975), Sivanandam (1974), Sohani (1975), Singh (1981), Rani (1980, 1981, 1983), Nagla (1982), Rao, Prasad, Sanyal and Agarwal, Ramadevi, Mohan and Singh, et al (all in 1982), Trivedi and Krishna (1983) etc.

This chapter presents a review of the studies which were undertaken by researchers both in India and abroad on the multifarious aspects of women criminality. The chapter has been divided into various sections.

1. Nature and Extent of Women Criminality

Women criminality is socially viewed as more serious and is reportedly on the increase. In recent years in India a few studies have been conducted on female criminality in general, like the studies conducted by Ahuja (1969, 1970, 1996), Bhanot and Mishra (1978), Nagla (1982) etc. Some studies focussed murder in particular like in the studies of Singh (1981, 1983), Trivedi and Krishna (1983), Sharma (1985) etc. In the case of female, specific crimes like abortion, assault, infanticide, molestation, prostitution, rape, etc., are more than in general crimes like, theft, murder, cheating, etc.

Kawale (1982) in his study of female offenders found that the offences committed by women were pick-pocketing, dacoity with arms, theft and forcible theft. These offences were committed either singly or in combination with others. They belonged to such communities, where they operated equally with men to commit crimes mostly involving force and trickery. In committing crimes like sale of illicit liquor, gambling, prostitution and dacoity the women were helped actively by their men folk.

Regarding the place for committing crimes, Wolfgang (1958) observed that most of the homicides committed by women took place within the home and kitchen.

Rani (1983) also found that women committed murders either in the bed room, kitchen, or in the backyard of the house. The analysis reveals that while committing murders women concentrate mostly on persons who lived closer to them. This was supported by the review findings of Pollak (1950), Smith (1962), Smart (1976) and empirical findings of Wolfgang (1958), West (1965) and in India, Ahuja (1970) and Rani (1983).

As regards the nature of assistance given by the accomplices, it was found by Rani (1983) that the accomplices assisted women at different phases of the offence. The accomplices include both men and women. Rani also found that women adopt either the same method or various methods differently in taking away the life of their victims of any age group, whether the victim is physically stronger or weaker than the women criminals.

Pollak (1950) also found that many times women made use of their kinship associations and roles in putting away the life of victims.

Ghosh (1986) found that murder was the most violent offence for which 95.65% have been apprehended in Nari Bandi Niketan, Lucknow, than other offences.

Saxena (1994) found in her study that 89.5% of the respondents were convicted for offences like murder, attempt to murder, kidnapping, thefts, cheating, etc., and only a small percentage of the respondents 10.5% committed the non-victim offences. In 73.2% cases, the offenders used weapons such as axes, swords, etc., for murdering the victim. Four-fifths of the victims, that is, 86.2% were members of the respondents' family of procreation, which indicates that the family is much significant in the life of a woman. In her study she found that most of the women committed serious crimes and that too against the person. It was further found that 53.5% cases assumed the role of accomplices and 83.2% played the main culprit's role.

The official statistics of crime substantiate the comparatively low rates of feminine criminality or the trend of female participation in cognizable offences under the Indian Penal Code of 1995.

According to Rao (1982), low criminality among women can be ascribed to their physical inequality or to the general preferential treatment in the criminal justice system itself.

Nagla (1982) observed that, in the last decade the proportion of female arrests among total number of persons has increased rapidly. However, the compound annual rate of growth among female offenders is increasing at the rate of 10% as compared nine per cent increase male offenders. The crime pattern among women varies from place to place and time to time.

Ahuja (1996) made a study of 325 female offenders, which showed that 63% offenders were convicted for murder, 14% for theft. Five per cent for excise offences, four per cent for kidnapping, four per cent for vagrancy, three per cent for causing hurt, two per cent for immorality, one per cent for attempt to commit suicide and four per cent for other offences. In 77% cases, the victim was a member of the offender's family, in five per cent cases, had kinship relationship with the criminal, in nine per cent cases, the victim was her neighbour, in eight per cent cases, or was a member of her village community and in less than one per cent cases, was a complete stranger. This shows that in 99% cases, the female offender had primary relationship with the victim. Of the 77% cases in which the victim was a member of the respondent's family of procreation and only in 7.8% cases, the victim was a member of the family of orientation, which shows that family life after marriage plays a very crucial role in women's criminality.

Nagla (1991) in his study conducted in Haryana found that the majority of the female offenders were convicted for murder, maximum crime incidence took place at the offender's or victim's house, that is, 68.66%, 33.33% offenders poured kerosene and set fire for the killing the victims, 37.03% females committed crime alone whereas 55.5% took help from others.

Ahuja (1996) also found that, 20.4% belonged to the frustrated type, 28.6% to the emotional type, 13.2% to the revengeful type, 27.5% to the accidental type and 10.3% to the misled type of women criminals.

Sharma (1993) in terms of nature of crime found 73% females were convicted for very serious crimes like murder (59%) and bride burning (14%), five per cent for drug trafficking, three per cent for dacoity and three per cent abatement to suicide.

The fact that the victim being usually a kin or a close associate of the offender in crimes of murder was also discovered by Bullock (1955) in his study of urban homicides in Texas, by Svalastoga (1956) in his study of 172 Danish cases and by Sutherland (1950) in his study of 324 murders by females. Wolfgang (1958), however, had found such relationships only in 23.13% cases in his study of 588 homicides in Philadelphia. In about four-fifths of the cases, husband-wife relationship proved quite an important factor in the causation of murder. This proves family maladjustment as the main cause of female criminality.

Rita Simon (1975) analysed various dimensions of female criminality like the extent and types of crimes committed and their treatment by the court and prison officials. However, she did not study the issue of etiology of female crime. According to her, the increase in female crime is due to the expanding occupational opportunities for women.

Pollak's study (1950) found that women would shoplift rather than commit armed robbery; they would use poison rather than use a weapon; they would kill a family member rather than a stranger. The woman, according to Pollak, was more likely to be the instigator than the actor; she was likely to be behind a male, urging and enticing him into criminal action. Pollak attributed this deceit to the biological and social factors. He did identify women as an oppressed class. He believed that women were trained from birth to hide such natural processes as menstruation, sexual desire and frustration.

Gluecks (1934) studied five hundred delinquent women in Massachusetts. The major problem involved in the criminality and delinquency of women and girls were their lack of control of their sexual impulses. More than 80% of these women committed acts of sexual or personal immorality and only 12.4% committed anti-social, illegal acts that did not involve sex or immorality, 68% had venereal disease before they were twenty one, 42% had the habit of drinking, 54% had illegitimate pregnancies, 68% had eight years or less of schooling and 72% were of dull intelligence.

2. Social Background of Women Criminals

The demographic and socio-economic variables in relation to the women prisoners have been analyzed by many researchers to identify whether there is a profile, in terms of social background or demographic and socio-economic status, that can be typically associated with this group of women criminals.

Ahuja (1969), Kawale (1982), Rani (1983), etc., found that women criminals were in the age group of 20 to 40 years. Therefore, this is the problem of young women. Mostly they were married and mentally immature to cope up with the expectations of their husbands and in-laws. This results in maladjustments between them and their family members and sometimes force them to indulge in deviant behaviour. Ahuja (1969) observed that the incidence of crime was low in low castes, while Rani (1983) found that slightly more than 50% women criminals belonged to the backward castes. However, it revealed that the incidence of crime is high in low economic classes (Ahuja, 1969) and higher in low social and economic class (Kawale, 1982). Rani (1983) found that more than 50% female criminals were dependent, whose household members' income was Rs.100 to Rs.150, while the other less than 50% independent earners, earned an income below Rs.100 per month. Prasad (1982) found that more than 90% female offenders came from Rs.50 to Rs.200 income group (low income). Thus a majority of the households were living with great difficulty on their meagre incomes. Most of the studies (Ahuja, 1969 ; Rani, 1983 etc.) revealed that urban areas provide more female offenders than rural areas. Prasad (1982) pointed that illiterate women tend to commit crime. This was supported in the studies of Ahuja (1969), as he found in his study, 79% female criminals were illiterate. His study also showed that 76% offenders were married. The five variables which he used in his study, that is, Marital status, Age, Income,

Education and Residence found in analysing that the role of family maladjustment is caused by early marriage, poverty and illiteracy in women's crime. His study pointed out that 85.7% offenders belonged to the families whose monthly income was less than Rs.300.

Misra and Gautam (1982) revealed that the female criminality increased as the level of education decreased and vice versa. Thus it may be said that women criminals are generally younger in age, married, illiterate and also come from low economic classes. This reflects women's nature (adjustment), need (economic and social condition) and situation (environmental) for the explanation of crime and criminality.

Ghosh (1986) found that 34.9% of inmates lie in the age range of 31 to 40 years, while 30.4% of criminals fall in the age group of 21 to 30 years, 17.4% of convicts are in the age group of 41 to 50 years and 13% that of 51 to 60 years. Regarding marital status, it showed that 97.1% are married. The majority, that is, 76.81% belonged to the backward and scheduled caste. She found crime rate is higher in rural areas than in urban areas, which is in contrast to the studies of Ahuja (1969), Rani (1983) and others.

Sohoni (1989) from her sample of 120 women criminals found that 60% of the sample came from the age group of 22 to 41 years, while those below 22 years and above 41 years accounted for 20% each; 93.33% were married and the sample include more persons of depressed or backward caste. The association of crime with urban living was also found.

Mathew (1992) in her study conducted in Kerala found that the majority of the women criminals were married. But among the women caught for immoral activities, as high as 60.71% were living as separated, 55% were deserted women among the offenders, who have to suffer the malady of quarrels among parents. The majority of the women (50.95%) reported that they are coming from urban areas, 85.71% are from lower income group, that is, less than Rs.1000/- per month. The majority of the offenders (51.42%) belong to Hindu backward community. The majority of the women, that is, 56.36% charged for theft belong to the Hindu backward community. In terms of level of education, the majority of the offenders, that is, 52.14% are found to have only primary education.

Nagla [1991] revealed that 60% female offenders belong to the age-group of 30 to 50 years. The study showed that a large number of female offenders are young and adult at the time of committing crimes, which means that the interpersonal relations in the family after marriage create adjustment problems for women and sometimes force them to indulge in deviant behaviour. Most of the female criminals, that is, 62.96% were married, 3.72% were divorced and 33.32% were widows who had frustration in their life because of family problems, 70.36% were from rural areas, that is, female crime in Haryana is a rural phenomenon, whereas Rani (1981) in her study in Andhra Pradesh views that urban centres produce a greater number of female offenders than those of rural areas. A high proportion, that is, 22.22% belonged to the Hindu Scheduled Castes and 11.11% belonged to the Backward Castes. Regarding the educational background of the convicts, a large number of female criminals, that is, 88.88% were illiterate and 51.88% were engaged in agriculture. The study also pointed that 51.85% offenders had Rs.400 as monthly income of the family.

Sharma (1993) studied 36 female offenders in Tihar Jail, Delhi and Borstal Jail, Hissar (Haryana). Of these, 39% were below 25 years of age, 39% belonged to the age group of 26 to 43 years, 16% belonged to the age group of 44 to 53 years and 6% were of 53 and more years. Further, 78% were illiterate, 78% were married, 56% were from the rural areas and 83% had a monthly income of less than Rs.2000.

Nirmala Adwani (1978) found out that age appears to be closely related to the frequency and type of the crime committed by female prisoners at Central Jail, Jaipur. It revealed that the crime rate was highest during the young age, that is, among female prisoners it was highest in the age of 16 to 20 years, that is, in the age group in which they were comparatively less grown up physically. The highest rate of offenders (65.07%) was of married women and the lowest rate (0.73%) of crime was found to be among deserted and divorced persons. The highest number of crimes was in the lower income group of female offenders.

Saxena (1994) found that nearly half of the offenders, that is, 49.0% belonged to middle age group of 31 to 50 years. The age pattern further revealed that little more than one third of the offenders, 37.0% were in the younger age group of 16 to 30 years. It revealed that 72.5% were married, 60.05 participated in different economic activities, 79.5% were illiterate and 65.5% belonged to the rural areas. A very high percentage of women offenders belonged to the economically lower class.

In a study conducted by Manuel Lopez-Rey (1970) among female offenders in England and Wales, it was found that for females, the greatest contribution to crime is made by the 21-30 age group followed by the 14-17 age group in the Magistrate's Courts and the 17-21 age group in the Sessions Courts.

West (1963) observed from the study conducted among habitual prisoners that there was an association between family background and age at the onset of crime. The worse the home background, the earlier the onset of crime.

In 1970, Gibbons observed from a study on delinquents, on official cases of female law-breaking that the girls are frequently from lower income backgrounds and situations of social inadequacy.

Bingham's (1923) intensive study of 500 cases on the determinants of sex delinquency in adolescent girls found that, in 19% of 300 girls, sex delinquents had one or more delinquent sibs. Parallel findings have been made by Beane (1931), Lumpkin (1931), Bagot Epps (1941), Merrill (1947), the Gluecks (1930, 1950), Epps (1951) and Ferguson (1952).

John Cowie and followers (1968) observed from their study conducted among Magdalen girls found that these girls suffered educational deprivation, their families tended to be unduly large, the home was more often than not 'broken' and delinquency was common in the sibship.

Watterberg and Saunders (1954) found a high proportion of broken homes among female than male juvenile offenders, 56% of the boys but only 41% of the girls came from intact families. Defects of interpersonal relations, especially conflicts within the family, play a larger role in the causing of delinquency in girls than boys.

Elizabeth Windschuttle (1981) found that women who live in restrictive, more anonymous urban environments, who are more independent of the male protectors but more dependent on the labour market and thus more subject to the vagaries of the industrial economy, are more likely to turn to crime. According to her finding, women's crime was greater in the urban areas than rural areas. Women's crime also accounted for a much higher proportion of the total crime in the city than in the countryside.

Weinberg (1973) studied 67 institutionalized female delinquents, 107 institutionalized male delinquents and 74 non-delinquent female school children (all between 11 and 16 years of age) in Accra, Ghana. Half the parents of the female delinquents were divorced or separated, compared with 29% of the female non-delinquents and 34% of the male delinquents.

3. Factors Leading to Women Criminality

Various studies conducted on women criminals throw some light on the different factors like biological, psychological, sociological and economic, which contribute to the criminal offences of the individual. Society tends to view the problems of female criminality with greater concern and anxiety. Crimes by women are supposed as more dysfunctional than the crimes by men, because the former will have greater disastrous consequences on the social structure than the latter. Crimes by women in India are a little studied phenomenon and the study of the causes and factors leading to women criminality is a question of vital criminological significance.

Misra and Gautam (1982) assume that the problem of female criminality originates from the rapid transformations of the society from past tradition to modernity. This process of transformation creates a changed new situation which is demanding on the individual for quick and proper adjustment. It calls for the reorientation and change of values in their day-to-day social interactions. The discrepancies between the cultural goals and the institutional means prescribed by the social structure fail to achieve it. The gap between the two creates frustration and aggression among the individuals in cultural situations which lead to the deviant behaviour. The contention strengthens the empirical findings of Rani (1983) and the theoretical interpretation of Cohen (1970) and Merton (1938).

Family Maladjustment

Prasad (1982) found in his study that all the female offenders were highly frustrated in their conjugal life and sexual relations.

Mathew (1992) found that uncongenial home background for the women and the influences of these when combined with broken marital bonds has paved the way for the offensive behaviour of the women.

Sohoni (1989) found that marital conflict was due to poverty, drunkenness and infidelity in the respondent herself or in her husband. In fact, when combined for the respondent and the spouses, both drunkenness and infidelity came out stronger than poverty as factors leading to marital conflict.

Ahuja's (1996) study of female offenders is a starting point for the discussion looking into situational and environmental variables compelling women to commit crime. Most of the crime committed by women are due to stressful family situation, marital mal-adjustment, disharmonious and often conflict-prone relationship with husband. It is clear that mal-adjustment in interpersonal relationships within the family is one of the most important causes of criminality amongst women. Ahuja's hypothesis of "family maladjustments" or "role conflict in family" was supported by Sharma, Rani Bilimoria, Mishra and Gautam, Eswar Shariff and Sekar, Sanyal and Agarwal and Neera Sohony.

Rani Bilimoria (1983) studied 120 female convicts in Andhra Pradesh and also supports the findings of Ahuja, by explaining crime in terms of unhealthy marital and family relations, and family maladjustment as the main cause of female crime. In her study, in more than 70% cases, domestic factors played an important role in disposing of women to entertain attitudes of victims, provocation, lover's/friends instigation played a major direct role in pulling out such criminal proneness.

Eswar Shariff and Sekar (1982) studied female inmates of Remand Home in Bangalore and pointed out defective family environment (pathological family patterns), faulty discipline by parents, broken homes, parental rejection, etc., as causes of deviant behaviour.

Broken Homes

Mishra and Gautam (1982) too in their study have pointed out that female criminality is largely due to broken homes and crisis of changing social values. Rani in her analysis of case histories showed that in 33 out of 35 cases, women were deprived of love of their parents, or husbands and in-laws, or a combination of both, adding to this an incessant ill treatment by the members of their family of procreation, their attitude to divorce or desert their husbands and various other unhappy incidents in their life had strengthened frustration leading to various deviant acts (like establishing illicit contacts with other persons) and aggressive acts (like committing murder) on their part.

Datesman and Scarpitti (1975) found in their studies that there is a relationship between female delinquency and broken homes. Wilkinson (1974) also concluded that the higher incidence of broken homes among female delinquents, irrespective of the types of offences, has shown their greater involvement in offences such as ungovernability, running away and promiscuity.

Family Influences

Mathew (1992) found that large families are found to be very much associated to the criminal tendencies. As 97.30% of offenders from very large families, in the sample experience uncongenial home atmosphere. Since the size of the family of women offenders increased the degree of uncongeniality also increased and this phenomenon influenced their women towards deviant life. In her study 90.91% of the women who committed theft has reported to be having uncongenial atmosphere at home. Thus the prevalence of high degree of uncongeniality at home is found to be one of the major channels of influences leading females to the commitment of crime. The majority (66.67%) of the offenders complained of poverty as the contributing factor to uncongeniality at home. The majority (62.04%) of the offenders from the above group has criminal relatives and 18.52% women have criminal career among the parents. A large part (69.81%) of the women admitted that it is their close relatives who co-operated with them to do the crime.

Sohoni (1989) revealed in her study that family size has little relevance to the type of offence. The findings also suggest that negative nurturing by parents was not overly experienced by any offence category in particular, although positive nurturing was more evident in murder and, to some extent, in theft than in miscellaneous crimes.

Mohon and Singh (1982) found that murderers often victimize friends, family members, close relatives or neighbours, under the peak of emotional stress to resolve conflict through extreme and uncontrollable aggression. Their criminal behaviour speaks of their mal-adjustment. The t-test results between the scores of male and females victimiser group revealed that females are significantly less adjusted both emotionally and in marital relations. In the sphere of home relations poorer adjustment trends of the female are observed also. In the Indian cultural set-up females tend to undergo a lot of stress specially in the post-marital period.

Prasad and Krishna (1982) have revealed that the major areas of their (female criminals) conflicts are :

- Husband having the habits like drinking, gambling, drug addiction.
- Lack of interest in the family and love.
- A forced marriage.
- Illegal connection with in-laws and others due to sexual incompatibility and husband's maladjustment.
- Jealousy due to husband's illegal connection with other women.
- Low income and excessive expenditure.
- Conflicts over sex.
- Sexual jealousy and jealousy over property.

Saxena (1994) found that 49.5% belonged to poor housing and living conditions. Over-crowding was prevalent in more than half of the families, giving tensions and conflicts, resulting in aggressive behaviour of women. A higher percentage of women (85.5%) had come from broken homes. It was also found that the presence of step-parents increased the possibility of women's involvement in aggressive behaviour, that is, 64.3%. As many as 46.5% felt that they were rejected by the parents and 26% felt that they were brought up under strict discipline, thus feeling rejection. A large number of offenders (40.3%) reported to have indifferent relations with siblings, while 17.7% experienced conflicting relationships with their siblings. The majority of the offenders experience the home environment as uncongenial and uncomfortable which included unhappy marital relations between parents, presence of frequent quarrels between parents and separation of parents either temporarily or permanently.

Relationships

Kathryn's (1973) research into the characteristics of women prisoners indicated that severe pathological problems were often present. In many cases, their lives have been based on rejection and exploitation by men and by inability to form lasting positive relationships.

An interesting experimental study was carried out by Ruth Morris (1964) on the relational problems among female delinquents. Since the life of the female is so much involved with personal relations, it was assumed that girls would be more likely than boys to suffer under relational problems. Three predictions were made: that delinquent girls would be, of all four groups, most likely to come from broken homes, to come from homes with many family tensions and to be at a disadvantage in personal attractiveness and grooming. Morris concluded that her results strongly support the view that girls are particularly susceptible to relational problems.

Peggy C Glordano's (1978) research on the social context in which females participate in delinquent acts shows that interaction with males, particularly in a non-romantic way, simply affords the most suitable environment in which girls will learn about, as well as actually engage in, delinquent acts.

Values

Singh, A.K.; Singh, S.K. and Singh, S.B. (1998), studied values among females convicted for different types of crimes committed in Bihar. They found that female criminals were fairly high in their value patterns. The female property criminals rated themselves desirably in terms of their value patterns, but on the whole, it revealed that criminals as a group possessed low social, economic, moral, religious value compared to the non-criminals.

4. Social Roles of Women

Studies of female criminality have so far ascribed the differential facets of anti - social behaviour in the two sexes to their "restrictive social roles", which have been institutionalized and perpetuated through continuance of the old myths of the fair sex's vulnerability, physical weakness and need for protection. The status of women in India has been laid down by ancient discriminatory laws, religious sanction and tradition. In Indian society, the lower social status and the underprivileged positions of women have certainly contributed to the liberal provisions relating to the arrest, bail and custody of female offenders. Even in sentencing, there is a greater degree of lenience. Although the existing criminal laws do not prohibit the imposition of capital punishment on women, in practice, no woman has been executed in the country since 1944, indicating that capital punishment has been virtually abolished in the case of women at least.

However, the female offender can be better understood on the basis of her social roles as has been determined by her constitutional differences, her psychological differences and her social position all of which are inter-related. A woman's role is of a home-maker dependent upon her husband. A married woman spends most of her life in devotion and service to her husband and family. Sometimes in order to get her wishes satisfied and to achieve her goals, out of frustration, a woman gets involved in crimes. Thus when women cannot control their anger, they give up their traditional role and express themselves by getting into criminality.

Nagla (1982) attributed to differences in the social roles ascribed to women and men by most cultures. The role of wife, lover or girl friend is important to a woman. Many female offenders engage in prostitution and property offences to earn money to support the drug habit or to get rid of debts of husband and lovers. When couples are involved in robberies, the woman is usually the girl friend or wife of the male robber. The criminal activity of women is influenced by the requirements of the men to whom they are emotionally attached. But today, the pattern of role behaviour is changing, so also the pattern of crime among women.

Ruth Hartley (1960) conducted a survey into the attitude of working women on their jobs and found that they perceived their work "as an extension of the nurturant, mothering role" and that 'they were working to improve the welfare of their families and this was seen as in concert with, rather than in conflict with, the wife-mother role'.

Davis and Olsen (1965) surveyed a group of college girls to ascertain their attitude to the female sex role. The results clearly indicated that the subjects took the conventional view. They considered the woman's primary role as being in the home, over 87% of the girls in the study ranking "home and family" as top priority.

Douvan and Adelson (1966) found in their attitudinal study of adolescents that girls listed marriage, home and family as their major long term aims.

Mabel Elliot (1952), a female criminologist, presented a review of theories on female crime, including sex role formulation to account for low rates of crime among women. She also discussed a number of socio-demographic characteristics of women offenders in the United States.

Case studies on female crime made by Jenkins (1949), Parker (1965), Franklin (1967), Edith de Rham (1969) and Sparrow (1970) accepted as facts Pollok's assumption that women commit many more crimes for which they are never arrested than do men and that the legitimate and traditional roles women perform in society provide excellent cover for the most devious types of crimes. In each of these case history studies, the woman as nurse, lover, companion, secretary or wife carefully and slowly poisons to death the person with whose life she has been entrusted. These studies strive to dramatize Pollak's basic assumption that women are no more endowed with morality and decency than are men, but the roles they perform in society assume goodness, charity and morality and it is those roles that serve as useful masks for hiding criminal activities, When a man commits a crime, it is more likely to be a public act than when a woman does.

These studies produced a consistent picture of women's perceptions of their sex role, the traditional view that their life should revolve around home-making and the pursuance of successful family relationships. These studies were, however, equally consistent in their failure to comment on the nature of the social conditioning necessary to produce such a homogeneous display of attitude.

5. Physiological Causes

Menstruation and Crime

Negative associations with menstruation and criminal behaviour have a long history. Singh (1980) concludes in the study that premenstruum is the most stressful period for women and about 53% of the sufferers committed their crimes at the time of these symptoms. The adverse effect of menstruation was greatest among sufferers of pre-menstrual tension which is defined as mood changes, headaches, tiredness and bloatedness during premenstruum. Premenstrual tension was present among 50% of the 95 prisoners. It was more common among those sentenced for offences of violence such as murder, attempt to murder, causing grievous hurt etc. The symptoms themselves may be responsible for certain crimes e.g. irritability and loss of temper may lead to violence and assault, lethargy may lead to child neglect and depression to suicide. Various other studies have highlighted the adverse effects of premenstrual tensions on women's behaviour.

Devi and Rao (1972) found 60% of the suicide were committed by women in the premenstruum.

Singh and Singh (1979) found that 61.6% murders were committed during the premenstrum. Thus Singh's (1982) study also fully co-relates these earlier things.

Nagla (1991) in his study found that 78.56% women committed crime who had irregular period of oestrus than those of regular (21.42%). Moreover, 62.94% female committed crime when they were in menopause, 14.8% each pre- and post-menstruation cycle and 74% were pregnant.

In the early studies Lombroso and Ferrero (1895) also linked menstruation to women's criminal behaviour. Cooke (1945) quotes the findings that 84% of violent crime by women in Paris was committed just before or during menstruation. Gibbens and Prince (1962) claimed that in their sample of shoplifters the offence usually took place just before menstruation. Marsh (1981) stated that 80% of all female crime occurs paramenstrually. Writers like Freud (1924) and Pollak (1961) attributed the underlying reason to revenge; menstruation was said to remind women of their inferior status.

Dalton (1961) presented data on a sample of female prisoners, 156 of those interviewed had committed their offences during the previous 28 days. Nearly half of all the crimes were committed by the women during menstruation or in the premenstruum. According to Dalton (1969), premenstrual tension often drives the women to war with the world, since it is also accompanied by irritability, lethargy, depression and water retention and these symptoms make women more ill-tempered, impatient, violent and emotionally deranged. These symptoms themselves may be responsible for certain crimes e.g. irritability and loss of temper may lead to violence and assault, lethargy may lead to child neglect and depression to suicide. Dalton also reported pre-menstrual tension to be the cause of habitual crimes.

Epps (1962) interviewed 200 women in Holloway prison soon after their admission. Fourteen per cent admitted to PMT (pre-menstrual tension) symptoms. These were feelings of irritability, depression or tension. Less than half of them had committed their offences during the paramenstruum.

Parlee (1982) studied a small sample of women and found that the women experienced increase in anxiety, irritability, depression and tension in the pre-menstrual phase.

Heredity

As regards excess of energy or physical development that may lead to delinquency, the same can be inherited. Though crime is not transmitted by heredity, certain peculiarities and characteristics that are constituent factors in the causation of crime can be inherited. An irritable temper is a vital factor in the causation of crime. Sethna (1980) in his study found that environmental conditions can make the child follow the same crime or crimes as her parent, which she learns by imitation.

Sethna (1980) also reports from his studies on offenders that ocular ailments, nose and throat obstructions, ear troubles, speech defects, enuresis, phimosis, physical irritations, headaches, excessive physical strength, menstrual disorders, ailments of adolescence and other physical ailments and under-nourishment are contributing to the condition of anti-social behaviour and crime among females in society.

Physical Characteristics and Female Offences

Mathew (1992) found in her studies that the female offenders (84.52%) are of normal appearance in bodily features. There are 14.05% of women offenders who are abnormal and a very few, i.e. 1.43% women are monstrous in appearance. Most of the prostitutes, i.e. 95.79% in the sample are of quite normal appearance. Among the offenders with abnormal appearance, the largest, i.e. 32.20% of them are found to have committed homicide, murder, infanticide, attempted suicide, murder, etc. About one-fourth, i.e. 27.27% of the thieves are of abnormal appearance. In the case of women with monstrous appearance, 66.66%, i.e. majority are found to commit homicide and murder. A major part, i.e. 83.33% of women charged for homicide, murder, infanticide, attempted suicide and murder are mentally handicapped. Among the women charged for theft, 66.67% are physically handicapped. Thus physical disabilities are found to be closely related to offensive behaviour among the females. This study reveals that women with unusual physical features are more prone to offensive behaviour.

Lombroso and Ferrero (1920) compared criminal women, found in prisons for women and the courts, to non criminal women. They recorded comparisons of physical features such as cranial capacities, facial anomalies, facial angles and brain weights. It was believed that criminal women could be categorized by their physical features. For instance, prostitutes were said to have heavy lower jaws, large nasal spines, simple cranial sutures, deep frontal sinuses and wormian bones. All criminal women could be identified by the higher percentage of physical abnormalities or atavistic qualities they possessed. Criminal women were believed to be deficient in moral sensibilities, to have unstable characters and to possess excessive vanity, irritability, desire for revenge and sexuality.

Dobash et al (1986) emphasized on the ugly and masculine characteristics of the female criminal. They described the criminal woman as "masculine, unsexed, ugly, abnormal women".

6. Psychological Causes

Sanyal and Agarwal (1982) studied a sample of 69 female convicts and found that about 75% criminals had a feeling of insecurity and 80% had a feeling of low self-esteem. Inmates with a longer length of stay in prisons have revealed lower self-esteem in comparison with those inmates with a shorter length of stay. High guilt feeling is evident in 30.43% of the inmates only. Negative self-esteem is found more in the convicts who belonged to low social and economic strata and class. It has been observed that the low self-esteem not only makes the convict self-critical and non-conformist, but also it creates unhealthy interpersonal behaviour.

Belle and Akran (1970) while studying the anti-social and pro-social offenders tried to study the guilt feeling in them. The findings revealed that the pro-social groups have a greater sense of guilt about anti-social activity than the anti-social group.

Paripurnanand Varma (1972) conducted a study on crime and delinquency and found that there are four factors which pre-dispose delinquent acting out :

a) Guilt, b) Lowered self esteem, c) Anger, d) Inability to establish meaningful mature personal relationships.

Ghosh (1986) in her study made an attempt to observe association between anxiety and insecurity among female convicts. She found out that of a population of 69, 73.91% inmates are highly insecure, while 26.09% suffer from less insecurity. On the other hand 92.75% have high anxiety in them and 7.25% in comparison have less anxiety. A relationship between insecurity and guilt was also studied, which revealed that, in the total population 30.43% are those categorized as suffering from high guilt and 69.57% of them are less guilty. Moreover, 73.91% in this population, are those who feel highly insecure and 26.09% experience less insecurity in them.

Mental Illness and Crime

Female offenders are, according to the statistics, less numerous than male offenders and so it is assumed that there must be "something" with them.

Goodman and Price (1967), Gibbens (1971), D'Orban (1971), Eysenck and Eysenck (1973), Worth (1981) pointed to high rates of psychiatric abnormality among women in prisons. Gibbens (1971) found in the 1967 Holloway Survey, that almost half of the women were suffering from some form of psychiatric disorder and that a quarter had previously been admitted to psychiatric hospitals.

Eysenck and Eysenck (1973) studied 264 female prisoners and found them to be characterized by high psychotism, high neurotism and high extraversion scores.

Turner and Tofler (1986) in a recent survey of psychiatric disorder among female prisoners at Holloway prison found that, from a random sample of 708 women, 18% had a history of psychiatric disturbance.

Singh (1986) compared 100 female delinquents with 100 female non-delinquents matched in term of socio-economic status, age and urban versus rural place of residence, he found that delinquents had higher scores on extraversion and neuroticism than did the non-delinquents.

Rehman and Hussain (1984) studying female criminals in Bangladesh, found them to have much higher psychotism and neuroticism scores than controls, those engaged in prostitution, fraud, kidnapping and possession of illegal arms also had high extraversion scores. Murderers were significantly introverted.

Sharma (1987) found that criminal women as compared to their counterparts were more reserved, emotionally unstable, had weaker super ego, tough minded, suspicious, apprehênsive, self-sufficient and less integrated.

7. Economic Causes

Financial difficulties have been one of the direct contributing causes for the acts of female crime. This factor is very common in a country like India, which hardly needs any detailed explanation. Financial factors give rise to different situations of stress and stress compelling the individuals to commit different types of deviant behaviour.

Mathew (1992) found in her study that the majority that is, 72.30% of the women offenders come from poor homes and have the problem of poverty at home. The analysis reveals that the intensity of poverty among female offenders is greater and this trend decreases with the increasing level of income of her sample.

Nagla (1991) in his study points out that, 15 female offenders were involved in financial matters. Of these 15 cases, 40% had disputes over agricultural land and related property and 40% had other financial matters, besides 20% had financial crisis for want of dowry.

Saxena (1994) found that due to poor economic condition, the family were under severe pressure to support the family. Hence, certain conditions and consequences of poverty such as economic insecurity, unemployment, under-nourishment, denial of basic necessities and lack of recreation motivated these women near to anti social behaviour. Her study showed that 79.3% were in the income group of below Rs.1000/-, which might have caused acute stresses and strains leading to anti-social behaviour.

Adler (1975) found that, where the economic disparity between men and women decreases, there has been a corresponding increase in rates of female criminality.

Klein (1973) in her study rejected economic causes as a possibility, denying its importance in criminal activity with as much certainty in close agreement to Lombroso, Freud, Davis, Pollak and most other writers.

Kellor (1900) found that many women criminals came from the ranks of domestic service; inadequate salaries spurred women to steal, as they were unskilled; they were unable to do anything else. Thus domestic service was an easy route to prostitution.

Pantazis and Gordon (1997) in their study explored the extent and nature of female criminality in a relatively minor offence in Great Britain television license evasion. By 1994, 64% of the prosecutions for these offences involved women. Data were obtained from agency records. The growth in poverty over the past two decades, women's domestic routines and the long term increase in female headed households account for the growing involvement of women in this offence. Poverty and financial hardship have forced more women, particularly single mothers, to break the law, because they are unable to afford the annual license fees. Recommended solutions are offered for alleviating the burden of these fees on poor households and decriminalizing sanctions.

Boritch (1997) explored the issues related to female crime and criminal justice in Canada. Women remain a small minority of those charged with criminal offences in Canada, although their numbers are increasing. The typical woman incarcerated in Canada is socially and economically disadvantaged, and is in custody for minor crimes. Imprisonment contributes to women's crimes by exacerbating their economic and social problems. Suggestions have been made to devote greater attention to redressing women's deprived economic and social conditions and re-evaluating laws that criminalize women.

Chesney-Lind (1997) found that the personal troubles experienced by girls create and facilitate their crimes, eliminate other choices and eventually result in crimes by women. These troubles include childhood victimization, as well as problems engendered by being raised in poverty. Thus the pathways into crime and violence are shaped by the experiences of the girls on the margin of impoverished communities. As adults, women have been disproportionately penalized by harsh sentences associated with the war on drugs, which has produced vast increases in the number of women in prison.

8. Social Causes

Various case histories reveal that the domestic causes include such as ill treatment by family members or lovers, unfaithful husband, unhappy marriage and unhappy family relations.

Nagla (1991) found that 40.7% respondents were compelled to take criminal acts because of their marital mal-adjustment and one was divorced who felt deserted all the time. Moreover, 29.6% female had illicit relations with other persons than their husbands whereas husbands of nine women criminals had illicit relations with other females. Thus breach of faith of both (husband-wife) to each other is also the main cause of offences. Furthermore, out of 16 offences which resulted from social causes other than domestic causes, 14.8% females committed offences due to instigation from intimate friends such as lovers, 11.11% due to dowry, 3.7% in self defence, 14.8% in fear of social contempt and 14.8% were provoked by the kinsmen. This shows that social causes are also important factors giving rise to criminal behaviour.

Punekar and Rao (1967) found in their study conducted among the prostitutes in Bombay, that the unscrupulous guardians or the superstitious mothers in the absence of the fathers, were perhaps responsible for the dedication of many of the girls towards offences.

Mathew (1992) found that a tempting situation, compulsion or persuasion by others, etc., are also significant to the problem of female offences. Chronic alcoholism of the family members diverted 68.75% towards deviant habits and consequently to punishments for theft. The majority of the offenders, that is, 60% in this study are unable to adjust themselves to their varying conditions due to troubled home environments. The neglect and indifferent behaviour of parents is another issue for many. Nearly 45.45% of the female offenders from very large families are found to experience neglect from parents and other family members.

Saxena (1994) found that women offenders had stressful relations with their husbands. Their marital life had undergone severe conflicting situations involving oppression, cruelty, rejection and humiliation. Husband's adultery, his illicit affairs with other women, immoral behaviour of husbands contributed significantly in motivating married women to resort to crimes of murderous violence. The majority of the women offenders convicted for homicidal activities, were poorly adjusted to the family settings.

Elliott and Voss (1974) found out from their researches that troubled parent-child relationships are more often reflected in female than in male delinquency, but that school factors are more directly linked than parental rejection to adolescent law violation.

Dae, H. Chang (1976) found out from his study on criminals, a cross-cultural perspective, that much crime and delinquency is derived from broken home, residence within disorganised areas such as slums, uneducated parents, hostility towards their children, unsuitable recreational facilities, undesirable play mates, poor educational systems, transiency and corrupt politicians dominating the community. He also found that inconsistent parental discipline as an influence of family on children has also been suggested as related to crime.

9. Correctional Institutions

The aim of the correctional institution is the restoration of the offender back to the law-abiding nature.

Mathew (1992) found in her study that 79.52% offenders admitted that their experience in the institutional life have influenced in their not retaining in the offensive career. Only one fifth, that is 20.48% of the whole women admitted that they are still retained in the offensive career. It was found that the younger women in the sample are more influenced by the correctional service towards improvement than older women. 99.44% of the unmarried women admitted that institutional life has corrected their criminal behaviour to a great extent. A very few women, that is, 9.76% complained that they suffered exploitations at the correctional institutions. Among these, physical torture and hard labour are the major complaints. Institutional authorities or officers are generally considerate towards the women offenders. The poor women in the sample thought that their personal problems are reduced after their incarceration. A good majority (77.14%) among the offenders do not support after care services as a means of improving their career after release. It was found that 89.17% of women aged 30 years and above are having this view. Among the women who do support after care services as good, 33.33% do not like to go back to their homes under the fear of either no admission to their homes or because they (17.17%) do not have any home at all. Regarding the nature of behaviour of women inside the institutions, 80% of authorities/officers admitted that female offenders behave well inside the institution. Only a very few (11.11%) of the authorities complained of uncontrollable behaviour of female offenders. The majority, that is, 86.36% of the officers admitted that female inmates behaved well. The majority, that is, 73.33% of the jail authorities opined that the institutional services rendered to the females are quite effective in the improvement of their career.

Ghosh (1986) found the majority of the female convicts have expressed a favourable attitude towards the convict officer, while the inmates have a negative attitude towards the warder. Convicts have a favourable attitude towards the authorities except for the warders whom they dislike. Convicts do perceive the society negatively, though a considerable number of inmates still perceive the members of the free community favourably. The convicts described the society to be bad and cruel, but at the same time, a group of convicts feel that there are members in this free community who are yet sympathetic to them and can forgive them for their offences. This group of convicts may see some chances of their rehabilitation in the free community once again, but the larger portion of the convicts believe that it would be extremely difficult for them to regain the former recognition from the free community once again. The maximum of the respondents' attitude towards education is highly favourable. A large proportion of the inmates believe it to be a good method to earn their livelihood. A majority of the inmates have given a favourable attitude towards the vocational skills, while the inmates have an ambivalent attitude towards the institutional programmes. A majority of the inmates possess a positive opinion about the jail environment, a large number of inmates also have a negative opinion about it. Very few inmates have expressed extremely favourable opinion towards the environment. Though the maximum number of respondents have given positive responses towards the recreational programme, yet a considerable number of the population have given their negative opinion towards the recreational programme. While studying the attitude of the inmates towards the fulfillment of their primary needs, that is, food, clothing, medical treatment, etc., it was found that the majority of the inmates have a positive response. Ghosh also found that the inmates with a longer confinement inside the prison need not have a positive attitude towards the institutional programme.

Sohoni (1989) found that prison life appeared to be harsh for 48% of the sample. While assessing prison life in comparison to their life outside, it revealed that a majority, that is, 59.16% found that prison life was worse, 17.5% felt that it was the same as life outside and 15% felt prison life was better, 62.5% stated that they were not satisfied with their life in prison, 93 respondents found prison life being difficult to adjust. A total of 35% believed that the employment skill gained in prison would enable them to obtain work or be self-employed, while 55.83% did not reply. Only 16 of the 36 respondents availing of educational facilities believed that education would help them to improve their lot on release. Only 22 respondents agreed that prison moral instruction helped them to adjust to life in prison, whereas 62 respondents did not believe it was helpful and 36 respondents did not reply. The respondents appreciated the prison staff but most of the respondents disliked the prison routine. Two-fifths of the sample were convinced of the correctional value of prison services. It was also found that 75% had no interaction with the fellow inmates and only 10.83% had made friendships in prison.

Saxena (1994) found that a significant number, that is, 70% of the respondents were long termers and had already spent a few years in the prison and hence were partially influenced by the process of prisonization. Most of the respondents, that is 52% had been receiving visitors too. While ascertaining the opinion of inmates towards prison officials, it was found that offenders convicted for the offences of transgression and vice offences were more aggressive in their attitude towards prison officials. Those inmates who were imprisoned for offences of aggression, expressed submissive attitudes. Those who were harbouring aggressive attitudes towards prison officials were short termers. A large number of transgressors, that is 63.2% and the vice offenders, that is 52.4% expressed hostile opinions towards other inmates. One third of the aggressors maintained good relations with co-inmates. About 70% of the convicts were extremely critical of the judicial system.

Vernon Fox (1972) could bring out from his researches on the major facets of correction services that first termers without any previous institutional experience adjust better in prison than those with previous institutionalization. First termers are more easily intimidated by other inmates and correctional officers and are more cautious and apprehensive of their behaviour and records.

Sagarin (1973) and others found that one of the biggest problems facing the offender after she is released is lack of community acceptance.

In the 1977 Federal Survey, administrators of women's institutions were asked their views concerning the special needs of women prisoners. Their comments indicate the range and the depth of the problem. The inmates' special role in society is home making, she needs a home like setting, even in prison (this is why women inmates turn to homosexuality). She needs stronger ties to institutions. About one-third of the women in institutions are enrolled in some type of vocational or academic programme. However, these vocational "rehabilitative" programmes are often geared to the stereotyped female tasks such as sewing, food service and laundry.

Burkhardt (1977) reports on women in prison says that only a handful of women prisoners throughout the country are trained to be such things as dental assistants, etc. Being "need of a household" is a big problem for many women inmates. Women inmates are unmotivated; they need more counseling and positive social involvement; they need to acquire problem-solving skills. Women inmates have low self-esteem because of social stigmas. Women have difficulty dealing with institutionalization. They need to learn to be self-sufficient. They seek more medical help often. The women have few skills and have employability problems.

Laura Crites (1976) studied women criminals but she made no important contribution in any respect except pointing out that women criminals are neglected and are given discriminatory treatment in prisons.

Dodd and Hunter (1992), analysing the National Prison Survey data, show that 47% of women prisoners compared with 32% of males had dependent children living them when they were imprisoned. The children of women in prison were far more likely to be looked after by other relatives or to be in the care of foster parents.

Peelo et al (1992) found that women are more at risk than men of losing stable accommodation while in prison, since they are more likely to have been the sole carers for dependent children and less likely to have left a partner behind who can be depended upon to pay the rent.

Wheeler (1961), studied 237 prisoners in a close-custody prison in the United States and found that the degree of prisonisation varies with the length of the time served.

Wolfgang (1961), found that : (a) young prisoners (below 35 years) adjust less than the middle-aged prisoners, (b) felons adjust less than misdemeanors, (c) short-termers (imprisoned for less than six months and between six months and two years) indicate high conformity to jail norms than long-termers (imprisoned for more than two years) and (d) marital status has no effect on prisonisation.

Women in the Criminal Justice System

Farmington and Morris (1983); Eaton (1986) found in their studies of sentencing of adults, in fact suggest either that women and men are treated more or less equally when factors such as offence seriousness and previous convictions are taken into account.

Moxon (1988) found in the study of Crown Courts, that women do benefit from leniency. Women were much more likely than men to be recommended for probation and less likely to be recommended for community service, a form of community penalty which does not entail any expectation of "help" with the offender's personal problems.

During and Roth (1996) compared the imprisonment of women in Germany and U.K. Imprisonment involves greater deprivation for women than men. Female prisoners do not receive the same work and educational opportunities as men and surveillance of women is often closer. Many female inmates do not need to be incarcerated. Suggestions have been made for a new structure for women's imprisonment to be adopted that involves minimizing security measures and loosening of controls.

Thus the following reviews of the studies on various variables are necessary in understanding the conceptual framework for psycho-socio-cultural research as well as helps in preparing strategies for the treatment, correction, reformation and rehabilitation of women criminals. The studies in women criminals in India are more sociological and demographic in nature than psycho-social or action-based evaluative studies. Most of these variables presented have been examined in the present study.

Though social work professionals evaluate the interventions and skills used by them in order to show their effectiveness and significant contributions, not much work has been done in this direction in India. Some of the social work institutions involved in teaching, training and practising have taken up research studies on various aspects of women criminality. These are the Faculties and Colleges of Social Work, Tata Institute of Social Sciences and Delhi School of Social Work. But these studies have not been presented by the researcher in this section. Most of the research studies conducted in India are by the sociologists and criminologist and thus do not focus much on social work perspectives.

4

Research Setting

Prisons in the shape of dungeons had existed from time immemorial in all the old countries of the world. Prison sentence or imprisonment, as a specific punishment, is of relatively recent origin. The prison which now came into existence, largely is an interim house of detention of an offender pending his trial and punishment. The prison sentence also satisfied the then twin purposes i.e. of inflicting pain on the offender in fair measure and protecting society by incarcerating him and deterring him from criminality. It was believed that rigorous isolation and custodial measures would reform the offenders, but with the changes in the society over a period of time, the functions of prisons have also changed from custodial, to coercive, to corrective.

In early India, jails functioned on the principle of custodial care. With the assertion that a jail is for confinement and not for punishment, prisons were concerned simply with holding prisoners while they waited for trial. During the medieval and early British periods, emphasis came to be laid on the retributive and deterrent aspects of punishment. Physical torture, social degradation and restrictions on freedom were among the programmes used for inflicting pain on criminals. Prisons were primarily used as penal institutions. No attention was paid to differences in age, sex, nature of crime, criminal background or mental status of the offenders. It was only after the recommendations of the Jail Reforms Committee of 1919 were accepted that conditions in prisons gradually improved and prisons came to be used for corrective purposes, i.e., for bringing offenders round to becoming good citizens through discipline of work, education and moral instructions.

The basic functions of the prisons today are as follows :

(1) Social isolation and confinement

(2) Repentance

(3) Punishment and deterrence

(4) Protection

(5) Reformation

Prisonisation

This concept was developed by Donald Clemmer in 1940. According to Clemmer, prisonisation is a process of assimilating prison culture or a process of taking on in a greater or a lesser degree the folkways, mores, customs and general culture of a prison in integrative steps. The main elements of prisonisation are :

(a) Every prisoner is prisoned.

(b) Prisonisation takes place in stages.

(c) Degree of prisonisation may be low, medium or high.

(d) Prisonisation depends upon several factors like age, cell – inmates, nature of crime, term of imprisonment, type of relationships before punishment and relations with the outside world.

(e) There could be deprisonization and reprisonization also.

The integrative steps in prisonisation are :

- Acceptance of an inferior role by wearing jail clothes and becoming an anonymous figure.
- Accumulation of facts concerning the structure, organisation and the norms of prison, i.e. learning about ranks, titles and authority of various officials.

- Development of somewhat new habits of eating, dressing, working and sleeping.
- Learning and adopting local language and nicknames, i.e. jail argot.
- Recognition that he is not obliged to anybody for the food, clothes, etc., he gets in jail.
- Demands more facilities and desires a good job.

The Supreme Court of India has recommended from time to time for improving prison conditions. These suggestions have been given for last 15 years or so in different cases from states like Andhra Pradesh, Maharashtra, Delhi, Kerala and Bihar (National Expert Committee Report on Women Prisoners, 1989).

1. Assigning Congenial Work

A prisoner should be assigned congenial work which gives job satisfaction. Supreme Court judges directed the state Government to see that within the framework of the jail rules, the prisoner is assigned work not of a monotonous, mechanical, degrading type but of a mental, intellectual or like type mixed with a little manual labour.

2. Remuneration

A prisoner must be paid a reasonable fraction of remuneration by way of wages for the work done, since unpaid work is bonded labour and humiliating.

3. Meditation, Sports and Games

Self-expression and self-realisation have a curative effect. Therefore, any sports and games, artistic activity or meditational course will stimulate the prisoner's creativity and sensitivity.

4. Parole Release

The Supreme Court judges gave thought to another humanizing strategy, namely, a guarded parole release every three months for at least a week, punctuating the total prison term. The jail authorities should periodically check whether the prisoner is making progress.

5. Therapeutic Outlook

The Supreme Court judges considered a therapeutic rather than a punitive outlook should prevail in the prisons since the brutal incarceration of the person merely produces laceration of a criminal's mind. The direction of prison reform is not towards dehumanisation but humanisation. These are designed to restore the dignity of the individual and the worth of the human person.

6. Legal Assistance

Legal assistance to a poor accused is a constitutional imperative. Thus it is made available to prisoners in jails, whether they be undertrials or convicted prisoners.

7. Human Treatment and Protection of Fundamental Rights

If a person is incarcerated, it does not mean that inhuman treatment may be meted out to him and he be deprived of his fundamental rights. The term "life" means something more than mere animal existence and the inhibition against its deprivation extends to all those limits and faculties by which life is enjoyed.

8. Handcuffs

A prisoner in transit between prison and court should not be handcuffed, except under special conditions which have to be justified before or after. Handcuffs are prima facie inhuman and repugnant. It is brutalising to handcuff a person in public.

9. Grievance Boxes

Grievance deposit boxes shall be maintained in the prisons which will be opened as is deemed fit, and suitable action taken on complaints made. Access to such boxes shall be accorded to all prisoners.

10. Visits by Magistrates

District magistrates and session judges shall personally

or through substitute, visit prisons in their jurisdiction and afford effective opportunities for ventilating legal grievances. They shall make necessary inquiries thereinto and take suitable remedial action.

Amnesty International Rules

The Amnesty International adopted certain rules for the treatment of prisoners. Some of the rules are quoted here from the National Expert Committee Report on Women Prisoners (1989).

1. No Discrimination

There shall be no discrimination among prisoners on grounds of sex, religion, political or other opinion, national or social origin and birth or other status. Prison authorities are supposed to respect the religious beliefs and moral precepts of the community to which a prisoner belongs.

2. Separation

Different categories of prisoners shall be kept in separate institutions or part of the institutions on the basis of their age, sex, criminal record and other circumstances.

3. Corporal Punishment

Corporal punishment by placing in dark cell and all cruel, inhuman, degrading punishments shall be completely prohibited.

4. Hygienic Conditions

Due consideration to hygienic conditions for living should be made. The food served must be of nutritional value. Services of qualified medical officers having some knowledge of psychiatry should also be made available.

5. Under Trials

Undertrials should be separated from the convicts. Young untried prisoners should also be kept separate from untried adults.

6. Social Relations and Aftercare

Before the completion of the sentence, it is desirable that necessary steps should be taken to ensure for the prisoner a gradual return to normal life in society. He should be permitted to correspond with and meet relatives from time to time.

Constitutional/ Statutory Rights of Prisoners

The Constitution of India incorporates certain rights to prisoners. Besides, statutes like Prisons Act 1894, Prisoners Act 1900 and Prisoners' Attendance in Courts Act 1955 also confer some rights on prisoners. Some of these constitutional/ statutory rights are :

1. Double Jeopardy

No person shall be punished/prosecuted for the same offence more than once.

2. Testimony

Jail authorities cannot compel prisoners to give testimony which is likely to expose them to criminal consequences.

3. Physical Protection

It is the duty of prison authorities to protect the person physically. The prisoners cannot be kept in prison in the open, exposed to sun, rain or cold. The authorities will provide accommodation in prisons. In case of overcrowding or outbreak of an epidemic, the authorities shall provide temporary accommodation. The medical officer shall be responsible for sanitary conditions. The medical officer is also required to examine the new inmates and shall advise the jailer regarding the nature of work to be carried out by the prisoner.

4. Separation

Male and female prisoners shall be kept in separate prisons or separate parts of the same building.

5. Solitary Confinement

Solitary confinement is used to ensure the safe custody of other prisoners or is inflicted as a punishment. Prisoners in solitary cells must be examined by a medical officer at least once a day if confined for a period of more than twenty four hours.

6. Under trials

Under trials may be permitted to have their own clothing, food and other accessories from their own sources and are entitled to be permitted to contact these sources at reasonable hours.

7. Civil Prisoners

Civil prisoners are also to be treated like the under trials. They are allowed to work in jail according to their will.

8. Work

A criminal who is sentenced to labour shall not be allowed to work for more than nine hours a day. The medical officer shall examine such prisoners every fortnight to record the effect of work on their health.

The issues relating to the condition of prisoners and jail reforms have been considered by a number committees from time to time and their reports have included special recommendations on women prisoners. The National Committee on women prisoners headed by Justice Krishna Iyer (1986-87) has made exhaustive recommendations exclusively for women prisoners covering various facets and even formulating a draft "Legislative-Cum-Administrative Code" for consideration of the Government. Similarly, 135th Report of The Law Commission (1989) was devoted entirely to the problems of women prisoners and it came up with a completely new draft Chapter XXXIII – A to be added to Criminal Procedure Code.

The major recommendations made by the National Expert Committee on women prisoners 1986-87 were :

(a) Provisions of a National Policy relating to the women prisoners in India.

(b) Formation of new rules and regulations relating to their punishment and conduct.

(c) Maintenance of proper co-ordination among the Police, Law and Prison for providing due justice to women prisoners.

(d) Provision of legal aid for them.

(e) Construction of separate prisons for women prisoners.

(f) Proper care of the baby born in jail to a woman prisoner and provision of nutrition diet for the mother and the child.

Until recently, female offenders did not receive enough attention since their number is small. They have been neglected and discriminated against at all stages of the criminal correctional process. Most of the undertrial female prisoners are lodged in separate enclosures of common jails. The All India Committee on Jail Reforms 1980-1983 headed by Justice A.N. Mulla expressed concern over the conditions of female prisoners. The committee said, "In view of the status of women in the family and the society, their special needs and problems and their vulnerability while in the prison, special consideration has to be given to the segregation, protection, care, treatment, training and rehabilitation of women offenders."

The committee made several recommendations and suggestions on various aspects of female prisoners :

(1) Revision of legislation relating to women prisoners.

(2) Establishment of homes for released women prisoners.

(3) Action against atrocities committed against women in prisons.

(4) Re-integration of ex-women prisoners into the family and community.

(5) Free legal aid to women prisoners.

(6) Welfare of women prisoner's family.

The All India Committee on Jail Reforms (1980-1983) highlighted in its report that, "Segregation of offenders on the basis of sex, age, criminal record, social background and sequence of criminal behaviour is an essential system of modern prison system."

National Commission for Women

One of the functions specifically assigned to the Commission under the provisions of the National Commission for Women Act, 1990, is to inspect jails or other places of custody where women are kept as prisoners or otherwise and make appropriate recommendations for the improvement of their condition. The subject of custodial justice for women has been one of the thrust areas of the Commission's activities. During the tenure of the first Commission between February, 1992 and January, 1995 some good work was done by the Commission.

The Commission has visited many jails all over the country to study first hand the condition of the women inmates. The report of the National Commission for Women on "Custodial Justice for Women" (1993) needs attention. The following are some of the important aspects, many of which do not cast any financial burden for their implementation.

(1) Women prisoners – like men – should be informed of their rights under the law.

(2) Searches should be conducted by women constables.

(3) Medical check-ups of women prisoners or undertrials, should be done by women doctors as soon as they come to prison.

(4) Women prisoners should be allowed to contact their families and communicate with their lawyers, women social workers and voluntary organisations.

(5) Women prisoners should be allowed to keep their children with them.

(6) Voluntary organisations of women should be encouraged to be associated with women prisoners.

(7) Separate jails should be provided for women.

(8) Special prosecution officers should be available to present the case of women prisoners.

Prison Institutions and Correctional Administration is one of the three main constituents of the Criminal Justice System. The most common and standard Jail Institutions which are in existence in the States/UTS are better known as Central Jails, District Jails and Sub Jails. The other types of Jail establishments are Women Jails, Children or Borstal Jails, Open Jails and Special Jails. Among the 30 States/UTS, only 12 States reported the existence of Women Jails that functioned exclusively for women inmates.

Gujarat

Gujarat is a leading State in India so far as its socio-economic performance and the level of development are concerned. It ranks above the average pertaining to all India on the basis of industrialization, per capita income, level of literacy, urbanization and infrastructural facilities are concerned.

Though the socio-economic profile of Gujarat reveals that it is a highly industrialized, urbanized and developed State of the country, yet the districtwise development pattern shows a low level of development i.e, in terms of the low level of literacy, low level of density of population, low level of per capita income, low level of daily employment, high level of rural population, and high level of scheduled caste and scheduled tribe population are predominant in the backward district of Gujarat namely Kutch, Banaskantha, Panchmahals, Dangs and Sabarkantha. Thus it implies that a higher degree of backwardness is the main cause of a higher degree of crimes in a backward region. The state, even being a highly developed one in the country, emerges with increasing number of crimes. The major crimes noticed in Gujarat are riot, house breaking, thefts and murder.

With the number of convicts and undertrials increasing over the years, most of the jails are finding it difficult to provide good living conditions and proper accommodation. The condition of even the Central Jails of Ahmedabad and

Baroda, as far as living space is concerned, needs to be looked into. There are about 8579 prisoners in 22 jails of the State, including the two Central Jails, against the capacity of 5266,

Table 4.1

Women Prison Population in Gujarat State

Sl. No.	Name of Jail	Convicted	Undertrial
1.	Ahmedabad C. Prison	0	13
2.	Baroda C. Prison	55	5
3.	Rajkot Dist. Prison	0	1
4.	Bhavnagar Dist. Prison	0	1
5.	Jamnagar Dist. Prison	0	4
6.	Junagadh Dist. Jail	0	6
7.	Surat Dist. Prison	0	14
8	Nadiad Dist. Prison	0	6
9.	Bhuj Special Prison	0	2
10.	Porbandar Special Prison	0	2
11.	Amreli Open Jail	0	0
12.	Ahmedabad Open Jail	0	0
13.	Navsari Sub Jail	0	2
14.	Bharuch Sub Jail	0	3
15.	Chhotaudepur Sub Jail	0	1
16.	Godhra Sub Jail	0	3
17.	Rajpipla Sub Jail	0	4
18.	Mehsana Sub Jail	0	6
19.	Himatnagar Sub Jail	0	0
20.	Palanpur Sub Jail	0	3
21.	Amreli Sub Jail	0	3
22.	Surendranagar Sub Jail	0	2
	Total	**55**	**81**

Total Female Polulation as on 1-12-99 = 136

Source : I.G.P. (Prison) office (Jan 2000)

Table 4.2

Women Arrested under Different IPC Crimes During 1995 and 1997

Sr. No.	Crime	Gujarat 1995	Gujarat 1997	Ahmedabad 1995	Ahmedabad 1997	Vadodara 1995	Vadodara 1997
1.	Murder	261	257	30	18	2	5
2.	Attempt to Commit Murder	158	139	22	10	6	3
3.	Dacoity	4	10	0	0	0	0
4.	Robbery	23	31	6	6	2	3
5.	Burglary	143	118	38	5	3	19
6.	Theft	362	427	38	56	32	24
7.	Breach of Trust	104	138	1	4	18	21
8.	Cheating	132	124	7	3	33	30
9.	Dowry Deaths	NR	92	5	4	3	0
10.	Narcotic Drugs & Psycho-Substances Act	16	9	1	1	2	1

Source : Crime in India – 1997.

which shows inadequate facilities to provide proper accommodation to the prisoners. According to the survey made by the Jail officials of I. G. Prison, Gujarat State (Dec, 1999), it was found that there are 2413 convicts and 4478 undertrials, 14 TADA convicted and 55 TADA undertrials, 273 NDPS convicted and 314 NDPS undertrials. Thus there are total 2700 convicted criminals, 4847 undertrials and 723 detenus in 2 Central Jails, 6 District Jails, 2 Special Jails, 2 Open Jails and 10 Sub Jails of Gujarat State. The figures thus give an understanding that the accommodation facilities, in 2 Central Jails, 20 district and sub–Jails and 116 taluka jails used for temporary lock-ups have prisoners more than their actual capacity. The total capacity of female prisoners in Gujarat is 227, while at the end of 1998 it was found to be 236, i.e. 68 convicts, 148 undertrials and 20 detenus in 22 jails.

Ahmedabad Central Jail

The Ahmedabad Central Jail was constructed in 1891–94 in Ahmedabad and was a historic prison like the Yerawada Jail of Pune, where Gandhiji and other veteran freedom fighters were kept during the British rule.

Very close to the entrance of the Jail, there is a separate cell for the women prisoners, which is used for only undertrials and detenus. The convicted women criminals are not imprisoned here. The strength of the cell is of 50 prisoners. The cell is under the care of a male Jailor and has a lady Hawaldar and a lady Matron.

Recently in a move to provide privacy and protection to the women prisoners in the historic Sabarmati Jail of Ahmedabad, the State Government has decided to create separate jails for them.

Baroda Central Jail

The Baroda Central Jail was constructed in 1881 by the then Gackwad ruler of Baroda State, Sir Sayajirao Gackwad. In the Central Jail special arrangements for having separate cells were made for undertrial prisoners and civil prisoners. Separate cells away from the other cells were constructed for notorious prisoners. While away from the male section a separate section of cells were constructed for the female prisoners. Thus arrangements were made to accommodate 639 male prisoners and 49 female prisoners. It also has the facilities of living quarters for all the staff members and jail Superintendent within the prison premises. In Gujarat, Baroda Central Jail is the only Jail, where convicted women criminals are kept. In all other jails including Ahmedabad only undertrials and detenus are kept. The Female Section of Baroda Central Jail has separate provision for the convicted, undertrials, detenus and for offenders of simple imprisonment under the supervision of a lady Jailor, 3 female Hawaldars and Matrons. Here female prisoners come from various District jails of Gujarat.

Women in Indian prisons constitute a small segment of the convict population and their problems do not receive the same priorities as available to male prisoners. Women in Indian jails live under pathetic conditions. Female wards in prisons are mostly over crowded with various types of offenders housed together. Facilities for education, vocational training and social uplift are greatly restricted. The rationale for sending people to prison tends to be rehabilitation, but what is found is that the society tends to separate and isolate the deviant person from the community, which largely hinders the rehabilitative process.

Prison Administration

The Executive head who is known as "Inspector General of Police (Prison)" is the head of the Jail Department and is entrusted with carrying out the policy framed by the Jail Minister. He has control over all the Jails of the state and holds the charge of several thousand prisoners. He supervises and controls the work of the superintendents, Jailors, Jail Cadre staff and medical staff.

The administrative set-up consists of one Superintendent, one deputy Superintendent, one deputy Senior Jailor, male Jailors and a female Jailor. Under them are guarding staff, Subedars, Hawaldars, Warders, Matron and Sepoys.

FIGURE – 4.1

Administrative Set-up of Central Jail

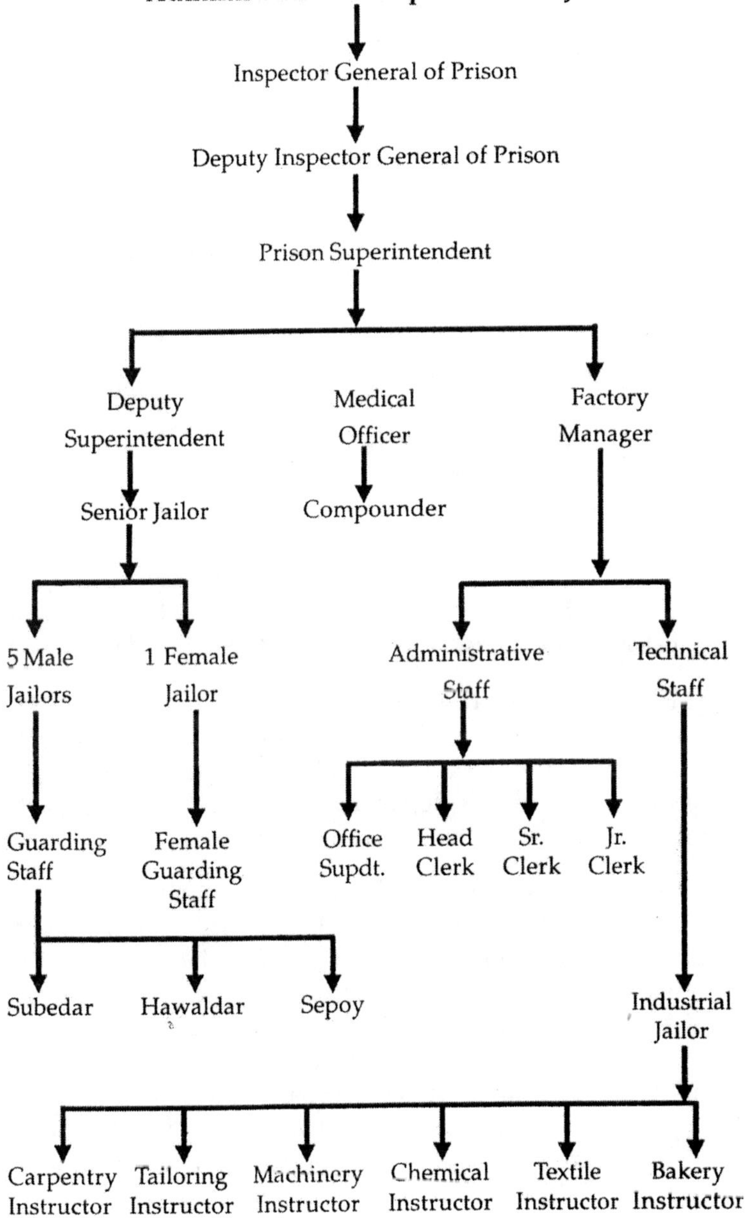

FIGURE - 4.2

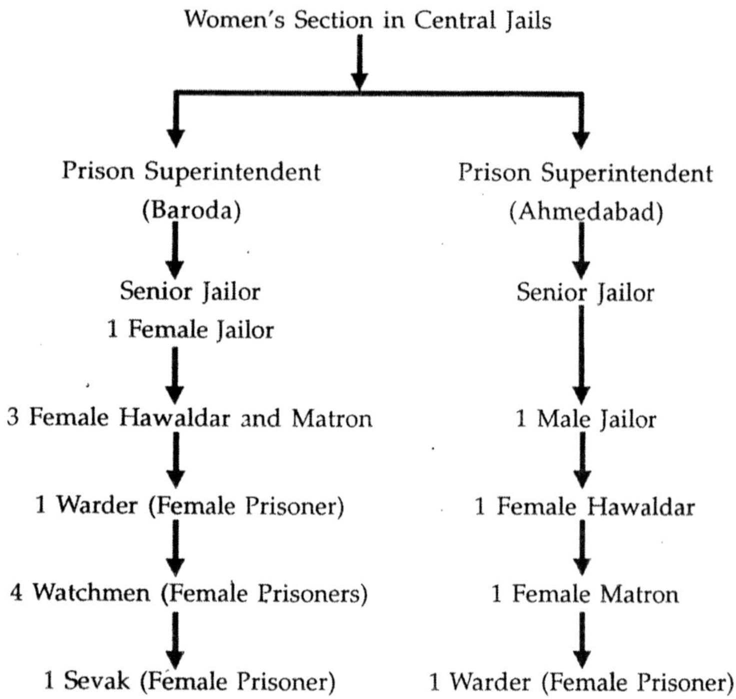

Medical officer provides medical care to the prisoners. He is assisted by pharmacist. There is also a factory manager working under the Superintendent, who supervises the jail factory and the various departments such as the Carpentry, Tailoring, Machinery, Textile, Bakery etc.

Superintendent is the head of the institution and manages the prison in all the matter relating to discipline, labour, expenditure, punishment and control. With the change in the administrative structure of the prison, the policy of the prison towards the prisoners gradually changed. The basic objective is not retribution or revenge any more but reformative and rehabilitation of both men and women who are imprisoned. While imprisoned, they are trained in such a way that after they are released from jail, they can settle down as honest, decent and useful citizens of the society.

Admission Procedure

When a female criminal is brought to the Central Jail, her name is recorded in the Register of the prison and then she is allowed to enter the prison with the security of a female guard, who takes her to the female yard. Here, her name is again recorded in the register of the female yard. The female warder of the female yard make a search of the offender, and if the offender has some expensive commodity, it is deposited with the Jailor, which will be handed over to her after the termination of her punishment. A convicted female offender is given the jail uniform.

Daily Routine

This was observed during data collection.

Morning : 7.00 am to 10.00 am

In the morning the female criminals are engaged in brooming and sweeping the rooms and the surrounding of the women cells. Some of them take care of the garden during the morning hours. Then they go for their wash and bath. After which a light breakfast of *gur, sing, chana* and tea is served to them. After this they settle down for cleaning of grains and cutting vegetables for the entire jail inmates as cooking is done by the male inmates for both the sections. In between at about 10.00 am lunch is served to the inmates.

Afternoon : 12.00 noon – 4.00 pm

In the afternoon the inmates carry on with their regular routine work. Lunch from outside is brought for the undertrials and detenus, which is checked by the Hawaldar in the presence of lady Jailor. Some of them retire to their cells for rest in the afternoon. The grains and the vegetables after cleaning are sent to the kitchen for dinner.

Evening : 4.00 pm to 6.00 pm

At this time freedom is given for half an hour to interact with visitors who came to meet them in the presence of a lady Jailor and other male and female jail staff, who keep vigilance on the visitors. After they leave, the gifts and food brought by them are first checked and then given to the inmates to keep. After this dinner is served to them at 5.00 p.m. Before 6.00 p.m. the women prisoners are gathered for taking attendance and then locked up in their cells throughout the night. During night no jail staff is present in the female yard and they are locked from outside.

Letters

Letters play an important role in maintaining continuity of contact between the prisoners and her family and the outside community. Two postcards are given free to all the inmates monthly. When the prisoners receive letters from the family, they are first read by the lady Jailor or jail official and then it is handed over to the respective person. The same procedure is followed, that is the lady Jailor reads the letter before it is to be despatched by the prisoners.

Visits

An effective aspect of the rehabilitative process is maintaining relationship and contact with the family of the prisoners. So visits from relations and friends and exchange of letters are permitted under certain rules and restrictions. Relatives and friends are permitted to visit at a specified time and place in the presence of a guard or official, for a limited time.

Canteen

The canteen has been organised in the prison with the objective of making available small amenities and articles of food to the prisoners, which are given to them at government cost and at the same time, they are not prohibited by law. The canteen provides the facilities of day-to-day requirements like, biscuits, snacks, *bidis*, matchbox, toothpaste, soaps, etc. The female prisoners are not allowed to visit the canteen and so once a week, a trolley from the canteen visits the female yards, where the inmates purchase all the required commodity for a week.

Medical Facility

Medical treatment as well medicines are given free to the inmates. There is no provision of a lady Medical Officer and so if the problem arises the Medical Officer is called to the female yard for any check-up. The hospital inside the jail provides 24 hours of service and consists of medical officers, two male nurses and two pharmacists. If required, female prisoners are allowed to go to the government hospital with the security staff.

Wages

In order to provide some motivation to the prisoners and considering that some monetary reward would develop interest in work and can use the earnings on herself or on her family, wages are given to the prisoners. From 1st Nov. 1998, the wages were increased in Gujarat jails. For an unskilled job they get Rs.12 per day, for a semi-skilled job they get Rs.13 per day, and for a skilled job they get Rs.14 per day. Thus for cleaning grains and cutting vegetables, the women prisoners earn Rs.12 per day. Besides, those convicted prisoners who have good character are given administrative work and other work in prison. Those female prisoners who work as Warden and Sevak earn Rs.14 per day, while a watchman receives Rs.13 per day.

Other Facilities

The children of the female prisoners are allowed to stay with their mothers up to the age of five years. Nursing mothers and children are provided with proper food under the advice of the Jail Medical officer.

Observance of individual religious practices is allowed.

A few voluntary organisations are working for the rehabilitation of the women criminals, such as Sahayog of Himatnagar, which gives shelter to those women who are not accepted by their families. Another organisation like Vikas Jyot is helping in cases, especially for the process of release work.

It has been observed that there is absence of any kind of vocational training being given to the women criminals for preparing their rehabilitative goals. Instead they are occupied with activities like cleaning grains and gardening, which is not of much value in the employment market. So most of the women inmates pass their leisure time without any constructive work or get mixed-up with hardened criminals and get corrupted by the insidious influence of the jail.

It can be understood that the government's and communities' participation in correctional programmes and offender's self-improvement is needed for the reformation of offenders.

Thus, in this chapter a total picture of the prison condition and reformative system has been highlighted. The physical lay-out of the setting has been presented in this chapter.

5

PROFILE OF WOMEN CRIMINALS

This chapter deals with the personal and social characteristics of the inmates. To understand the realities of the criminals' social life, we need to look into the socio-cultural background and personal qualities such as age, caste, education, religion, occupation, etc., of the criminals. These background data of information are equally significant in understanding and determining the criminal's social attitudes and behaviour patterns and this can also have an important impact on the mode of their perceptions. The following data of information of the women criminals were gathered based on the data collected from intensive interviews.

1. Personal Background

Age

From the analysis of the data shown in Table 5.1, it can be seen that the women between the age of 31 and 50 years get more involved in crime, i.e., about 60 per cent of the women criminals fall into this category. A small number of 19.6 per cent of women criminals were below 30 years of age. The findings of the present study indicated that the predominance of women offenders was in the middle age group i.e. 31-50 years.

Education

The data also show the educational background of the women criminals. It has highlighted that majority of the criminals, i.e., 66 (64.7%) of the women criminals were illiterate. Only 24 (23.5%) and 10 (9.8%) had primary and secondary education respectively. Thus it shows that illiteracy is more predominant in women criminals.

Table 5.1

Personal Background of the Respondents

Background Characters	Frequency	Percentage
Present Age		
Below 30	20	19.6
31 – 40	37	36.3
41 – 50	25	24.5
51 – 60	14	13.7
61 above	6	5.9
	102	100.0
Education		
Illiterate	66	64.7
Primary	24	23.5
Secondary	10	9.8
Graduate	1	1.0
Primary Teacher's Certificate	1	1.0
	102	100.0
Caste		
S.T.	29	28.3
S.C.	12	11.8
SEBC	16	15.7
General	33	32.4
Minority	12	11.8
	102	100.0

Contd...

Background Characters	Frequency	Percentage
Religion		
Hindu	89	87.3
Muslim	11	10.7
Christian	1	1.0
Jain	1	1.0
	102	100.0
Ordinal Position of the Respondent		
Order Number one	39	38.2
Order Number two	22	21.6
Order Number three	17	16.7
Order Number above three	24	23.5
	102	100.0
Marital Status		
Married	68	66.6
Unmarried	1	1.0
Deserted	2	2.0
Widowed	25	24.5
Divorced	4	3.9
Separated	2	2.0
	102	100.0
Occupation Prior to Imprisonment		
House wife	42	41.2
Self Employed	20	19.6
Petty shopkeeper	5	4.9
Service	6	5.9
Labour	18	17.6
Illicit business	11	10.8
	102	100.0

Contd...

Background Characters	Frequency	Percentage
Income of Respondents (Monthly)		
Below Rs.500	17	16.7
Rs.501-1000	28	27.4
Rs.1001-5000	15	14.7
Nil	42	41.2
Total N =	102	100.0

Religion and Caste

Table 5.1 shows that, 89 (87.3%) women criminals were from Hindu families, while only 12 (11.8%) were from families belonging to the minority communities. Since the proportion of Hindu women is much more in the total population than in other religions, thus Hindu women were found more in the criminal women population too.

Further the data have also shown that the percentage of women belonging to backward caste are relatively high. It shows that more than 50 i.e. about 55 per cent of women were from the scheduled tribe, scheduled caste and from the socially and economically backward caste. Only 33 (32.4%) were from the general category of caste group.

Ordinal Position of the Respondent

Table 5.1 shows that a large number i.e. 39 (38.2%) were first born in the order of the sibling structure, then comes the second and the third born i.e. 22 (21.6%) and 17 (16.7%) respectively.

Marital Status

It can be seen from the Table that married women show a higher crime rate than other categories of marital status. The majority of women criminals were married i.e. 68 (66.6%), while 25 (24.5%) fell into the category of widow in marital status.

A high rate of married women involved in crime commission may be, due to the adjustment problems with in-laws and husbands. As coming from lower socio-economic and illiterate families, their marriages were arranged by parents without taking into consideration of these women, at an early age.

Occupation Prior to Imprisonment

In the present study the data have shown that about 60 per cent of the women criminals were engaged in different types of economic activities. About 19.6 per cent were self employed in different small jobs are domestic/household work, 18 (17.6%) of them worked as labourers, 5 (4.9%) of them had business of small shops and were the sole earners of their families. About 11 (10.8%) were engaged in illicit liquor business. Most of these women belonged to a particular community called *Chhara* in Gujarat, usually engaged in anti-social activities, prepare liquor and sell them to earn their living. These women were habitual criminals since they had adapted crime as their profession. They were involved in the traditional profession of their family and in some cases were convicted earlier also on the same charges.

Income of Respondents

As shown in the Table, it shows that, 17 (16.7%) have earning below Rs.500, while 28 (27.4%) of the women criminals had an income of Rs.501 to Rs.1000. Only 15 (14.7%) earned more than Rs.1001 to Rs. 5000. The remaining 42 (41.2%) had no occupation and thus did not have any earning. It can be observed that, more than 50 per cent of these women either had no income or had very little income of their own.

2. Family Background

It is important to understand the role of family in influencing the personality of a person. The family is one of the primary agents for the socialization of children. A child's first experience with social life usually comes from within the family. The quality of this experience helps to determine whether the person will engage in normal or criminal pattern. The types of behaviour exhibited by the youngsters with other community institutions depend on the socialization pattern and social control of the family. In the present study an attempt has been made to analyse some relevant aspects of the families of the respondents and evaluate the relations between the family conditions and criminal behaviour of women criminals.

Education of Parents

The data in Table 5.2 show that majority of the parents i.e both father and mother of the respondents are very poorly educated. The Table indicates that

Table 5. 2

Family Background of the Respondents

Family Background	Frequency		Percentage	
Education of Parents	**F**	**M**	**F**	**M**
Illiterate	61	86	59.8	84.3
Primary	26	8	25.5	7.8
Secondary	8	2	7.8	2.0
Graduate	1	0	1.0	0
Do not know	6	6	5.9	5.9
	102	102	100.0	100.0
Occupation of Father				
Labour	36		35.2	
Farmer	20		19.6	
Service	12		11.8	
Self employed	11		10.8	
Business	12		11.8	
Not working	5		4.9	
Do not know	6		5.9	
	102		100.0	

Contd...

Family Background	Frequency	Percentage
Income of Father (Monthly)		
Below Rs. 500	11	10.8
Rs. 501 – 1000	19	18.6
Rs. 1001 – 2000	4	3.9
Rs. 2001 – 3000	2	2.0
Rs. 3001 – 4000	1	1.0
No income	5	4.9
Do not know	60	58.8
	102	100.0
Economic Status of Father		
Low	65	63.7
Middle	35	34.3
High	2	2.0
	102	100.0
Type of Family Background		
Intact Family	45	44.1
Broken Family	57	55.9
	102	100.0
Nature of home conditions		
Congenial	76	74.5
Uncongenial	26	25.5
	102	100.0
Childhood Experiences (of Respondents)		
Happy Experiences	92	90.2
Unhappy Experiences	10	9.8
Total N =	102	100.0

62 (59.8%) of the respondents' fathers and 86 (84.3%) of the respondents mothers were illiterate, while 26 (25.5%) of the fathers had primary education. Only 8 (7.8%) of the fathers and 2 (2.0%) of the mothers had secondary education, none of the mothers had any college education. About 6 of the respondents were not aware of the educational qualifications of their parents. Thus it can be seen that poor education must have affected their socio-economic condition and the economic status of the family.

Occupation of Father

The data presented in the Table 5.2 show that the women criminals were drawn from the various types of occupational pattern in the families. Table 5.2 indicates that 36 (35.2%) of the fathers of the respondents were labours in the industries. About 20 (19.6 %) had their own business. Few of them i.e. 5 (4.9%) were not working as they have become very old.

The occupational pattern of the family shows that the families of these women were economically very poor and were overburdened with liabilities to support the family with such small income.

Monthly Income and Economic Status of Father

From the responses presented in Table 5.2, it appears that nearly sixty per cent of the respondents were not aware of the income of their father. Table 5.2 shows that 19 (18.6%) of the fathers of the respondents were having income of Rs.501 to Rs.1000, while 11 (10.8%) of them had income below Rs.500. A very few of them had income above Rs.2000 per month.

The Table also shows that 65 (63.7%) of the respondents' families had low economic status, while only 2 (2.0%) had high economic status in the society.

From both the Tables it can be analysed that the majority of the families suffered from poverty and economic strain. Therefore, it indicates that economic status of a family is conducive to anti-social behaviour.

Type of Family Background

The family is considered as the chief socializing agent of the early childhood of a child. The basic reaction pattern in terms of values, norms, feeling, thought process and life style develops through the family. It is said that the family should be structurally complete, i.e. where both the natural parents are present.

In the present study, an attempt has been made to understand the family structure of the respondent's background. It was found that 57 (55.9%) of the respondents belonged to broken families, while 45 (44.1%) were from intact family. Either both the parents or one of the parents was dead. In some cases the parents were divorced or the father left the home and the family. It shows that the family might have undergone economic stress, insecurity and responsibilities only on one parent. Thus the presence of both parents is required for proper socialization.

Nature of Home Conditions

The study also revealed that 76 (74.5%) of the respondents had congenial home conditions, while 26 (25.5%) belonged to uncongenial home conditions. The reasons for un-congeniality at home were due to quarrels among parents, quarrels with other family members, poverty in the family, alcoholic parents, etc. It is a widely accepted fact that parent-child relationship is the basis of the child's security, which depends largely on a harmonious marriage relationship between the parents and proper family environment.

Childhood Experience

Lastly, the Table 5.2 reveals that, 92 (90.2%) of the respondents had a happy childhood, while only 10 (9.8%) had unhappy childhood experiences. It shows that the respondents were contended in their family of orientation.

3. Marital History

In the present study a large majority of the respondents were married and came from Hindu families. Thus it becomes important to discuss the marital relations among the respondents and their family of procreation. Marriage is considered as an important institution and it is the most complex involvement of human relations and a part of the social system. Marital mal-adjustments and the disruption of family manifests a crisis of deviation from expectations. The present study makes an attempt to learn the situations affecting the intra-familial interactions and to identify the motivational factors that might have been responsible for the disruption of family relationships.

Education of Husband

It can·be observed from Table 5.3 that 38 (37.3%) of the respondents' husbands were illiterate, 33 (32.3%) had primary education and 25 (24.5%) had secondary education. Only 5 (4.9%) of the respondents' husbands were graduate. Thus it shows that about 70 per cent of them were either illiterate or had elementary education.

Table 5.3

Marital History of Respondents

Marital History	Frequency	Percentage
Education of Husband	**38**	**37.3**
Illiterate	33	32.3
Primary	25	24.5
Secondary	5	4.9
Graduate	1	1.0
N.A.	**102**	**100.0**
Occupation of Husband		
Labour	23	22.5
Farmer	10	9.8
Service	32	31.3
Self employed	17	16.7
Business	10	9.8
Illicit Business	2	2.0
Not working	7	6.9
N.A.	1	1.0
	102	**100.0**

Contd...

Marital History	Frequency	Percentage
Income of Husband		
Below Rs. 500	8	7.8
Rs. 501 – 1000	26	25.5
Rs. 1001 – 2000	23	22.5
Rs. 2001 & above	11	10.8
Not Working	7	6.9
N.A.	1	1.0
Do not Know	26	25.5
	102	**100.0**
Economic Status of Husband		
Low	64	62.7
Middle	34	33.3
High	3	2.9
N.A.	1	1.0
	102	**100.0**
Size of Present Family		
Small Family	15	14.7
Medium Family	47	46.1
Large Family	40	39.2
	102	**100.0**
Type of Marital Life		
Happy Life	75	73.5
Unhappy Life	26	24.5
N. A (unmarried)	1	1.0
	102	**100.0**
Reasons for Marital Conflict		
Husband's relation with another women	5	4.9
Alcoholism/Gambling Habit of Husband	11	10.8
Financial Crisis/Poverty	3	2.9
Quarrel with husband/in-laws	6	5.9
Disliking of husband	1	1.0
N.A.	76	77.5
Total N =	**102**	**100.0**

Contd...

Marital History	Frequency	Percentage
Nature of Cruelty by Husband		
Beating	20	19.6
Neglect	4	3.9
Denying respondent any access to money	2	2.0
Over-demanding work	6	5.9
Verbal abuse	23	22.5
Any other (unmarried)	1	1.0
Not applicable	75	73.5
(Multiple responses)		
	131	

Occupation of Husband

Table 5.3 shows that 32 (31.3%) were employed in government organization or in industries, 23 (22.5%) were working as un-skilled labourers, 10 (9.8%) were having their own land and were engaged in cultivation. Further 17 (16.7%) were self-employed and 10 (9.8%) were engaged in small business. Few of them were also engaged in illicit business. This shows that most of them occupationally were of low economic level and of lower status, as they worked as peons, factory workers, rickshaw or tempo drivers, cobblers, washermen, construction workers, etc.

Income of Husband

The data reveals that 34 (33.3%) of the respondents' husbands earned below Rs.1000, while 23 (22.5%) belonged to the income group of Rs.1001 – 2000, only 4 (3.9%) were having an earning of more than Rs.5000. Further 26 (25.5%) of the respondents were not aware of their husband's earning. Thus the table indicates that majority of the families belonged to the lower income group.

Economic Status of Husband

The analysis of the data highlights that the majority i.e. 64 (62.7%) of the respondents' husbands were of low economic status, 34 (33.3%) belonged to middle class economic status, while only 3 (2.9%) were of higher class status. All these indicate the inadequate socio-economic condition of the husband, which results in dissatisfaction and unhappiness in married life.

Size of the Present Family

The table 5.3 shows the size of the family, which explains that 47 (46.1%) of the respondents were having families of medium sized and 40 (39.2%) of them were having large sized families. Only 15 (14.7%) were having small families of 1-3 members.

Type of Marital Life

Table 5.3 shows that majority i.e. 75 (73.5%) of the respondents were having happy married life. 26 (24.5%) were having unhappy marital life. Thus the study indicates that the relationships of the respondents with their husbands were harmonious, but the nature of their relationship with sister-in-laws and daughter-in-laws was conflicting in many of cases. Some of the respondents though had a happy married life with their husbands, yet were dominating and had strained relationships with their daughter-in-laws.

Reasons for Marital Conflict

From Table 5.3 it can be seen that there are various factors that caused tensions and disharmony in marital relationships. The Table reveals that 11 (10.8%) reported that their husbands were having habits of alcoholism or gambling as the primary cause of conflict. Further it shows that, 6 (5.9%) had often quarrel with their husbands or in-laws, 5 (4.9%) reported that their husbands had relations with other women. Only 3 (2.9%) revealed that the financial condition or poverty was the cause for marital conflict.

Nature of Cruelty by Husband

Table 5.3 also reveals the nature of cruelty shown by their husbands. These findings show that 23 (22.5%) suffered from verbal abuse of their husbands and 20 (19.6%) of the respondents were beaten by their husbands. All these factors lead to conflicting intra-familial patterns, which produce maladjustment among the inter-personal relations of the family. This makes the women to deviate and to take to non-conformist behaviour to overcome the strained and stressful situations at the family level.

Thus there was a need to examine the involvement of women criminals and the situational and motivational factors that may resort them to various forms of deviant behaviour.

4. Causes Leading to Crime

Various scholars have attempted to build different theories to explain systematically the causes of crime. The theoretical explanations of criminal behaviour have been classified as follows : (i) classical and neo-classical theories, (ii) biological and constitutional theories, (iii) psychological, psychiatric and psychoanalytical theories, (iv) economic theory (v) geographical or topographical theory, (vi) sociological theories, and (vii) multiple factor theory. A very few of these theories have dealt with female criminality. An attempt has been made in the present study to understand the etiology of female crime and thus a few of the theories have been tested.

Aspirations/ Goals in Childhood

The researcher tried to explore this with the help of Robert Merton's "Social Structure and Anomie Theory". The main thrust of Merton's efforts was "in discovering how some social structures exert a definite pressure upon certain persons in a society to engage in nonconformist rather than conformist conduct". He made a threefold distinction in his theory of deviant behaviour. They are (1) the cultural goals or aspirations that people learn from their culture, (2) the norms that people employ when attempting to achieve the goals, and (3) the institutionalized means or the facilities that are available for goal achievement.

Table 5.4 reveals that, 34 (33.3%) of the respondents had some or the other aspirations in their childhood, while 68 (66.7%) did not have any aspirations in their childhood and were contended with whatever they had. Merton feels that, when there is a discrepancy between the institutionalized means that are available within the environment and the goals that individuals have learned to aspire to in their environment, strain or frustration is produced, norms break down, and deviant behaviour can result. When a life style is difficult to attain because of lack of institutionalized means, Merton feels, it will create strain and frustration. This strain and frustration can produce the behaviour that is deviant and contrary to the norms or the rules that generally govern that behaviour.

Table 5.4

Causes Leading to Crime

Causes	Frequency	Percentage
Aspirations/ Goals in Childhood		
Having aspirations	34	33.3
Not having aspirations	68	66.7
	102	**100.0**
Criminal Association before crime		
Association with Anti-social person in Neighborhood	11	10.8
Association with gangs/Liquor dons	3	2.9
Association with deviant family members	6	5.9
Association with deviant relatives	2	2.0
Had no criminal association	80	78.4
	102	**100.0**
Environmental Pressure before Crime		
Social pressure	68	66.7
Economic pressure	29	28.4
Psychological pressure	5	4.9
Total N =	**102**	**100.0**

Criminal Association before Crime

This was explored with the theory of Sutherland's "Differential Association". This theory is one of the most systematic and complete theory. It states that criminal behaviour is learned in interaction with other persons in the process of communication.

Table 5.4 shows that 11 (10.8%) of the respondents had association with anti-social people in the community, 6 (5.9%) had association with deviant family members, who were involved in criminal acts, 2 (2.0%) had association with relatives, who were involved in anti-social activities, while 3 (2.9%) were associated with gangs or liquor dons. Thus it can be seen that if individuals associate mostly with criminals, the chances are that they will become involved in criminal activity. The table shows that 80 (78.4%) of the women criminals were not having any criminal association. Thus in the present study though not many but some of them had criminal association.

Environmental Pressure before Crime

Ohlin and Cloward, Cohen, Durkheim, Merton, Shaw and Mckay, and Thrasher have all either stated or implied that crime is the result of the strain produced by a lack of environmental opportunity or system and is therefore more prevalent among the lower socio-economic classes.

Table 5.4 shows that, 68 (66.7%) of the respondents had social pressure within their environment and committed the act, 29 (28.4%) of them had economic pressure for which they took to criminal activity and 5 (4.9%) suffered from psychological pressure and got themselves involved in crime. Thus the hostile manifestation of criminal behaviour is generally felt to be a reaction to the psychological or economic and social conditions, as well as to those institutions that set normative standards.

5. Nature and Patterns of Crime

A few decades ago, it was believed that crime is predominantly a male phenomenon and the world of crime is only a man's world. Statistically speaking, crime amongst females is not a significant problem in India. There are more female crimes in Western countries in comparison to India. But recent studies show that the pattern of crime among the women are moving out of traditional crimes like sex offences and shoplifting to thefts, burglary and crimes of violence like murder, abduction, etc. Therefore there has been an increase in female criminality in India since 1971. In the present study an effort has been made to explore into the nature and pattern of female criminality.

Table 5.5

Nature and Patterns of Crime

Nature and Pattern	Frequency	Percentage
Nature of Crime		
Murder of daughter-in-law	27	26.5
Murder of husband	8	7.8
Murder of close relatives	14	13.7
Murder of children	2	2.0
Murder of others	18	17.6
For Stealing/Thefts	3	2.9
Violation of Public laws	2	2.0
Violation of Narcotic Act	7	6.9
Violation of Liquor Prohibition	18	17.6
Eloping with minor girls	3	2.9
	102	**100.0**
Motive behind Crime Commission		
Revenge	3	2.9
Temptation	5	4.9
Accidental	10	9.8
Situational	26	25.5
Need to overcome economic stress	21	20.6
Need to overcome social stress	37	36.3
	102	**100.0**

Contd...

Nature and Pattern	Frequency	Percentage
Method of Crime		
Burnt	43	42.2
Hanged	5	4.9
Drowned	2	2.0
Strangulated	1	1.0
Use of weapons	9	8.8
Poison	3	2.9
Any other method	6	5.9
N.A.	33	32.3
	102	**100.0**
Type of Companion		
Crime performed alone	39	38.2
Crime performed with Companion	63	61.8
	102	**100.0**
Place of Crime		
Rural and Tribal	35	43.3
Urban	67	65.7
	102	**100.0**
Time of Crime		
Day time	63	61.8
Night time	19	18.6
Evening	17	16.7
Refused to say	3	2.9
	102	**100.0**
Living with at the time of committing offence		
Parents	7	6.9
Husband	70	68.6
Relative	8	7.8
Friend	2	2.0
On the street	3	2.9
Children	12	11.8
	102	**100.0**
Acceptance of Crime		
Accepting the crime committed	26	25.5
Not accepting the crime committed	76	74.5
Total N =	**102**	**100.0**

Nature of Crime

It has been found from the data of the present study that the majority of the respondents, i.e. 69 (67.6%) were in the jail for the offence of murder. Further interpretation of the Table 5 reveals that 27 (26.6%) of the respondents were in the jail for killing their daughters-in-law, 8 (7.8%) for murdering their husbands, 14 (13.7%) for murdering their close relatives, while only 2 (2%) of them for killing their children, and 18 (17.6%) of the respondents murdered any other person other than close relations i.e. neighbours, any acquaintance or an enemy. Murder of this type was committed either after a sudden quarrel or in the heat of passion.

Data further indicates that 18 (17.6%) of the respondents violated the liquor Prohibition Act and were serving jail terms under the Prevention of Antisocial Activities Act. While 7 (6.9%) violated the Narcotic Act i.e. Narcotics Drugs and Psychotropic Substances Act. About 3 (2.9%) committed theft, the same number for eloping with minor girls and only 2 (2%) violated Public Laws, like travelling without tickets, etc.

Motive behind Crime Commission

It is rather difficult to determine or pinpoint any particular factor as a cause for a crime. The researcher, based on the interviews as expressed by the criminals, analysed the motives behind their crime commission. The degree of involvement of the women in various crimes varies from individual to individual. Though it is very difficult to understand the processes which led her to commit a violent act, an attempt has been made to understand the dynamics of her criminal behaviour.

Table 5.5 shows that 37 (36.3%) of the respondents had social stress in the families, like domestic quarrels, strained intra-personal relationships, etc., while 21 (20.6%) of them had economic stress in the families and had financial difficulties. For 26 (25.5%) of the women criminals, the crime was committed in a particular situation, which compelled them to do so, while 10 (9.8%) felt it was accidental and they did not have any intention to do it. The other factors reported were the desire for revenge in cases of 3 (2.9%) and temptation in 5 (4.9%) of the respondents.

The main factors responsible as a motive were unhappy marital relations, domestic quarrels, husband's relations with other women, enmity, land dispute, financial strains, etc.

Method of Crime

Table 5.5 reveals that 43 (42.2%) of the respondents used the method of burning for killing their victims. As has been already mentioned, most of the murder victims were daughters-in-law. Thus it seems bride burning is becoming a serious problem in Gujarat. In 9 (8.8%) of the cases, the offenders hand used weapons like axes, stone, knives, etc., for killing the victims; in 5 (4.9%) of the cases, the victims were found hanging from the roof and in 1 (1%), the death of the victim was due to strangulation. Further, it can be seen that in 2 (2%) cases, the victims were thrown into water tanks or a river and were drowned, while in 3 (2.9%) cases, the offenders had used poison to get rid of their victims. It was found that the offender used poison for killing all three of her children. In the majority of the cases, before murder took place, there was a lot of heated arguments and fights, which provoked the criminals to take such a step as killing the victims.

The women criminals who fall into the category of 'not applicable' were arrested for theft, illicit drug or liquor business or any other offences, other than murder. A total of 67 (65.7%) of the respondents were either convicted or were under custody for murder charges, while 25 (24.5%) were again either convicted or were PASA detenus.

Type of Companion

Table 5.5 reveals that in the majority of the cases, i.e. 63 (61.8%) the crime was performed in the company of family members or non-family members. In the present study it shows that, in most of the cases, the respondents committed the crime along with her spouse, son or any other family members, while in very few cases the respondents took the assistance of non-family members.

It was further found that 39 (38.2%) of the respondents performed the crime alone and did not have any accomplices for committing the crime.

Place and Time of Crime

It can be seen from Table 5.5 that most of the crime i.e. 67 (65.7%) were committed in urban areas and 35 (34.3%) in rural areas. Thus it shows that though the majority of them were born in rural areas, they got into criminality after migrating to the urban areas. Social depravity, emotional insecurity and economic strain might have indulged them into criminality. It was also noticed that 63 (61.8%) of the crimes were committed during daytime, 19 (18.6%) at night and 17 (16.7%) in the evening, while 3 of them refused to talk about it.

Living with at the Time of Committing Offence

It was found that a large number of the respondents i.e. 70 (68.6%) were living with their husbands at the time of committing the offence. This shows that women after marriage have to make lots of adjustment with their new environment. Her life becomes strictly confined to domestic affairs, where she has to adjust in the beginning with parents-in-law and later on with daughters-in-law, the treatment they received, the nature, habits, temperaments of their new relatives and the expectations which they demand from them, many a time either provoke or become motivational factors for committing crime.

Acceptance of Crime

It was quite interesting to find that a majority of the women criminals in the present study i.e. 76 (74.5%) refused to accept the crime. Not only the undertrials but even those who were serving life-terms or convicted for murder said that they have not committed the crime, but because of the dying declaration of the victim, they have been convicted. Only 26 (25.5%) of the respondents, who were mostly detained under PASA, accepted their crime and tried to defend their criminality by giving economic needs as the cause for their crime.

6. History of Imprisonment

Women in Indian prisons constitute a small segment of the convict population, and their problems do not receive the same priorities as available to male prisoners. Women in Indian jails live under pathetic conditions. The female wards in prisons were mostly over-crowded with various types of offenders housed together. The facilities for education, vocational training and social uplift are not adequate. These women are sent to prison with the rationale of rehabilitation, but actually they are separated and isolated from the community. The National expert committee of women prisoners proposed for a proper classification system which should include the medical, criminological and social assessment of the inmates and serve as basis for care, treatment, employment, training, education and rehabilitation of the inmates. In the present study an attempt has been made to reveal the nature and degree of prisonization.

Status as a Prisoner

It can be observed from Table 5.6 that the majority of the respondents i.e. 56 (54.9 percent) were convicted, 17 (16.7%) were detained in the jail under the prevention of Anti-social Act, while 29 (28.4%) were kept in the jail as undertrials.

Nature of Present Punishment

The table 5.6 further reveals that the majority of the respondents 54 (52.9%) were serving rigorous imprisonment, while 2 (2%) were on simple imprisonment. It was observed during data collection that the respondents serving life imprisonment were well adjusted than those who were under detention or were undertrials. The majority of the convicted criminals were first time offenders, while those under detention, came second or third time in the jail.

Table 5.6

History of Imprisonment

History of Imprisonment	Frequency	Percentage
Status as a Prisoner		
Convicts	56	54.9
Detenus	17	16.7
Undertrial	29	28.4
	102	**100.0**
Nature of Present Punishment		
Rigorous imprisonment	54	52.9
Simple imprisonment	2	2.0
1 year detention	17	16.7
under custody	29	28.4
	102	**100.0**
Reaction to Jail Routine		
Not adjusting	23	22.5
Trying to adjust	35	34.3
Adjusted	43	42.2
No reaction	1	1.0
	102	**100.0**
Suggestion for Reformation		
Job and Education	48	47.0
Vocational Training & Guidance	28	27.5
Family should accept them	26	25.5
Total N =	**102**	**100.0**

Reaction to Jail Routine

An attempt has been made to find out the feelings of prison experience and adjustment with the daily routine of the jail. Once a person has been put in a prison, it leads to physical isolation, which may result in other kinds of deprivations. The prison tends to deprive the prisoners of liberty for years. This is regarded as a deterrent measure. To face this reality, they undergo anxiety caused by pains and losses. Deprivations refer strictly to the dispossession or loss of privileges, opportunities, material goods, etc. Thus the inmates' social behaviour and relationships within the prison are affected by their opinion regarding prison experience and their reaction to that experience.

Table 5.6 shows that 43 (42.2%) of the respondents could adjust the Jail routine, 35 (34.3%) of the respondents were trying to adjust, while 23 (22.5%) were having difficulties to adjust. These were mostly the undertrials, who were mentally not prepared for their stay in the prison and having hopes that they would be released or will get bail.

The majority of the respondents were satisfied with the attitudes of their co-inmates, jail officers, guarding staff and Superintendent. They found them cordial and sympathetic towards them. Most of the prisoners were spending their leisure time by gossiping or through recreational activities. Very few had the habit of reading books and could spend their time by reading books from the Jail library. More than 50 per cent of the criminals participated in vocational programmes of envelope making, stitching, embroidery, etc. The convicted women worked for the Jail kitchen, while morning and afternoon hours were used for cleaning grains and cutting vegetables for all the male and female inmates of the Jail.

For doing these activities they get daily wages as per the rules of the Jail. They use this money for buying things for their daily use.

It was also found that usually the primary relatives of the prisoners visit them regularly, while very few secondary relatives or family of procreation visit them.

Suggestion for Reformation

Table 5.6 also reveals that 48 (47.1%) of the respondents felt that they should have some education and after release they must get employed somewhere to be on their own. While 28 (27.5%) felt that vocational training and guidance could have improved their condition after release, as that would facilitate their rehabilitation. Further it was observed that 26 (25.5%) were keen to go back to their families and felt all their problems and insecurity will be over if their family members accept them back.

To conclude, it may be said that due to lower occupations, insufficient income, these women were economically distressed and frustrated, and in order to meet their needs, they got involved in crimes. Then the family life along with environmental surrounding, neighbourhood, living conditions, social customs might have affected their behaviour in childhood and finally their behaviour in adulthood. From the above discussion, it can be seen that all the factors of the family situation, such as the type of the family, the size of the family and economic conditions play a vital role in promoting intra-familial relationships. Conflicting intra-familial patterns produce maladjustment among the inter-personal relations of the family and create complexities and conflicts in the family. Thus the continuous process of the socialization of women in a variety of interacting situations and circumstances is found to be the most important factor causing female criminality. Lastly, the objective of the punishment is the protection of society through the control and prevention of crime and treatment and rehabilitation of the criminals. The imprisonment brings not only punishment but also deprivation, pains and losses to an accused. Right from the arrest, till her release, the woman convict undergoes harassment, mental tensions, social and economic losses. Thus it can be analysed that the social background and personal qualities of the inmates have an important impact on the way they perceive their prison environment, patterns of adjustment and social life in prison.

6

DATA ANALYSIS

In the previous chapters, a theoretical and methodological framework has been developed from the remarkable work done by various criminologists, sociologists and psychologists.

This chapter is concerned with the various results analysed pertaining to the data collected from the two Central Prisons of Gujarat i.e Baroda and Ahmedabad Central Jails. A total number of 102 women criminals, who were undergoing imprisonment as convicts, detenus or undertrials, were interviewed to understand their social, economic, psychological and cultural background so that a picture of their life style could be explored. Besides, in order to understand the influence and impact of the imprisonment environment on them, their own assessment and perceptions of the prison culture have been analysed.

The previous chapter has given the analysis of the profile and socio-economic background of the women offenders. While in this section an attempt has been made to study the relationships of socio-economic conditions and patterns of crime variable with temperament, life style, family environment and correctional institutions environment. The main variables used in the study are :

(1) Age.
(2) Education.
(3) Income of respondent.
(4) Type of family.
(5) Place of residence at birth.
(6) Place of crime.
(7) Reasons for arrest.
(8) Motive behind crime commission.
(9) Nature of crime.
(10) Length of conviction.
(11) Length of time spent in prison.
(12) Moral values.
(13) Guilt feelings.
(14) Causes of crime.
(15) Temperament.
(16) Life style.
(17) Family environment.
(18) Institutional environment.

In the present study bi-variate and master tables have been used for analysis. Association of variables were computed through statistical analyses like chi-square, ANOVA-LSD, and T value. Two social climate scales of Dr. Moos were used in the study. The Correctional Institutions Environmental Scale (CIES) having nine subscales assess three underlying domains or sets of dimensions i.e. Relationship dimensions, Personal growth and System Maintenance dimensions. These subscales consist of i.e. Involvement, Support, Expressiveness, Autonomy, Practical Orientation, Personal Problem Orientation, Order and Organisation, Clarity and Staff Control, that is, three subscales in each dimension.

The Family Environment Scale (FES) comprises ten subscales that measure the social environmental characteristics of all types of families. The ten FES subscales assess three underlying domains or sets of dimensions. i.e Relationship dimensions, Personal growth and System Maintenance dimensions. The Subscales are Cohesion, Expressiveness, Conflict, Independence, Achievement Orientation, Intellectual–Cultural Orientation, Active-Recreational Orientation, Moral Religious Orientation, Organisation and Control. The score of each component was computed and the total score of all the components was taken into consideration in presenting the picture of Institutional and Family Environment. Below mean score and above mean score was taken into consideration while deciding the criteria on high and low levels of Family Environment and Institutional Environment.

The nine areas of Temperament Scale such as, Active, Impulsive, Dominant, Emotional, Sociable, Reflective, Nervous, Introvert/Extrovert and Aggression and eight areas of Life Style Scale like Individualistic, Exploitive, Explosive, Resistive, Domineering, Conforming, Escapist and Evasive were also computed, to find out the below mean score and above mean score in order to decide the high and low levels of Temperament and Life Style.

This chapter has been divided into different sections to give a total picture of the data analysis, such as, socio-economic background, patterns of crime, history of imprisonment, Guilt feelings, moral values, temperament, life style, family environment and correctional institutions environment.

SECTION – 1

Socio–Economic Background

It is very important to understand the effect of the socio-economic background on women criminals. Thus an effort has been made to understand the personal social characteristics of the inmates, such as, age, education, income, type of family, place of birth and their association with temperament, life style, family environment and institutional environment.

Table–6.1 : Association between Age and Life Style – Individualistic

Present Age	Life Style-Individualistic		Row Total
	Low	High	
Below – 30	7 12.7	13 27.7	20 19.6
31 – 40	16 29.1	21 44.7	37 36.3
41 – 50	16 29.1	9 19.1	25 24.5
51 & above	16 29.1	4 8.5	20 19.6
Respondents Total	55 53.9	47 46.1	102 100.0

Chi-Square	D.F.	Significance
11.07636	3	.0113

Referring to the table 6.1 it can be seen that the Chi-square value is significant at .05 level of confidence. Therefore there is a strong association between Age and Life Style.

Further it can be interpreted that, "Individualistic" Life style is found more among 31–40 age group.

Table–6.2: Association between Age and Correctional Institutions Environment - Staff Control

Present Age	C.I.E. – Staff Control		Row Total
	Low	High	
Below – 30	7 17.9	13 20.6	20 19.6
31 – 40	15 38.5	22 34.9	37 36.3
41 – 50	5 12.8	20 31.7	25 24.5
51 & above	12 30.8	8 12.7	20 19.6
Respondents Total	39 38.2	63 61.8	102 100.0

Chi-Square	D.F.	Significance
7.70377	3	.0525

Referring to the table 6.2 it can be seen that the Chi-square value is significant at .05 level of confidence. Therefore there is a strong association between Age and Staff Control.

The Data shows that 62 respondents i.e. 60.8 per cent fall into the category of 31–50 age group, out of that 38.5% of respondents fall on low "Staff Control".

GRAPH 6.1: AGE OF RESPONDENTS

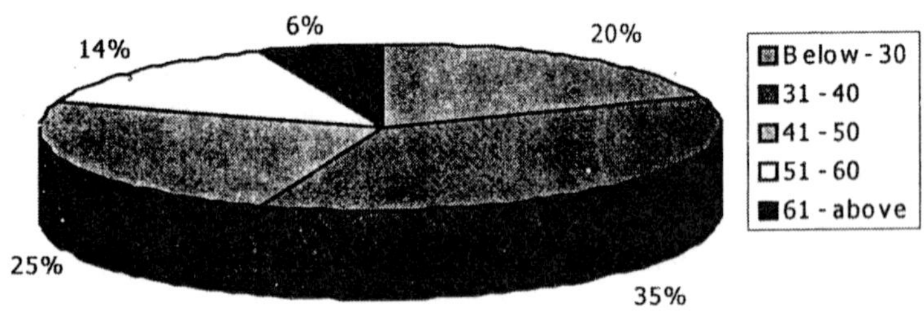

GRAPH 6.2: EDUCATION OF RESPONDENTS

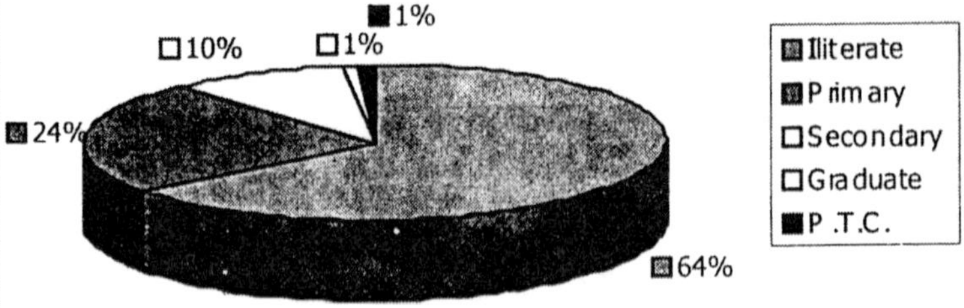

Table – 6.3: Association between Education and Temperament – Impulsive

Education	Temperament – Impulsive		Row Total
	Low	High	
Illiterate	44 73.3	22 52.4	66 64.7
Primary	8 13.3	16 38.1	24 23.5
Secondary & above	8 13.3	4 9.5	12 11.8
Respondents Total	60 58.8	42 41.2	102 100.0

Chi-Square	D.F.	Significance
8.41905	2	.0149

Referring to the table 6.3 it can be seen that the Chi-square value is significant at .05 level of confidence. Therefore there is a strong association between Education and Temperament.

Further it can be noted that 66 respondents fall into the category of illiterate, out of that 77.3% respondents fall on low "impulsive" Temperament.

Table – 6.4 : Association between Education and Family Environment – Expressiveness

Education	F.E. – Expressiveness		Row Total
	Low	High	
Illiterate	51 73.9	15 45.5	66 64.7
Primary	11 15.9	12 39.4	24 23.5
Secondary & above	7 10.1	5 15.2	12 11.8
Respondents Total	69 67.6	33 32.4	102 100.0

Chi-Square	D.F.	Significance
8.48778	2	.0144

Referring to the table 6.4 it can be seen that the Chi-square value is significant at .05 level of confidence. Therefore there is a strong association between Education and Family Environment i.e. Expressiveness.

The table 6.4 also reveals that 66 respondents fall into the category of illiterate, out of that 51 i.e. 73.9% of respondents fall on low "Expressiveness" Family Environment.

Table – 6.5

Association between Education and Family Environment – Personal Growth

Education	FE – Personal Growth		Row Total
	Low	High	
Illiterate	42 75.0	24 52.2	66 64.7
Primary	11 19.6	13 28.3	24 23.5
Secondary & above	3 5.4	9 19.6	12 11.8
Respondents Total	56 54.9	46 45.1	102 100.0

Chi-Square	D.F.	Significance
7.16423	2	.0278

Referring to the table 6.5 it can be seen that the Chi-square value is significant at .05 level of confidence. Therefore there is a strong association between Education and Family Environment.

It can be observed that 66 respondents fall into the category of illiterate group, out of that 75.0% respondents fall on low "Personal Growth" Family Environment.

Table – 6.6 :

Association between Income of Respondent and Family Environment – Moral-Religious Orientation

Income of Respondent	F.E. – Moral RO		Row Total
	Low	High	
Below 500	3 6.1	14 26.4	17 16.7
501 – 1000	14 28.6	14 26.4	28 27.5
1001-5000	10 20.4	5 9.4	15 14.7
Nil	22 44.9	20 37.7	42 41.2
Respondents Total	49 48.0	53 52.0	102 100.0

Chi-Square	D.F.	Significance
8.73612	3	.0330

Referring to the table 6.6 it can be seen that the chi-square value is significant at .05 level of confidence. Therefore there is a strong association between Income of Respondents and Family Environment.

Further it can be interpreted that 42 respondents fall into the category of Nil Income; out of that 44.9% of respondents fall on low "Moral-Religious Orientation" Family Environment.

GRAPH 6.3: CASTE

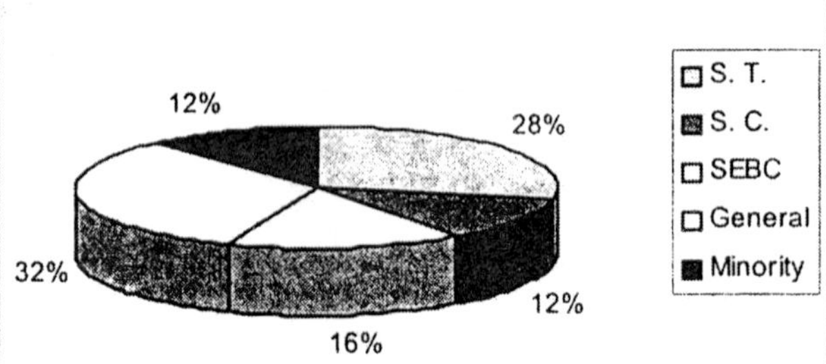

GRAPH 6.4: MARITAL STATUS

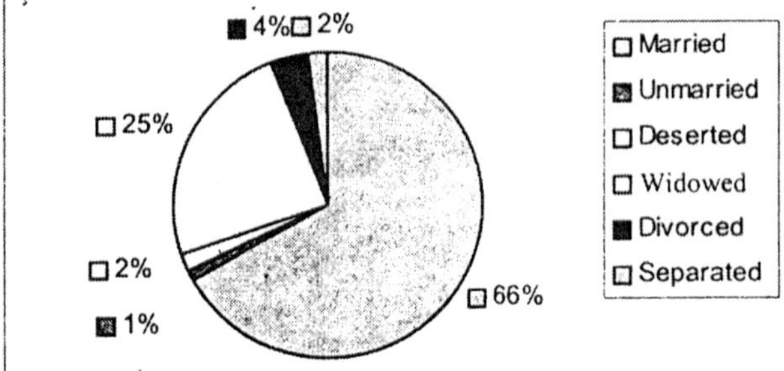

Table – 6,7: Difference Between Type of Family and Temperament – Active

T-test for :

Type of Family		Number of cases		Mean	Standard Deviation		Standard Error
Group – 1 Nuclear		51		12.2549	1.481		.207
Group – 2 Joint		51		11.3333	2.471		.346
		Pooled Variance Estimate			Separate Variance Estimate		
F Value	2–Tail Prob.	T Value	Degrees of Freedom	2–Tail Prob.	T Value	Degrees of Freedom	2–Tail Prob.
2.78	.000	2.28	100	.024	2.28	81.82	.025

From the table 6.7 it can be interpreted that two groups of respondents i.e. Type of Family (Nuclear/Joint) differ significantly from each other at .05 level of confidence with reference to "Active" Temperament.

Referring to the mean score, further it could be inferred that group 1 has higher mean score than group 2 or it means that group 1 i.e. nuclear families are more active than group 2, i.e. joint families.

Table – 6.8

Difference Between Type of Family and Temperament – Reflective

T-test for :

Type of Family		Number of cases		Mean	Standard Deviation		Standard Error
Group – 1 Nuclear		51		10.6275	1.469		.206
Group – 2 Joint		51		9.8235	1.621		.227
		Pooled Variance Estimate			Separate Variance Estimate		
F Value	2-Tail Prob.	T Value	Degrees of Freedom	2-Tail Prob.	T Value	Degrees of Freedom	2-Tail Prob.
1.22	.489	2.62	100	.010	2.62	99.05	.010

From the table 6.8 it can be interpreted that two groups of respondents i.e. Type of Family (Nuclear/Joint) differ significantly from each other at .05 level of confidence with reference to "Reflective" Temperament.

Referring to the mean score, further it could be inferred that group 1 has higher mean score than group 2 or it means that a nuclear family is more reflective than a joint family.

GRAPH 6.5: TYPE OF FAMILY AND TEMPERAMENT–REFLECTIVE

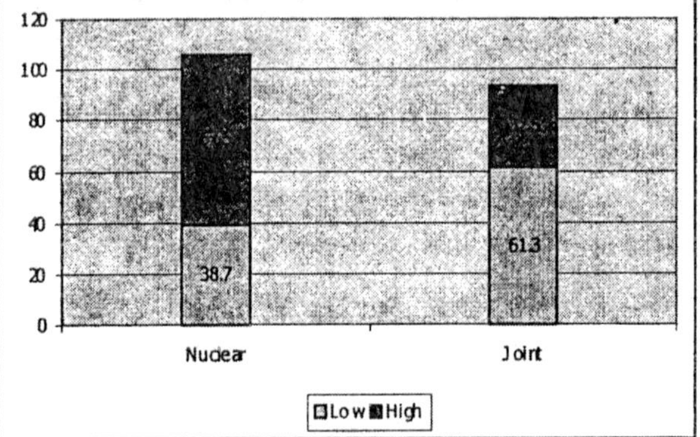

GRAPH 6.6: AGE & LIFE STYLE INDIVIDUALISTIC

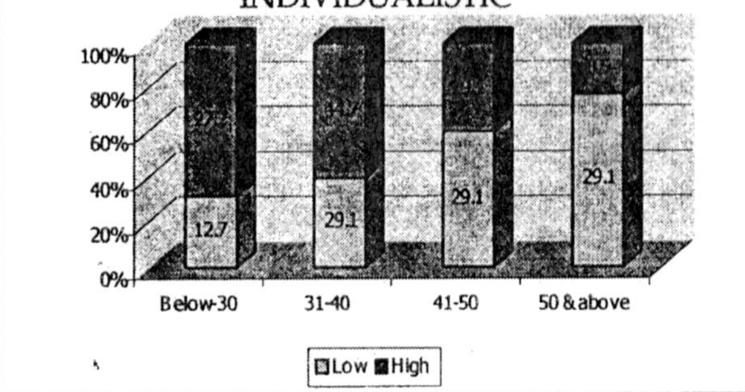

Table – 6.9: Difference Between Type of Family and Temperament – Aggression

T-test for :

Type of Family		Number of cases		Mean	Standard Deviation		Standard Error
Group – 1 Nuclear		51		9.1373	2.771		.388
Group – 2 Joint		51		8.0392	2.821		.395
		Pooled Variance Estimate			Separate Variance Estimate		
F Value	2–Tail Prob.	T Value	Degrees of Freedom	2–Tail Prob.	T Value	Degrees of Freedom	2–Tail Prob.
1.04	.901	1.98	100	.050	1.98	99.97	.050

From the table 6.9 it can be interpreted that two groups of respondents i.e. Type of Family (Nuclear/Joint) differ significantly from each other at .05 level of confidence with reference to "Aggression" Temperament.

Referring to the mean score, further it could be inferred that group 1 has higher mean score than group 2 or it means that members of a nuclear family are more aggressive than members of a joint family.

Table – 6.10

Difference Between Type of Family and Life Style – Exploitive

T-test for :

Type of Family		Number of cases		Mean	Standard Deviation		Standard Error
Group – 1 Nuclear		51		7.9020	1.285		.180
Group – 2 Joint		51		7.3333	1.071		.150
		Pooled Variance Estimate			Separate Variance Estimate		
F Value	2-Tail Prob.	T Value	Degrees of Freedom	2-Tail Prob.	T Value	Degrees of Freedom	2-Tail Prob.
1.44	.202	2.43	100	.017	2.43	96.86	.017

From the table 6.10 it can be interpreted that two groups of respondents i.e. Type of Family (Nuclear/Joint) differ significantly from each other at .05 level of confidence with reference to "Exploitive" Life Style.

Referring to the mean score, further it could be inferred that group 1 has higher mean score than group 2 or it means that group 1 is more exploitive than group 2.

Table – 6.11: Difference Between Type of Family and Family Environment – Relationship

T-test for :

Type of Family		Number of cases		Mean	Standard Deviation		Standard Error
Group – 1 Nuclear		51		13.2745	1.801		.252
Group – 2 Joint		51		12.4706	1.554		.218
		Pooled Variance Estimate			Separate Variance Estimate		
F Value	2-Tail Prob.	T Value	Degrees of Freedom	2-Tail Prob.	T Value	Degrees of Freedom	2-Tail Prob.
1.34	.300	2.41	100	.018	2.41	97.90	.018

From the table 6.11 it can be interpreted that two groups of respondents i.e. Type of Family (Nuclear/Joint) differ significantly from each other at .05 level of confidence with reference to "Relationship " Family Environment.

Referring to the mean score, further it could be inferred that group 1 has higher mean score than the group 2 or it means that group 1 is more relative than group 2.

Table – 6.12: Difference Between Type of Family and Correctional Institutions Environment – Expressiveness

T-test for :

Type of Family		Number of cases		Mean	Standard Deviation		Standard Error
Group – 1 Nuclear		51		5.2353	1.210		.169
Group – 2 Joint		51		5.7059	1.082		.152
		Pooled Variance Estimate			Separate Variance Estimate		
F Value	2-Tail Prob.	T Value	Degrees of Freedom	2-Tail Prob.	T Value	Degrees of Freedom	2-Tail Prob.
1.25	.435	-2.07	100	.041	-2.07	98.79	.041

From the table 6.12 it can be interpreted that two groups of respondents i.e. Type of Family (Nuclear/Joint) differ significantly from each other at .05 level of confidence with reference to "Expressiveness " Correctional Institutions Environment.

Referring to the mean score, further it could be inferred that group 2 has higher mean score than group 1 or it means that group 2 is more expressive than group 1.

Table – 6.13

Difference Between Type of Family and Correctional Institutions Environment – Autonomy

T-test for :

Type of Family		Number of cases		Mean	Standard Deviation		Standard Error
Group – 1 Nuclear		51		6.1765	1.014		.142
Group – 2 Joint		51		6.6275	1.113		.156
		Pooled Variance Estimate			Separate Variance Estimate		
F Value	2-Tail Prob.	T Value	Degrees of Freedom	2-Tail Prob.	T Value	Degrees of Freedom	2-Tail Prob.
1.20	.513	-2.14	100	.035	-2.14	99.15	.035

From the table 6.13 it can be interpreted that two groups of respondents i.e. Type of Family (Nuclear/Joint) differ significantly from each other at .05 level of confidence with reference to "Autonomy " Correctional Institutions Environment.

Referring to the mean score, further it could be inferred that group 2 has higher mean score than group 1 or it means that group 2 is more autonomous than group 1.

Table – 6.14 : Association between Place of Residence at Birth and Temperament – Dominant

Place of Residence at Birth	Temperament – Dominant		Row Total
	Low	High	
Rural, Tribal	35 52.2	26 74.3	61 59.8
Urban	32 47.8	9 25.7	41 40.2
Respondents Total	67 65.7	35 34.3	102 100.0

Chi-Square	D.F.	Significance
3.77673	1	.0520
4.64863	1	.0311

Referring to the table 6.14 it can be seen that chi-square value is significant at .05 level of confidence. Therefore there is a strong association between Place of Residence at Birth and Temperament.

Data in table 6.14 indicates that 61 respondents fall into the category of Rural and Tribal, out of that 74.3% of respondents fall on high "Dominant" Temperament.

Table – 6.15: Difference Between Place of Residence at Birth and Life Style – Conforming

T-test for :

Place of Birth	Number of cases	Mean	Standard Deviation	Standard Error
Group – 1 Rural	61	6.9016	1.012	.130
Group – 2 Urban	41	7.4390	.923	.144

		Pooled Variance Estimate			Separate Variance Estimate		
F Value	2–Tail Prob.	T Value	Degrees of Freedom	2–Tail Prob.	T Value	Degrees of Freedom	2–Tail Prob.
1.20	.544	-2.72	100	.008	-2.77	91.07	.007

From the table 6.15 it can be interpreted that two groups of respondents i.e. Place of Birth (Rural/Urban) differ significantly from each other at .01 level of confidence with reference to "Conforming" – Life Style.

Referring to the mean score, further it could be inferred that group 2 has higher mean score than group 1 or it means that group 2 is more conforming than group 1.

Table – 6.16

Association between Place of Residence at Birth and Family Environment – Expressiveness

Place of Residence at Birth	F. E. Expressiveness		Row Total
	Low	High	
Rural, Tribal	47 68.1	14 42.4	61 59.8
Urban	22 31.9	19 57.6	41 40.2
Respondents Total	69 67.6	33 32.4	102 100.0

Chi-Square	D.F.	Significance
5.10747	1	.0238
6.12964	1	.0133

Referring to the table 6.16 it can be seen that chi-square value is significant at .05 level of confidence. Therefore there is a strong association between Place of Residence at Birth and Family Environment.

Table 6.16 shows that 61 respondents fall into the category of Rural and Tribal, 68.1% fall on low "Expressiveness" Family Environment.

Table – 6.17: Difference Between Place of Residence at Birth and Family Environment –Independence

T-test for :

Place of Birth		Number of cases		Mean		Standard Deviation		Standard Error
Group – 1 Rural		61		4.9508		1.217		.156
Group – 2 Urban		41		5.4634		1.027		.160
		Pooled Variance Estimate			Separate Variance Estimate			
F Value	2 –Tail Prob.	T Value	Degrees of Freedom	2 –Tail Prob.	T Value	Degrees of Freedom	2–Tail Prob.	
1.40	.257	-2.22	100	.029	-2.29	94.82	.024	

From the table 6.17 it can be interpreted that two groups of respondents i.e. Place of Birth (Rural/Urban) differ significantly from each other at .05 level of confidence with reference to "Independence" Family Environment.

Referring to the mean score, further it could be inferred that group 2 has higher mean score than group 1 or it means that group 2 is more independent than group 1.

Table – 6.18: Association between Place of Residence at Birth and Family Environment – Intellectual–Cultural Orientation

Place of Residence at Birth	FE – Intellectual C.O.		Row Total
	Low	High	
Rural, Tribal	36 69.2	25 50.0	61 59.8
Urban	16 30.8	25 50.0	41 40.2
Respondents Total	52 51.0	50 49.0	102 100.0

Chi-Square	D.F.	Significance
3.16232	1	.0754
3.92151	1	.0477

Referring to the table 6.18 it can be seen that chi-square value is significant at .05 level of confidence. Therefore there is a strong association between Place of Residence at Birth and Family Environment.

The data show that out of 61 respondents falling into the category of Rural and Tribal, 69.2% fall on low "Intellectual–Cultural Orientation" Family Environment.

Table – 6.19

Difference Between Place of Residence at Birth and Family Environment –Organization

T-test for :

Place of Birth		Number of cases		Mean	Standard Deviation		Standard Error
Group – 1 Rural		61		6.6885	.941		.120
Group – 2 Urban		41		7.1707	1.138		.178
		Pooled Variance Estimate			Separate Variance Estimate		
F Value	2-Tail Prob.	T Value	Degrees of Freedom	2-Tail Prob.	T Value	Degrees of Freedom	2-Tail Prob.
1.46	.178	-2.33	100	.022	-2.25	74.67	.028

From the table 6.19 it can be interpreted that two groups of respondents i.e. Place of Birth (Rural/Urban) differ significantly from each other at .05 level of confidence with reference to "Organization" Family Environment.

Referring to the mean score, further it could be inferred that group 2 has higher mean score than group 1 or it means that group 2 is more organized than group 1.

Table – 6.20: Association between Place of Residence at Birth and Correctional Institutions Environment – Autonomy

Place of Residence at Birth	CIE – Autonomy		Row Total
	Low	High	
	25	36	61
Rural, Tribal	48.1	72.0	59.8
	27	14	41
Urban	51.9	28.0	40.2
Respondents	52	50	102
Total	51.0	49.0	100.0

Chi-Square	D.F.	Significance
5.11429	1	.0237
6.06868	1	.0138

Referring to the table 6.20 it can be seen that chi-square value is significant at .05 level of confidence. Therefore there is a strong association between Place of Residence at Birth and Correctional Institutions Environment.

The data presented in table shows that 61 respondents are falling into the category of Rural and Tribal, out of that 72% of respondents fall on high "Autonomy" Correctional Institutions Environment.

SECTION - 2

Patterns of Crime

The patterns of criminality have been already discussed in the previous chapter of Profile of Women Criminals. In recent times, the processes of industrialization, urbanization and liberation of women's movement have changed the rate of criminality among women in India. An indepth analysis has been made to find the relationships between reasons of arrest, motive, nature, place of crime and temperament, life style, family environment and correctional institutions environment.

Table – 6.21

Association between Reasons for Arrest and Temperament – Reflective

Reasons for Arrest	Temperament –Reflective		Row
	Low	High	Total
Murder of daughter-in-law	18 34.6	9 27.3	27 31.8
Murder of husband	7 13.5	1 3.0	8 9.4
Murder of close relatives	12 23.1	2 6.1	14 16.5
Murder of others	7 13.5	11 33.3	18 21.2
Violation of Liquor	8 15.4	10 30.3	18 21.2
Respondents Total	52 61.2	33 38.8	85 100.0

Chi-Square	D.F.	Significance
12.11209	4	.0165

Referring to the table 6.21 it can be seen that chi-square value is significant at .05 level of confidence. Therefore there is a strong association between Reasons for Arrest and Temperament.

The analysis of data shows that 52 respondents fall into the category of low "Reflective" Temperament, out of that 34.6% of respondents fall in the category of Murder of daughter-in-law as Reason for Arrest.

Table – 6.22

Association between Reasons for Arrest and Family Environment – Cohesion

Reasons for Arrest	FE – Cohesion		Row Total
	Low	High	
Murder of daughter-in-law	13 28.9	14 35.0	27 31.8
Murder of husband	2 4.4	6 15.0	8 9.4
Murder of close relatives	9 20.0	6 12.5	14 16.5
Murder of others	14 31.1	4 10.0	18 21.2
Violation of Liquor	7 15.6	11 27.5	18 21.2
Respondents Total	45 52.9	40 47.1	85 100.0

Chi-Square	D.F.	Significance
9.36262	4	.0526

Referring to the table 6.22 it can be seen that chi-square value is significant at .05 level of confidence. Therefore there is a strong association between Reasons for Arrest and Family Environment.

The data distributed in the table 6.22 show that 45 respondents fall into the category of low "Cohesion" Family Environment, out of that 38 respondents fall into the category of murder as reason for arrest.

GRAPH 6.7 : ENVIRONMENTAL PRESSURE BEFORE CRIME

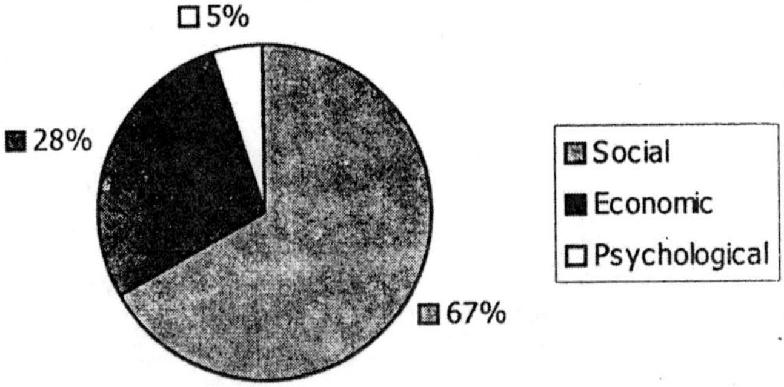

Table – 6.23

Association between Reasons for Arrest and Correctional Institutions Environment - Order and Organization

Reasons for Arrest	CIE – Order and Org.		Row Total
	Low	High	
Murder of daughter-in-law	6 17.1	21 42.0	27 31.8
Murder of husband	3 8.6	5 10.0	8 9.4
Murder of close relatives	3 8.6	11 22.0	14 16.5
Murder of others	8 22.9	10 20.0	18 21.2
Violation of Liquor	15 42.9	3 6.0	18 21.2
Respondents Total	35 41.2	50 58.8	85 100.0

Chi-Square	D.F.	Significance
19.58999	4	.0006

GRAPH 6.8 : MOTIVE BEHIND CRIME COMMISSION

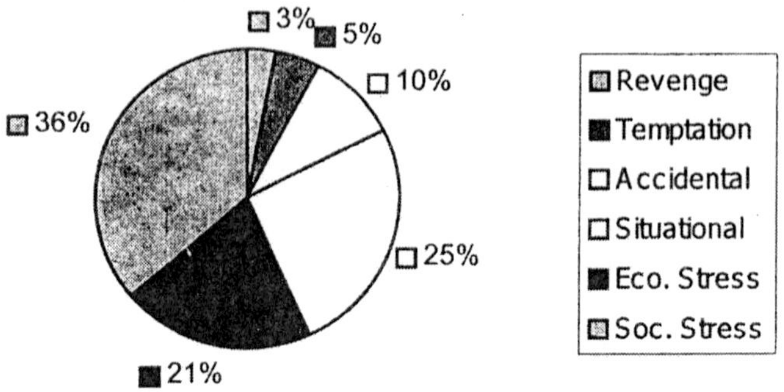

Referring to the table 6.23 it can be seen that chi-square value is significant at .05 level of confidence. Therefore there is a strong association between Reasons for Arrest and Correctional Institutions Environment.

The data presented in the table 6.23 shows that 50 respondents fall into the category of high "Order and Organization" Correctional Institutions Environment, out of that 42% of respondents fall into the category of murder of daughter-in-law as Reason for Arrest.

Table – 6.24: Association between Nature of Crime and Life Style – Explosive

Nature of Crime	Life Style – Explosive		Row Total
	Low	High	
Murder	39 84.8	28 60.9	67 72.8
Illicit liquor + Drugs	7 15.2	18 39.1	25 27.2
Respondents Total	46 50.0	46 50.0	92 100.0

Chi-Square	D.F.	Significance
5.49254	1	.0191
6.64597	1	.0099

Referring to the table 6.24 it can be seen that chi-square value is significant at .01 level of confidence. Therefore there is a strong association between Nature of Crime and Life Style.

The analysis of data shows that 67 respondents fall into the category of Murder, out of that 84.8% of respondents fall on low "Explosive" Life Style.

Table – 6.25: Difference Between Place of Crime and Life Style – Conforming

T-test for :

Place of Crime		Number of cases		Mean	Standard Deviation		Standard Error
Group – 1 (Rural)		35		6.8000	1.052		.178
Group – 2 (Urban)		67		7.2836	.950		.116
		Pooled Variance Estimate			Separate Variance Estimate		
F Value	2–Tail Prob.	T Value	Degrees of Freedom	2–Tail Prob.	T Value	Degrees of Freedom	2–Tail Prob.
1.22	.476	-2.35	100	.021	-2.28	63.27	.026

From the table 6.25 it can be interpreted that two groups of respondents i.e. Place of Crime (Rural/Urban) differ significantly from each other at .05 level of confidence with reference to "Conforming" – Life Style.

Referring to the mean score, further it could be inferred that group 2 has higher mean score than group 1 or it means that group 2 is more conforming than group 1.

Table – 6.26: Difference Between Place of Crime and Family Environment – Expressiveness

T-test for :

Place of Crime		Number of cases		Mean	Standard Deviation		Standard Error
Group – 1 (Rural)		35		3.8571	.845		.143
Group – 2 (Urban)		67		4.2836	.794		.097
		Pooled Variance Estimate			Separate Variance Estimate		
F Value	2–Tail Prob.	T Value	Degrees of Freedom	2–Tail Prob.	T Value	Degrees of Freedom	2–Tail Prob.
1.13	.652	-2.52	100	.013	-2.47	65.42	.016

From the table 6.26 it can be interpreted that two groups of respondents i.e. Place of Crime (Rural / Urban) differ significantly from each other at .05 level of confidence with reference to "Expressiveness" – Family Environment.

Referring to the mean score, further it could be inferred that group 2 has higher mean score than group 1 or it means that group 2 is more expressive than group 1.

SECTION - 3

History of Imprisonment

In the study an attempt has been made to explore the assumption that every inmate in prison is influenced by the social and physical surroundings of the jail and these influence their opinions, attitudes, behaviour and perceptions. An attempt has been made to find out the impact of prisonization on the inmates in relation to their length of conviction, duration of time spent in prison and temperament, life style, family environment and correctional institutions environment.

Table – 6.27: Association between Length of Conviction and Life Style – Escapist

Length of Conviction	Life Style – Escapist		Row Total
	Low	High	
10 yrs.	3 20.0	12 13.8	15 14.7
20 yrs. / Life Imp.	10 66.7	31 35.6	41 40.2
PASA / 1 yr. Detention	-	17 19.5	17 16.7
Under Trial	2 13.3	27 31.0	29 28.4
Respondents Total	15 14.7	87 85.3	102 100.0

Chi-Square	D.F.	Significance
7.74180	3	.0517

Referring to the table 6.27 it can be seen that Chi-square value is significant at .05 level of confidence. Therefore there is a strong association between Length of Conviction and Life Style.

Further it can be interpreted that 41 respondents fall into the category of Life Imprisonment, out of that 31 respondents fall on high "Escapist" Life Style.

It can also be seen that 87 respondents (85.3%) falling in different categories of Length of Conviction are having high "Escapist" Life Style.

Table – 6.28

Association between Length of Time Spent in Prison and Temperament – Reflective

Length of Time Spent in Prison	Temperament – Reflective		Row Total
	Low	High	
Less than 1 month	10 16.1	16 40.0	26 25.5
Less than 9 months	20 32.3	7 17.5	27 26.5
Less than 2 years	10 16.1	6 15.0	16 15.7
Less than 14 years	22 35.5	11 27.5	33 32.4
Respondents Total	62 60.8	40 39.2	102 100.0

Chi-Square	D.F.	Significance
7.93456	3	.0474

Referring to the table 6.28 it can be seen that Chi-square value is significant at .05 level of confidence. Therefore there is a strong association between Length of Time Spent in Prison and Temperament.

It can be observed from table 6.28 that 33 respondents fall into the category of less than 14 years stay in prison, out of that 35.5% of respondents fall on low "Reflective" Temperament.

It can also be seen that out of the total respondents 60.8% fall into the category of low "Reflective" Temperament".

Table – 6.29

Association between Length of Time Spent in Prison and Life Style – Explosive

Length of Time Spent in Prison	Life Style – Explosive		Row Total
	Low	High	
Less than 1 month	7 13.5	19 38.0	26 25.5
Less than 9 months	14 26.9	13 26.0	27 26.5
Less than 2 years	10 19.2	6 12.0	16 15.7
Less than 14 years	21 40.4	12 24.0	33 32.4
Respondents Total	52 51.0	50 49.0	102 100.0

Chi-Square	D.F.	Significance
8.99429	3	.0294

Referring to the table 6.29 it can be seen that the Chi-square value is significant at .05 level of confidence. Therefore there is a strong association between Length of Time Spent in Prison and Life Style.

The above Data reveal that 33 respondents fall into the category of less than 14 years stay in prison, out of that 40.4% of respondents fall on low "Explosive" Life Style.

Those respondents whose stay is less than one month in the prison, in that out of 26 respondents, 38% of respondents fall on high "Explosive" Life Style.

GRAPH 6.9: STATUS AS A PRISONER

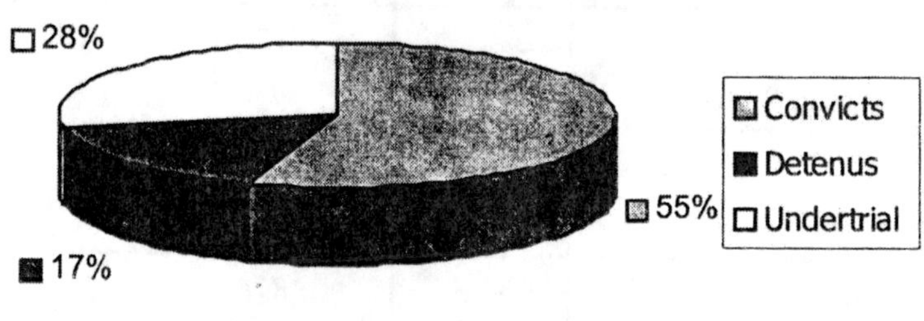

GRAPH 6.10: STATUS AS A PRISONER

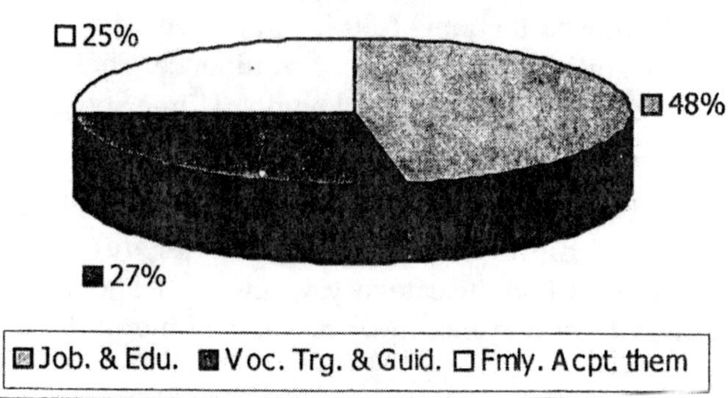

Table – 6.30

Association between Length of Time Spent in Prison and Life Style – Escapist

Length of Time Spent in Prison	Life Style – Escapist		Row Total
	Low	High	
Less than 1 month	2 13.3	24 27.6	26 25.5
Less than 9 months	1 6.7	26 29.9	27 26.5
Less than 2 years	3 20.0	13 14.9	16 15.7
Less than 14 years	9 60.0	24 27.6	33 32.4
Respondents Total	15 14.7	87 85.3	102 100.0

Chi-Square	D.F.	Significance
7.98873	3	.0462

Referring to the table 6.30 it can be seen that chi-square value is significant at .05 level of confidence. Therefore there is a strong association between Length of Time Spent in Prison and Life Style.

The Data interprete that 87 respondents fall into the category of high "Escapist" Life Style, out of that 50 respondents fall on the category, where the respondents have spent less than one month or less than nine months in the prison.

Table – 6.31

Association between Length of Time Spent in Prison and Family Environment – Intellectual Cultural Orientation

Length of Time Spent in Prison	FE – Intellectual Cultural Orientation		Row Total
	Low	High	
Less than 1 month	20 38.5	6 12.0	26 25.5
Less than 9 months	10 19.2	17 34.0	27 26.5
Less than 2 years	9 17.3	7 14.0	16 15.7
Less than 14 years	13 25.0	20 40.0	33 32.4
Respondents Total	52 51.0	50 49.0	102 100.0

Chi-Square	D.F.	Significance
11.05316	3	.0114

Referring to the table 6.31 it can be seen that chi-square value is significant at .05 level of confidence. Therefore there is a strong association between Length of Time Spent in Prison and Family Environment.

It can be observed that 52 respondents fall into the category of low and 50 respondents fall into the category of high "Intellectual Cultural Orientation" Family Environment.

Table – 6.32

Association between Length of Time Spent in Prison and Family Environment – Organization

Length of Time Spent in Prison	FE – Organization		Row Total
	Low	High	
Less than 1 month	17 40.5	9 15.0	26 25.5
Less than 9 months	10 23.8	17 28.3	27 26.5
Less than 2 years	7 16.7	9 15.0	16 15.7
Less than 14 years	8 19.0	25 41.7	33 32.4
Respondents Total	42 41.2	60 58.8	102 100.0

Chi-Square	**D.F.**	**Significance**
10.43234	3	.0152

Referring to the table 6.32 it can be seen that chi-square value is significant at .05 level of confidence. Therefore there is a strong association between Length of Time Spent in Prison and Family Environment.

Table 6.32 shows that 60 respondents fall into the category of high "Organization" Family Environment, out of that 41.7% of respondents fall into the category of less than 14 years stay in prison.

Table – 6.33

Association between Length of Time Spent in Prison and Correctional Institutions Environment – Autonomy

Length of Time Spent in Prison	CIE – Autonomy		Row Total
	Low	High	
Less than 1 month	7 13.5	19 38.0	26 25.5
Less than 9 months	16 30.8	11 22.0	27 26.5
Less than 2 years	10 19.2	6 12.0	16 15.7
Less than 14 years	19 36.5	14 28.0	33 32.4
Respondents Total	52 51.0	50 49.0	102 100.0

Chi-Square	**D.F.**	**Significance**
8.18589	3	.0423

Referring to the table 6.33 it can be seen that chi-square value is significant at .05 level of confidence. Therefore there is a strong association between Length of Time Spent in Prison and Correctional Institutions Environment.

Table 6.83 shows that 26 respondents fall into the category of less than one month stay in prison, out of that 38% of respondents fall on high "Autonomy" Correctional Institutions Environment.

Table – 6.34

Association between Length of Time Spent in Prison and Correctional Institutions Environment – Practical Orientation

Length of Time Spent in Prison	CIE – Practical Orientation		Row Total
	Low	High	
Less than 1 month	4 10.5	22 34.4	26 25.5
Less than 9 months	12 31.6	15 23.4	27 26.5
Less than 2 years	9 23.7	7 10.9	16 15.7
Less than 14 years	13 34.2	20 31.3	33 32.4
Respondents Total	38 37.3	64 62.7	102 100.0

Chi-Square	D.F.	Significance
8.45140	3	.0375

Referring to the table 6.34 it can be seen that chi-square value is significant at .05 level of confidence. Therefore there is a strong association between Length of Time Spent in Prison and Correctional Institutions Environment.

Table 6.34 shows that 64 respondents fall into the category of high "Practical Orientation" Correctional Institutions Environment.

SECTION – 4

Guilt Feeling

Guilt is a negative emotional trait which is expected to be significant among women criminals. Guilt from the psychological point of view always implies an inner sense of wrong doing or self blame. In the case of women criminals, as expressed by Frend (1950) fear of conscience has become the additional content of guilt feeling. The person with a well developed superego tends to feel guilty when he does something or even thinks of doing something that is contrary to the moral code by which she has been raised. She is said to feel conscience-stricken. After the commission of a crime, a woman offender may remain in fear of the consequences that she would confront, foremost among which is deprivation of her dependence on her family members, by being separated from them and placed in prison for prolonged periods.

In India, studies conducted on delinquents and adult male criminals by Shanmugam (1969), Mukerjee (1968), Rath and Pati (1969), Singh (1968) have revealed that delinquent and adult male criminals are emotionally unstable and suffer from feelings of guilt. While, except the study conducted by Ghosh (1986), no study has been done on women convicts to observe whether they equally suffer from guilt or not. Shanmugam (1956, 1958) conducted a study on delinquent girls, in which he mentioned that they suffer from insecurity, rejection and guilt.

As it is assumed that women criminals suffer from acute guilt also, therefore an association between criminality and guilt has been studied in the present research.

Table - 6.35

Feelings After Committing the Crime

Guilt Feelings	**Frequency**	**Percentage**
Sad and shocked	29	28.4
Worried and scared	13	12.7
Repents for the act	14	13.7
Ashamed of the act	12	11.8
Denial of committing the Crime	29	28.4
Knowingly involved	5	5.0
Reasons for Repenting		
Repent for what happened	20	19.6
Repent for getting labelled	7	6.9
Repent as unknowingly indulged in crime	7	6.9
Repent as family got disturbed	14	13.7
Repent for getting arrested	11	10.7
Repent as trapped by others	9	8.9
Do not repent	34	33.3
Ways of Repenting		
By praying to god	66	64.7
Keep aloof from others	2	2.0
Do nothing	34	33.3
Total	102	100.0

The analysis of the table 6.35 reveals that 29 (28.4%) were suffering from being sad and shocked after committing the crime, 13 (12.7%) were worried and scared, 14 (13.7%) were repenting for the act which they did, while 12 (11.8%) were ashamed of the act. Further 29 (28.4%) of the respondents denied that they have committed the crime and blamed others for their situation. It was also observed that 5 (5.0%) of the prisoners were involved in the crime knowingly. These were the women who were involved in illicit liquor business.

Table 6.35 also shows that 68 (66.7%) were repenting for their crime and gave various reasons for their repenting like, 20 (19.6%) were repenting for all that happened, 7 (6.9%) felt that they got labelled and the same per cent felt they got unknowingly indulged in crime. While 14 (13.7%) repent as they feel that family got disturbed, because of their imprisonment, 11 (10.7%) repent for getting arrested and 9 (8.9%) thought that they were trapped by others. Further, 34 (33.3%) were not suffering from guilt any feeling and thus were not repenting.

It was found that, 66 (64.7%) of them were praying to god, 2 (2.0%) kept themselves away from others, as a way to repent for their guilt.

Table – 6.36

Opinion on Reactions of Society Towards Criminals as felt by Respondents

Types of Prejudice people	Frequency	Percentage
Look down upon	6	6.0
Labelled/Stigmatised	19	18.6
Think bad of criminals	5	4.9
Hate criminals	3	2.9
No respect for criminals	3	2.9
People unaware of Prisoner's Problem/sufferings	6	6.0
Do not care of Society's prejudice	3	2.9
In confused state	57	55.8
Total	102	100.0

Table 6.36 reveals that, when the women criminals were asked about their opinion on the reactions of the society towards criminals, 19 (18.6%) felt that society labels them as deviant and thus a stigma is attached with them. That society looks down upon them was felt by 6 (6.0%) of prisoners, while the same number of prisoners also felt that people are unaware of prisoners' problems and sufferings. Further it can be seen that 5 (4.9%) felt that the society thinks bad about criminals, 6 (5.8%) thought people in the society hate criminals and have no respect for them. A few of them i.e. 3 (2.9%) did not care for the prejudice of the society. A large number of them i.e. 57 (55.8%) of the inmates were in a confused state at the reactions of the society towards the women criminals.

Table – 6.37

Reasons for not being able to face the Society

Reasons	Frequency	Percentage
Situation not same as before/ difficulties in living	5	4.9
Husbands & in-laws will not accept	1	1.0
Ashamed of staying in jail	7	6.9
People will criticize	5	4.9
Bad name will harm daughter's marriage	3	2.9
Difficult to get work due to bad name	2	2.0
Stigma will create problem for free movement	2	2.0
If not society, family will accept them	77	75.4
Total	102	100.0

Table 6.37 reveals that only 25 (24.6%) gave various reasons for not being able to face the society after release like: situations would not be the same as before or would have difficulties in living; husbands and in-laws will not accept

them; they are ashamed of staying in jail; people will criticize them; stigma will create problem for free movement in society; stigma will create problem for getting daughters' marriage or will be difficult to get a job. A large number i.e. 77 (75.4%) were confident that if not society, family will certainly accept them back.

SECTION – 5

Moral Value

Values originate from the society of which a person is a part. If individuals are thought of as evil, it is difficult to believe that individuals have worth and dignity. Values are seen as guides to behaviour, growing out of personal experiences, modified as experiences accumulate and evolving in nature. Factors that influence the values individuals hold include their cultural heritage, the values held by individuals and groups with which they are associated or to which they aspire to associate, personal experience and the views they hold about human beings and the nature of the human situation. Values provide a base for making judgements.

Thus, in the present study, an effort was made by the researcher to study the moral and religious values of the women criminals. It can be noted that data was collected after commission of crime, when the inmates were imprisoned in different categories as convicts, detenus and undertrials and were passing through the phase of repentance and guilt feeling for their crime. The women criminals mostly do not belong to the hard-core criminals or habituals but it is the environment and circumstances that forced them into a situation for which they become criminal. The Jail authorities from time to time are also conducting various spiritual activities like meditation, Vipasana, etc., for their reformation and correction. Thus when data was collected, many have had some impact of these programmes made on them, which was reflected in the data.

Table – 6.38: Moral Values and Education

Education	Moral Values		Row Total
	Low	High	
Illiterate	15 60.0	51 66.2	66 64.7
Primary	8 32.0	16 20.8	24 23.5
Secondary & above	2 8.0	10 13.0	12 11.8
Total	25 24.5	77 75.5	102 100.0

Table 6.38 indicates that out of 66 (64.7%) women criminals belonging to the illiterate group, 51 (66.2%) were having high moral values, while out of 24 (23.5%) of them belonging to the primary group of education, 16 (20.8%) were having high moral values. In all, 77 (75.5%) out of the total sample were having high moral values in the present study. It can be seen that, though these women criminals were illiterate or less educated, yet they were morally high, which might be because of the situational crime or the feelings of guilt.

SECTION – 6

Temperament

Temperament refers to those dispositions that are closely linked to the biological or physiological determinants and which consequently show relatively little modifiability with development. The role of heredity is somewhat greater here than in the case of some other aspects of personality. For Allport, temperament is a special subsection within the broader domain of personality. According to him, Temperament refers to the characteristic phenomena of an individual's emotional nature, including his susceptibility to emotional stimulation, his customary strength and speed of response, the quality of his prevailing mood and all peculiarities of fluctuation and intensity of mood, these phenomena being regarded as dependent upon constitutional make-up and therefore largely heredity in origin.

While Hilgard (1962) defined that temperament is the pre-dominance of a particular kind of emotional reaction. The person's prevailing emotional state determines his personality.

Thus, in the present study an attempt has been made to study the personality of the women criminals. To understand the nature and character, which permanently affects behaviour, nine temperament traits, such as active, impulsive, dominant, emotional, sociable, reflective, nervous, introvert / extrovert and aggressive were studied to find the association with women criminality.

Table – 6.39

Association Between Temperament – Active and Education of Women Criminals

Analysis of Variance

Source	D.F	Sum of Squares	Mean Squares	F Ratio	F Prob.
Between Groups	2	29.1386	14.5693	3.5392	.0328
Within Groups	99	407.5379	4.1165		
Total	101	436.6765			

Mean	Group	Grp 1	Grp 2	Grp 3
11.4242	Grp 1			
12.2500	Grp 2			
12.9167	Grp 3	*		

Group 1 – Illiterate

Group 2 – Primary

Group 3 – Secondary & above

(*) Denotes pairs of groups significantly different at the .050 level.

It can be interpreted from the table 6.39 that F ratio 3.5 is significant at .05 level of confidence. Therefore it can be said that there is a strong association between Active – Temperament and Education of Women Criminals.

It can further be interpreted that group 1 (Mean score–11.4242) differs significantly from group 3 (Mean score–12.9167). It means that the Illiterate group differs from the 'secondary and above' education groups with reference to Temperament–Active.

Table – 6.40

Association Between Temperament – Impulsive and Nature of Crime by Women Criminals

Analysis of Variance

Source	D.F	Sum of Squares	Mean Squares	F Ratio	F Prob.
Between Groups	1	20.8156	20.8156	4.3736	.0393
Within Groups	90	428.3475	4.7594		
Total	91	449.1630			

It can be interpreted from the table 6.40 that F ratio 4.3 is significant at .05 level of confidence. Therefore it can be said that there is a strong association between Impulsive – Temperament and Nature of Crime by Women Criminals.

It can be interpreted from the table 6.41 that F ratio 5.7 is significant at .01 level of confidence. Therefore it can be said that there is a strong association between Dominant – Temperament and Length of Time Spent in Prison by Women Criminals.

It can further be interpreted that group 2 (Mean score–6.7407) and group 5 (Mean score – 6.8125) differ significantly from group 7 (Mean score – 8.6970) and group 1 (Mean score–9.2692)

Table – 6.41

Association Between Temperament – Dominant and Length of Time Spent in Prison by Women Criminals

Analysis of Variance

Source	D.F	Sum of Squares	Mean Squares	F Ratio	F Prob.
Between Groups	3	123.2040	41.0680	5.7850	.0011
Within Groups	98	695.7078	7.0991		
Total	101	818.9118			

Mean	Group	Grp 2	Grp 5	Grp 7	Grp 1
6.7407	Grp 2				
6.8125	Grp 5				
8.6970	Grp 7	*	*		
9.2692	Grp 1	*	*		

Group 1 – Less than 1 month

Group 2 – Less than 9 months

Group 5 – Less than 2 years

Group 7 – 3 years and above

(*) Denotes pairs of groups significantly different at the .05 level.

It means that 'Less than 9 months' and 'Less than 2 years' groups differ from '3 years and above' and 'Less than 1 month' groups with reference to Temperament – Dominant.

Table – 6.42

Association Between Temperament – Emotional and Reasons for Arrest of Women Criminals

Analysis of Variance

Source	D.F	Sum of Squares	Mean Squares	F Ratio	F Prob.
Between Groups	3	11.4939	3.8313	2.7845	.0480
Within Groups	63	86.6852	1.3760		
Total	66	98.1791			

Mean	Group	Grp 3	Grp 2	Grp 1	Grp 5
11.5000	Grp 3				
12.0000	Grp 2				
12.4815	Grp 1	*			
12.5556	Grp 5	*			

Group 1 – Murder of daughter-in-law

Group 2 – Murder of husband

Group 3 – Murder of close relatives

Group 5 – Murder of others

(*) Denotes pairs of groups significantly different at the .05 level.

It can be interpreted from the table 6.42 that F ratio 2.7 is significant at .05 level of confidence. Therefore it can be said that there is a strong association between Emotional – Temperament and Reasons for Arrest of Women Criminals.

It can further be interpreted that group 3 (Mean score–11.5000) differs significantly from group 1 (Mean score–12.4815) and group 5 (Mean score–12.5556).

It means that 'Murder of close relatives' group differs from 'Murder of daughter-in-law' and 'Murder of others' groups with reference to Temperament – Emotional.

Table – 6.43

Association Between Temperament – Sociable and Reasons for Arrest of Women Criminals

Analysis of Variance

Source	D.F	Sum of Squares	Mean Squares	F Ratio	F Prob.
Between Groups	3	22.4681	7.4894	3.6945	.0163
Within Groups	63	127.7110	2.0272		
Total	66	150.1791			

Mean	Group	Grp 2	Grp 3	Grp 5	Grp 1
10.8750	Grp 2				
11.9286	Grp 3				
123889	Grp 5	*			
12.7037	Grp 1	*			

Group 1 – Murder of daughter-in-law

Group 2 – Murder of husband

Group 3 – Murder of close relatives

Group 5 – Murder of others

(*) –Denotes pairs of groups significantly different at the .05 level.

It can be interpreted from the table 6.43 that F ratio 3.6 is significant at .05 level of confidence. Therefore it can be said that there is a strong association between Sociable – Temperament and Reasons for Arrest of Women Criminals.

It can further be interpreted that group 2 (Mean score – 10.8750) differs significantly from group 5 (Mean score – 12.3889) and group 1 (Mean score – 12.7037).

It means that 'Murder of husband' group differs from 'Murder of others' and 'Murder of daughter-in-law' groups with reference to Temperament – Sociable.

Table – 6.44

Association Between Temperament – Reflective and Reasons for Arrest of Women Criminals

Analysis of Variance

Source	D.F	Sum of Squares	Mean Squares	F Ratio	F Prob.
Between Groups	3	20.1534	6.7178	2.6516	.0563
Within Groups	63	159.6078	2.5335		
Total	66	179.7612			

Mean	Group	Grp 3	Grp 2	Grp 1	Grp 5
9.3571	Grp 3				
9.3750	Grp 2				
10.1481	Grp 1				
10.7778	Grp 5	*	*		

Group 1 – Murder of daughter-in-law
Group 2 – Murder of husband
Group 3 – Murder of close relatives
Group 5 – Murder of others

(*) Denotes pairs of groups significantly different at the .05 level.

It can be interpreted from the table 6.44 that F ratio 2.6 is significant at .05 level of confidence. Therefore it can be said that there is a strong association between Reflective – Temperament and Reasons for Arrest of Women Criminals.

It can further be interpreted that group 3 (Mean score – 9.3571) and group 2 (Mean score – 9.3750) differs significantly from group 5 (Mean score – 10.7778).

It means that 'Murder of close relatives' group and 'Murder of husband' group differ from 'Murder of others' group with reference to Temperament – Reflective.

Table – 6.45

Association Between Temperament – Reflective and Motive behind Crime Commission by Women Criminals

Analysis of Variance

Source	D.F	Sum of Squares	Mean Squares	F Ratio	F Prob.
Between Groups	3	22.1539	7.3846	2.9917	.0351
Within Groups	90	222.1546	2.4684		
Total	93	244.3085			

Mean	Group	Grp 6	Grp 4	Grp 5	Grp 3
9.7027	Grp 6				
10.2308	Grp 4				
10.7619	Grp 5	*			
11.0000	Grp 3	*			

Group 3 – Accidental
Group 4 – Situational
Group 5 – To Overcome Economic Stress
Group 6 – To Overcome Social Stress

(*) Denotes pairs of groups significantly different at the .05 level

It can be interpreted from the table 6.45 that F ratio 2.9 is significant at .05 level of confidence. Therefore it can be said that there is a strong association between Reflective – Temperament and Motive behind Crime Commission by Women Criminals.

It can further be interpreted that group 6 (Mean score – 9.7027) differs significantly from group 5 (Mean score – 10.7619) and group 3 (Mean score – 11.0000).

It means that 'To overcome social stress' group differs from 'To overcome Economic Stress' and 'Accidental' Groups with reference to Temperament – Reflective.

Table – 6.46

Association Between Temperament – Reflective and Length of Time Spent in Prison by Women Criminals

Analysis of Variance

Source	D.F	Sum of Squares	Mean Squares	F Ratio	F Prcb.
Between Groups	3	28.2045	9.4015	4.0479	.0093
Within Groups	98	227.6092	2.3225		
Total	101	255.8137			

Mean	Group	Grp 7	Grp 5	Grp 2	Grp 1
9.8485	Grp 7				
9.8750	Grp 5				
10.0370	Grp 2				
11.1154	Grp 1	*	*	*	

Group 1 – Less than 1 month

Group 2 – Less than 9 months

Group 5 – Less than 2 years

Group 7 – 3 years and above

(*) Denotes pairs of groups significantly different at the .05 level.

It can be interpreted from the table 6.46 that F ratio 4.0 is significant at .01 level of confidence. Therefore it can be said that there is a strong association between Reflective – Temperament and Length of Time Spent in Prison by Women Criminals.

. It can further be interpreted that group 7 (Mean score – 9.8485), group 5 (Mean score –9.8750) and group 2 (Mean score – 10.0370) differ significantly from group 1 (Mean score – 11.1154).

It means that '3 years and above', 'Less than 2 years' and 'Less than 9 months' groups differ from 'Less than one month' group with reference to Temperament – Reflective.

Table – 6.47

Association Between Temperament – Nervous and Motive behind Crime Commission by Women Criminals

Analysis of Variance

Source	D.F	Sum of Squares	Mean Squares	F Ratio	F Prob.
Between Groups	3	73.0691	24.3564	2.9381	.0375
Within Groups	90	746.0904	8.2899		
Total	93	819.1596			

Mean	Group	Grp 3	Grp 5	Grp 4	Grp 6
9.1000	Grp 3				
10.6190	Grp 5				
11.4231	Grp 4	*			
11.9459	Grp 6	*			

Group 3 – Accidental

Group 4 – Situational

Group 5 – To Overcome Economic Stress

Group 6 – To Overcome Social Stress

(*) Denotes pairs of groups significantly different at the .05 level.

It can be interpreted from the table 6.47 that F ratio 2.9 is significant at .05 level of confidence. Therefore it can be said that there is a strong association between Nervous – Temperament and Motive behind Crime Commission by Women Criminals.

It can further be interpreted that group 3 (Mean score – 9.1000) differs significantly from group 4 (Mean score – 11.4231) and group 6 (Mean score – 11.9459).

It means that 'Accidental' group differs from 'Situational' and 'To overcome Social Stress' groups with reference to Temperament – Nervous.

Table –.6.48

Association Between Temperament – Introvert/ Extrovert and Reasons for Arrest of Women Criminals

Analysis of Variance

Source	**D.F**	**Sum of Squares**	**Mean Squares**	**F Ratio**	**F Prob.**
Between Groups	3	1438.3788	479.4596	2.9440	.0397
Within Groups	63	10260.2480	162.8611		
Total	66	11698.6269			

Mean	Group	Grp 3	Grp 5	Grp 2	Grp 1
94.5714	Grp 3				
98.6111	Grp 5				
99.3750	Grp 2				
106.2222	Grp 1	*			

Group 1 – Murder of daughter-in-law

Group 2 – Murder of husband

Group 3 – *Murder of close relatives*

Group 5 – Murder of others

(*) Denotes pairs of groups significantly different at the .05 level.

It can be interpreted from the table 6.48 that F ratio 2.9 is significant at .05 level of confidence. Therefore it can be said that there is a strong association between Introvert/Extrovert – Temperament and Reasons for Arrest of Women Criminals.

It can further be interpreted that group 3 (Mean score – 94.5714) differs significantly from group 1 (Mean score – 106.2222).

It means that 'Murder of close relatives' group differs from 'Murder of daughter-in-law' group with reference to Temperament – Introvert/Extrovert.

SECTION – 7

Life Style

Life style is the over-all pattern of living, whereby an individual attempts to meet his or her biological, social and emotional needs. It is the system principle by which the individual personality functions. The person perceives, learns and retains what fits the style of life and ignores everything else. Each person, early in childhood, develops his own individual style for solving the special problems of living. The basic element in understanding a person is the discovery of his implicit concept of life – his life style.

To understand the individual's way of life, i.e. his social, socio-cultural, economic and psychological aspects, a need was felt by the researcher to study the life style of women criminals. Eight life style traits such as, individualistic, exploitive, explosive, resistive, domineering, conforming, escapist and evasive were used in the present study to find association between life style and women criminals.

Table – 6.49

Association Between Life Style – Individualistic and Education of Women Criminals

Analysis of Variance

Source	D.F	Sum of Squares	Mean Squares	F Ratio	F Prob.
Between Groups	2	24.6560	12.3280	3.4834	.0345
Within Groups	99	350.3636	3.5390		
Total	101	375.0196			

Mean	Group	Grp 1	Grp 3	Grp 2
8.5455	Grp 1			
9.3333	Grp 3			
9.6667	Grp 2	*		

Group 1 - Illiterate

Group 2 – Primary

Group 3 – Secondary & above

(*) Denotes pairs of groups significantly different at the .05 level.

It can be interpreted from the table 6.49 that F ratio 3.4 is significant at .05 level of confidence. Therefore it can be said that there is a strong association between Individualistic – Life Style and Education of Women Criminals.

It can further be interpreted that group 1 (Mean score – 8.5455) differ significantly from group 2 (Mean score – 9.6667). It means that 'Illiterate' group differs from 'Primary education' group with reference to Life Style - Individualistic.

Table – 6.50

Association Between Life Style – Individualistic and Reasons for Arrest of Women Criminals

Analysis of Variance

Source	D.F	Sum of Squares	Mean Squares	F Ratio	F Prob.
Between Groups	3	49.1034	16.3678	4.9768	.0037
Within Groups	63	207.1951	3.2888		
Total	66	256.2985			

Mean	Group	Grp 1	Grp 3	Grp 2	Grp 5
7.5926	Grp 1				
8.7857	Grp 3				
9.3750	Grp 2	*			
9.5556	Grp 5	*			

Group 1 – Murder of daughter-in-law

Group 2 – Murder of husband

Group 3 – Murder of close relatives

Group 5 – Murder of others

(*) Denotes pairs of groups significantly different at the .05 level.

It can be interpreted from the table 6.50 that F ratio 4.9 is significant at .01 level of confidence. Therefore it can be said that there is a strong association between Individualistic – Life Style and Reasons for Arrest of Women Criminals.

It can further be interpreted that group 1 (Mean score – 7.5926) differs significantly from group 2 (Mean score – 9.3750) and group 5 (Mean score – 9.5556).

It means that 'Murder of daughter-in-law' group differs from 'Murder of husband' group and 'Murder of others' group with reference to Life Style – Individualistic.

Table – 6.51

Association Between Life Style – Individualistic and Nature of Crime by Women Criminals

Analysis of Variance

Source	D.F	Sum of Squares	Mean Squares	F Ratio	F Prob.
Between Groups	1	20.3763	20.3763	5.8767	.0173
Within Groups	90	312.0585	3.4673		
Total	91	332.4348			

It can be interpreted from the table 6.51 that F ratio 5.8 is significant at .05 level of confidence. Therefore it can be said that there is a strong association between Individualistic – Life style and Nature of Crime by women Criminals.

GRAPH 6.11: MOTIVE BEHIND CRIME COMMISSION AND LIFE STYLE EXPLOSIVE

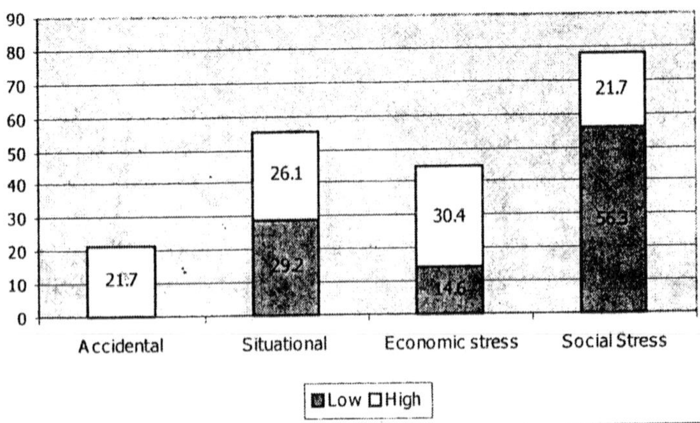

GRAPH 6.12: LIFE STYLE INDIVIDUALISTIC AND TEMPERAMENT-DOMINANT

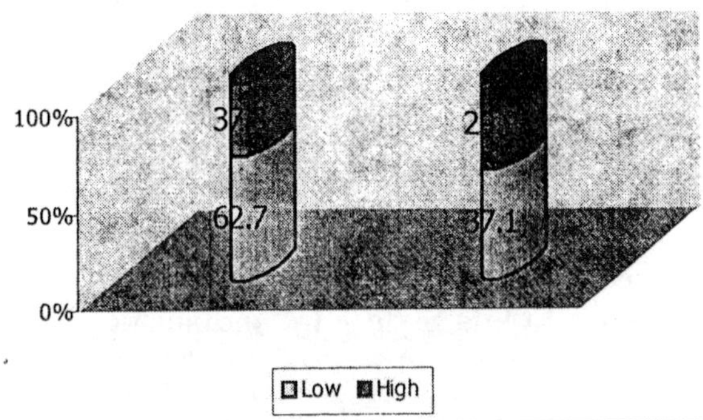

Table – 6.52

Association Between Life Style – Individualistic and Motive behind Crime Commission by Women Criminals

Analysis of Variance

Source	D.F	Sum of Squares	Mean Squares	F Ratio	F Prob.
Between Groups	3	48.8581	16.2860	4.8522	.0036
Within Groups	90	302.0781	3.3564		
Total	93	350.9362			

Mean	Group	Grp 6	Grp 3	Grp 5	Grp 4
8.0270	Grp 6				
9.1000	Grp 3				
9.3333	Grp 5	*			
9.6923	Grp 4	*			

Group 3 – Accidental
Group 4 – Situational
Group 5 – To Overcome Economic Stress
Group 6 – To Overcome Social Stress

(*) Denotes pairs of groups significantly different at the .05 level.

It can be interpreted from the table 6.52 that F ratio 4.8 is significant at .01 level of confidence. Therefore it can be said that there is a strong association between Individualistic – Life Style and Motive behind Crime Commission by Women Criminals.

It can further be interpreted that group 6 (Mean score – 8.0270) differs significantly from group 5 (Mean score – 9.3333) and group 4 (Mean score – 9.6923).

It means that 'To Overcome Social Stress' group differs from 'To Overcome Economic Stress' and 'Situational' groups with reference to Life Style – Individualistic.

Table – 6.53

Association Between Life Style – Individualistic and Length of Time Spent in Prison by Women Criminals

Analysis of Variance

Source	D.F	Sum of Squares	Mean Squares	F Ratio	F Prob.
Between Groups	3	30.0038	10.0013	2.8408	.0418
Within Groups	98	345.0158	3.5206		
Total	101	375.0196			

Mean	Group	Grp 7	Grp 2	Grp 5	Grp 1
8.3333	Grp 7				
8.7037	Grp 2				
9.0625	Grp 5				
9.7308	Grp 1	*	*		

Group 1 - Less than one month

Group 2 – Less than 9 months

Group 5 – Less than 2 years

Group 7 – 3 years and above

(*) Denotes pairs of groups significantly different at the .05 level.

It can be interpreted from the table 6.53 that F ratio 2.8 is significant at .05 level of confidence. Therefore it can be said that there is a strong association between Individualistic – Life Style and Length of Time Spent in Prison by Women Criminals.

It can further be interpreted that group 7 (Mean score – 8.3333) and group 2 (Mean score – 8.7037) differ significantly from group 1 (Mean score – 9.7308).

It means that '3 years and above' and 'Less than 9 months' groups differ from 'Less than one month' group with reference to Life Style - Individualistic.

Table – 6.54

Association between Life Style – Individualistic and Temperament–Active

Life Style Individualistic	Temperament Active		Row Total
	Low	High	
Low	8 88.9	47 50.5	55 53.9
High	1 11.1	46 49.5	47 46.1
Respondents Total	9 8.8	93 91.2	102 100.0

Chi-Square	D.F.	Significance
3.43670	1	.0638
4.85763	1	.0275

Referring to the table 6.54 it can be seen that chi-square value is significant at .05 level of confidence. Therefore there is a strong association between Life Style and Temperament.

Further it can be interpreted that 93 respondents fall into the category of high "Active" Temperament, out of that 50.5% of respondents fall on low "Individualistic" Life Style.

Table – 6.55: Association between Life Style – Individualistic and Temperament–Dominant

Life Style Individualistic	Temperament – Dominant		Row Total
	Low	High	
Low	42 62.7	13 37.1	55 53.9
High	25 37.3	22 62.9	47 46.1
Respondents Total	67 65.7	35 34.3	102 100.0

Chi-Square	D.F.	Significance
5.05310	1	.0246
6.03741	1	.0140

Referring to the table 6.55 it can be seen that chi-square value is significant at .05 level of confidence. Therefore there is a strong association between Life Style and Temperament.

It can be observed that 67 respondents fall into the category of low "Dominant" Temperament, out of that 62.7% of respondents fall on low "Individualistic" Life Style.

It can also be seen that 47 respondents fall into the category of high "Individualistic" Life Style, out of that 62.9% of respondents fall on high "Dominant" Temperament.

Table – 6.56: Association between Life Style – Individualistic and Temperament– Introvert/ Extrovert

Life Style Individualistic	Temperament – I/ E		Row Total
	Low	High	
Low	7 22.6	48 67.6	55 53.9
High	24 77.4	23 32.4	47 46.1
Respondents Total	31 30.4	71 69.6	102 100.0

Chi-Square	D.F.	Significance
15.84073	1	.0001
17.60625	1	.0000

Referring to the table 6.56 it can be seen that chi-square value is significant at .01 level of confidence. Therefore there is a strong association between Life Style and Temperament.

The data reveals that 71 respondents fall into the category of high "Introvert/Extrovert" Temperament, out of that 67.6% of respondents fall on low "Individualistic" Life Style.

Table – 6.57

Association between Life Style – Individualistic and Temperament– Aggression

Life Style Individualistic	Temperament – Aggression		Row Total
	Low	High	
Low	35 64.8	20 41.7	55 53.9
High	19 35.2	28 58.3	47 46.1
Respondents Total	54 52.9	48 47.1	102 100.0

Chi-Square	D.F.	Significance
4.58827	1	.0322
5.48034	1	.0192

Referring to the table 6.57 it can be seen that chi-square value is significant at .05 level of confidence. Therefore there is a strong association between Life Style and Temperament.

Table 6.57 shows that 54 respondents fall into the category of low "Individualistic" Life Style, out of that 64.8% of respondents fall on low "Aggression" - Temperament. While 47 respondents fall on high "Individualistic" Life Style, out of that 58.3% fall on high "Aggression" Temperament.

Table – 6.58: Association between Life Style – Individualistic and Family Environment Intellectual – Cultural Orientation

Life Style Individualistic	FE-Intellectual – C. O.		Row Total
	Low	High	
Low	22 42.3	33 66.0	55 53.9
High	30 57.7	17 34.0	47 46.1
Respondents Total	52 51.0	50 49.0	102 100.0

Chi-Square	D.F.	Significance
4.84466	1	.0277
5.75874	1	.0164

Referring to the table 6.58 it can be seen that chi-square value is significant at .05 level of confidence. Therefore there is a strong association between Life Style and Family Environment.

The data presented in the table 6.58 shows that 55 respondents fall into the category of low "Individualistic" Life Style, out of that 66% of respondents fall on high "Intellectual – Cultural Orientation".

Table – 6.59: Association between Life Style – Individualistic and Family Environment - Moral Religions Orientation

Life Style Individualistic	FE – Moral – R.O.		Row Total
	Low	High	
Low	20 40.8	35 66.0	55 53.9
High	29 59.2	18 34.0	47 46.1
Respondents Total	49 48.0	53 52.0	102 100.0

Chi-Square	D.F.	Significance
5.54296	1	.0186
6.51854	1	.0107

Referring to the table 6.59 it can be seen that chi-square value is significant at .05 level of confidence. Therefore there is a strong association between Life Style and Family Environment.

The data interpret that 55 respondents fall into the Category of low "Individualistic" Life Style, out of that 66% of respondents fall on high "Moral Religions Orientation" Family Environment.

Table – 6.60

Association between Life Style – Individualistic and Correctional Institutions Environment–Order and Organization

Life Style Individualistic	CIE – Order & Org.		Row Total
	Low	High	
Low	18 40.9	37 63.8	55 53.9
High	26 59.1	21 36.2	47 46.1
Respondents Total	44 43.1	58 56.9	102 100.0

Chi-Square	D.F.	Significance
4.39252	1	.0361
5.27333	1	.0217

Referring to the table 6.60 it can be seen that chi-square value is significant at .05 level of confidence. Therefore there is a strong association between Life Style and Correctional Institutions Environment.

Data indicates that 55 respondents fall into the category of low "Individualistic" Life Style, out of that 63.8% of respondents fall on high "Order and Organization" Correctional Institutions Environment.

Table – 6.61: Association between Life Style–Exploitive and Temperament – Active

Life Style Exploitive	Temperament – Active		Row Total
	Low	High	
Low	7 77.8	34 36.6	41 40.2
High	2 22.2	59 63.4	61 59.8
Respondents Total	9 8.8	93 91.2	102 100.0

Chi-Square	D.F.	Significance
4.21168	1	.0401
5.79962	1	.0160

Referring to the table 6.61 it can be seen that chi-square value is significant at .05 level of confidence. Therefore there is a strong association between Life Style and Temperament.

The data reveal that 93 respondents fall into the category of high "Active" Temperament, out of that 63.4% of respondents fall on high "Exploitive" life style.

Table – 6.62 : Association between Life Style –Exploitive and Temperament – Reflective

Life Style Exploitive	Temperament – Reflective		Row Total
	Low	High	
Low	34 54.8	7 17.5	41 40.2
High	28 45.2	33 82.5	61 59.8
Respondents Total	62 60.8	40 39.2	102 100.0

Chi-Square	D.F.	Significance
12.59073	1	.0004
14.10122	1	.0002

Referring to the table 6.62 it can be seen that chi-square value is significant at .01 level of confidence. Therefore there is a strong association between Life Style and Temperament.

The data distributed in the table 6.62 shows that 61 respondents fall into the category of high "Exploitive" life style, out of that 82.5% of respondents fall on high "Reflective" Temperament.

Table – 6.63

Association between Life Style – Exploitive and Temperament – Nervous

Life Style Exploitive	Temperament - Nervous		Row Total
	Low	High	
Low	7 20.6	34 50.0	41 40.2
High	27 79.4	34 50.0	61 59.8
Respondents Total	34 33.3	68 66.7	102 100.0

Chi-Square	D.F.	Significance
6.97911	1	.0082
8.15674	1	.0043

Referring to the table 6.63 it can be seen that chi-square value is significant at .01 level of confidence. Therefore there is a strong association between Life Style and Temperament.

The data in the table 6.63 indicate that 61 respondents fall into the category of high "Exploitive" life style, out of that 79.4% of respondents fall on low "Nervous" Temperament.

Table – 6.64: Association between Life Style –Exploitive and Temperament – Aggression

Life Style Exploitive	Temperament – Aggression		Row Total
	Low	High	
Low	27 50.0	14 29.2	41 40.2
High	27 50.0	34 70.8	61 59.8
Respondents Total	54 52.9	48 47.1	102 100.0

Chi-Square	D.F.	Significance
3.76244	1	.0524
4.58816	1	.0322

Referring to the table 6.64 it can be seen that chi-square value is significant at .05 level of confidence. Therefore there is a strong association between Life Style and Temperament.

Further it can be interpreted that 61 respondents fall into the category of high "Exploitive" life style, out of that 70.8% of respondents fall on high "Aggression" Temperament.

Table – 6.65: Association between Life Style –Exploitive and Family Environment Achievement - Orientation

Life Style Exploitive	FE – Achievement – O.		Row Total
	Low	High	
Low	20 54.1	21 32.3	41 40.2
High	17 45.9	44 67.7	61 59.8
Respondents Total	37 36.3	65 63.7	102 100.0

Chi-Square	D.F.	Significance
3.77794	1	.0519
4.63847	1	.0313

Referring to the table 6.65 it can be seen that chi-square value is significant at .05 level of confidence. Therefore there is a strong association between Life Style and Family Environment.

It can be seen that 61 respondents fall into the category of high "Exploitive" life style, out of that 67.7% of respondents fall on high "Achievement Orientation" Family Environment.

Table – 6.66: Association Between Life style – Explosive and Income of Women Criminals

Analysis of Variance

Source	D.F	Sum of Squares	Mean Squares	F Ratio	F Prob.
Between Groups	3	10.7206	3.5735	3.1649	.0279
Within Groups	98	110.6520	1.1291		
Total	101	121.3725			

Mean	Group	Grp 1	Grp 7	Grp 2	Grp 3
6.5294	Grp 1				
7.0238	Grp 7				
7.1786	Grp 2	*			
7.6667	Grp 3	*	*		

Group 1 – Below 500

Group 2 – 501 - 1000

Group 3 – 1001 - 5000

Group 7 – No income (Nil)

(*) Denotes pairs of groups significantly different at the .05 level.

It can be interpreted from the table 6.66 that F ratio 3.1 is significant at .05 level of confidence. Therefore it can be said that there is a strong association between Explosive – Life Style and Income of Women Criminals.

It can further be interpreted that group 1 (Mean score – 6.5294) and group 7 (Mean score – 7.0238) differ significantly from group 3 (Mean score – 7.6667), while group 1 (Mean score – 6.5294) also differs significantly from group 2 (Mean score – 7.1786).

It means that 'Below Rs.500/-' Income group and 'no income' differ from 'Rs.1001/- to Rs. 5000/-' income group with reference of Life Style–Explosive, also 'Below Rs.500/-' Income group differs from 'Rs. 501/- to Rs. 1000/-' Income group with reference to Life Style – Explosive.

Table – 6.67

Association between Life style –Explosive and Motive behind Crime Commission by Women Criminals

Analysis of Variance

Source	D.F	Sum of Squares	Mean Squares	F Ratio	F Prob.
Between Groups	3	20.4985	6.8328	7.2247	.0002
Within Groups	90	85.1186	.9458		
Total	93	105.6170			

Mean	Group	Grp 6	Grp 4	Grp 5	Grp 3
6.5946	Grp 6				
7.0385	Grp 4				
7.4762	Grp 5	*			
8.0000	Grp 3	*	*		

Group 3 – Accidental

Group 4 – Situational

Group 5 – To Overcome Economic Stress

Group 6 – To Overcome Social Stress

(*) Denotes pairs of groups significantly different at the .05 level.

It can be interpreted from the table 6.67 that F ratio 7.2 is significant at .01 level of confidence. Therefore it can be said that there is a strong association between Explosive – Life Style and Motive behind Crime Commission by Women Criminals.

It can further be interpreted that group 6 (Mean score – 6.5946) and group 4 (Mean score – 7.0385) differ significantly from group 3 (Mean score – 8.0000), while group 6 (Mean score – 6.5946) also differs significantly from group 5 (Mean score – 7.4762).

It means that 'To overcome Social Stress' group and 'Situational' group differ from 'Accidental' group with reference to Life Style – Explosive.

Also 'To overcome Social Stress' group differs from 'To overcome Economic Stress' group with reference to Life Style–Explosive.

Table – 6.68

Association between Life Style –Explosive and Temperament - Active

Life Style Explosive	Temperament – Active		Row Total
	Low	High	
Low	8 88.9	44 47.3	52 51.0
High	1 11.1	49 52.7	50 49.0
Respondents Total	9 8.8	93 91.2	102 100.0

Chi-Square	D.F.	Significance
4.13442	1	.0420
5.67623	1	.0172

Referring to the table 6.68 it can be seen that chi-square value is significant at .05 level of confidence. Therefore there is a strong association between Life Style and Temperament.

Further it reveals that 93 respondents fall into the category of high "Active" Temperament out of that 52.7% of respondents fall on high "Explosive" Life Style.

Table – 6.69

Association between Life Style –Explosive and Temperament - Dominant

Life Style Explosive	Temperament – Dominant		Row Total
	Low	High	
Low	40 59.7	12 34.3	52 51.0
High	27 40.3	23 65.7	50 49.0
Respondents Total	67 65.7	35 34.3	102 100.0

Chi-Square	D.F.	Significance
4.96909	1	.0258
5.94260	1	.0148

Referring to the table 6.69 it can be seen that chi-square value is significant at .05 level of confidence. Therefore there is a strong association between Life Style and Temperament.

Table shows that 67 respondents fall into the Category of low "Dominant" Temperament out of that 59.7% of respondents fall on low 'Explosive" Life Style.

Table – 6.70: Association between Life Style –Explosive and Temperament - Reflective

Life Style Explosive	Temperament – Reflective		Row Total
	Low	High	
Low	40 64.5	12 30.0	52 51.0
High	22 35.5	28 70.0	50 49.0
Respondents Total	62 60.8	40 39.2	102 100.0

Chi-Square	D.F.	Significance
10.25102	1	.0014
11.59105	1	.0007

Referring to the table 6.70 it can be seen that chi-square value is significant at .01 level of confidence. Therefore there is a strong association between Life Style and Temperament.

The analysis of data shows that 62 respondents fall into the category of low "Reflective" Temperament, out of that 64.5 % of respondents fall on low "Explosive" Life Style.

Table – 6.71: Association between Life Style – Explosive and Temperament-Nervous

Life Style Explosive	Temperament – Nervous		Row Total
	Low	High	
Low	12 35.3	40 58.8	52 51.0
High	22 64.7	28 41.2	50 49.0
Respondents Total	34 33.3	68 66.7	102 100.0

Chi-Square	D.F.	Significance
4.12413	1	.0423
5.02154	1	.0250

Referring to the table 6.71 it can be seen that chi-square value is significant at .05 level of confidence. Therefore there is a strong association between Life Style and Temperament.

The data in the table indicates that 68 respondents fall into the category of high "Nervous" Temperament, out of that 58.8% of respondents fall on low "Explosive" Life Style.

Table – 6.72

Association between Life Style –Explosive and Family Environment – Conflict

Life Style Explosive	FE – Conflict		Row Total
	Low	High	
Low	26 41.3	26 66.7	52 51.0
High	37 58.7	13 33.3	50 49.0
Respondents Total	63 61.8	39 38.2	102 100.0

Chi-Square	D.F.	Significance
5.24241	1	.0220
6.21714	1	.0127

Referring to the table 6.72 it can be seen that chi-square value is significant at .05 level of confidence. Therefore there is a strong association between Life Style and Family Environment.

Table 6.72 shows that 63 respondents fall into the category of low "Conflict" Family Environment, out of that 58.7% of respondents fall on high "Explosive" Life Style.

Table – 6.73: Association between Life Style – Explosive and Family Environment – Active–Recreational Orientation

Life Style Explosive	FE – Active – R.O.		Row Total
	Low	High	
Low	16 37.2	36 61.0	52 51.0
High	27 62.8	23 39.0	50 49.0
Respondents Total	43 42.2	59 57.8	102 100.0

Chi-Square	D.F.	Significance
4.72886	1	.0297
5.64131	1	.0175

Referring to the table 6.73 it can be seen that chi-square value is significant at .05 level of confidence. Therefore there is a strong association between Life Style and Family Environment.

Further it can be observed that 59 respondents fall into the category of high "Active Recreational Orientation" Family Environment, out of that 61.0% of respondents fall on low "Explosive" Life Style.

Table – 6.74: Association between Life Style –Explosive and Correctional Institutions Environment – Practical Orientation

Life Style Explosive	CIE – Practical O.		Row Total
	Low	High	
Low	27 71.1	25 39.1	52 51.0
High	11 28.9	39 60.9	50 49.0
Respondents Total	38 37.3	64 62.7	102 100.0

Chi-Square	D.F.	Significance
8.52574	1	.0035
9.76388	1	.0018

Referring to the table 6.74 it can be seen that chi-square value is significant at .05 level of confidence. Therefore there is a strong association between Life Style and Correctional Institutions Environment.

The data represent that 64 respondents fall into the category of high "Practical Orientation" Correctional Institutions Environment, out of that 60.9% of respondents fall on high "Explosive" Life Style.

Table – 6.75

Association between Life Style –Explosive and Correctional Institutions Environment – Order and Organization

Life Style Explosive	CIE – Order & Org.		Row Total
	Low	High	
Low	13 29.5	39 67.2	52 51.0
High	31 70.5	19 32.8	50 49.0
Respondents Total	44 43.1	58 56.9	102 100.0

Chi-Square	D.F.	Significance
12.75801	1	.0004
14.22644	1	.0002

Referring to the table 6.75 it can be seen that chi-square value is significant at .01 level of confidence. Therefore there is a strong association between Life Style and Correctional Institutions Environment.

Further it can be interpreted that 52 respondents fall into the Category of low "Explosive" Life Style, out of that 67.2%

of respondents fall on high "Order and Organization" Correctional Institutions Environment.

While 50 respondents fall into the category of high "Explosive" Life Style, out of that 70.5% of respondents fall on low "Order and Organization" Correctional Institutions Environment.

Table – 6.76

Association between Life Style – Resistive and Family Environment– Intellectual-Cultural Orientation

Life Style Resistive	FE - Intellectual - C.O.		Row Total
	Low	High	
Low	-	5 10.0	5 4.9
High	52 100.0	45 90.0	97 95.1
Respondents Total	52 51.0	50 49.0	102 100.0

Chi-Square	D.F.	Significance
5.46804	1	.0194

Referring to the table 6.76 it can be seen that chi-square value is significant at .05 level of confidence. Therefore there is a strong association between Life Style and Family Environment.

The data distributed in the table 6.76 shows that 97 respondents fall on high "Resistive" Life Style, out of that 52 respondents fall into the category of low "Intellectual-Cultural Orientation" Family Environment.

Table – 6.77
Association between Life Style – Resistive and Family Environment – Organization

Life Style Resistive	FE – Organization		Row Total
	Low	High	
Low	- -	5 8.3	5 4.9
High	42 100.0	55 91.7	97 95.1
Respondents Total	42 41.2	60 58.8	102 100.0

Chi-Square	D.F.	Significance
2.10985	1	.1464
3.68041	1	.0551

Referring to the table 6.77 it can be seen that chi-square value is significant at .05 level of confidence. Therefore there is a strong association between Life Style and Family Environment.

The data reveal that 97 respondents fall into the category of high "Resistive" Life Style, out of that 91.7% of respondents fall on high "Organization" Family Environment.

Table – 6.78

Association Between Life style – Domineering and Length of Time Spent in Prison by Women Criminals

Analysis of Variance

Source	D.F	Sum of Squares	Mean Squares	F Ratio	F Prob.
Between Groups	3	19.8400	6.6133	9.8766	.0000
Within Groups	98	65.6207	.6696		
Total	101	85.4608			

Mean	Group	Grp 2	Grp 5	Grp 7	Grp 1
6.0370	Grp 2				
6.1875	Grp 5				
6.5455	Grp 7	*			
7.1923	Grp 1	* * *			

Group 1 - Less than one month

Group 2 – Less than 9 months

Group 5 – Less than 2 years

Group 7 – 3 years and above

(*) Denotes pairs of groups significantly different at the .05 level

It can be interpreted from the table 6.78 that F ratio 9.8 is significant at .01 level of confidence. Therefore it can be said that there is a strong association between Domineering – Life Style and Length of Time Spent in Prison by Women Criminals.

It can further be interpreted that group 2 (Mean score – 6.0370) group 5 (Mean score – 6.1875) and group 7 (Mean score – 6.5455) differ significantly from group 1 (Mean score – 7.1923). Further group 7 (Mean score – 6.5455) differs significantly from group 2 (6.0370).

It means that 'Less than 9 months', 'Less than 2 years' and '3 years and above' groups differ from 'Less than one month' group with reference to Life Style – Domineering. Also 'three years and above' group differs from 'Less than 9 months' group with reference to Life Style – Domineering.

Table – 6.79

Association between Life Style – Domineering and Temperament – Nervous

Life Style Domineering	Temperament – Nervous		Row Total
	Low	High	
Low	19 55.9	55 80.9	74 72.5
High	15 44.1	13 19.1	28 27.5
Respondents Total	34 33.3	68 66.7	102 100.0

Chi-Square	D.F.	Significance
5.91349	1	.0150
7.11342	1	.0077

Referring to the table 6.79 it can be seen that chi-square value is significant at .05 level of confidence. Therefore there is a strong association between Life Style and Temperament.

Further it can be interpreted that 74 respondents fall into the category of low "Domineering" Life Style, out of that 80.9% of respondents fall on high "Nervous" Temperament.

Table – 6.80: Association between Life Style – Domineering and Temperament – Introvert/ Extrovert

Life Style Domineering	Temperament – I/ E		Row Total
	Low	High	
Low	15 48.4	59 83.1	74 72.5
High	16 51.6	12 16.9	28 27.5
Respondents Total	31 30.4	71 69.6	102 100.0

Chi-Square	D.F.	Significance
11.37023	1	.0007
13.05501	1	.0003

Referring to the table 6.80 it can be seen that chi-square value is significant at .05 level of confidence. Therefore there is a strong association between Life Style and Temperament.

The analysis of the data shows that 74 respondents fall on low "Domineering" Life Style, out of that 83.1% of respondents fall on high "Introvert/Extrovert" Temperament.

Table – 6.81: Association between Life Style – Domineering and Temperament – Aggression

Life Style Domineering	Temperament – Aggression		Row Total
	Low	High	
Low	45 83.3	29 60.4	74 72.5
High	9 16.7	19 39.6	28 27.5
Respondents Total	54 52.9	48 47.1	102 100.0

Chi-Square	D.F.	Significance
5.59983	1	.0180
6.70113	1	.0096

Referring to the table 6.81 it can be seen that chi-square value is significant at .05 level of confidence. Therefore there is a strong association between Life Style and Temperament.

The data reveal that 74 respondents fall into the category of low "Domineering" Life Style, out of that 83.3% of respondents fall on low "Aggression" Temperament.

Table – 6.82

Association between Life Style – Domineering and Family Environment – Active – Recreational Orientation

Life Style Domineering	FE – Active – R.O.		Row Total
	Low	High	
Low	25 58.1	49 83.1	74 72.5
High	18 41.9	10 16.9	28 27.5
Respondents Total	43 42.2	59 57.8	102 100.0

Chi-Square	D.F.	Significance
6.55001	1	.0105
7.75040	1	.0054

Referring to the table 6.82 it can be seen that chi-square value is significant at .05 level of confidence. Therefore there is a strong association between Life Style and Family Environment.

The data interpret that 74 respondents fall into the category of low "Domineering" Life Style, out of that 83.1% of respondents fall on high "Active – Recreational Orientation" Family Environment.

Table – 6.83: Association between Life Style – Domineering and Family Environment – Organization

Life Style Domineering	F.E – Organization		Row Total
	Low	High	
Low	26 61.9	48 80.0	74 72.5
High	16 38.1	12 20.0	28 27.5
Respondents Total	42 41.2	60 58.8	102 100.0

Chi-Square	D.F.	Significance
3.20420	1	.0734
4.06200	1	.0439

Referring to the table 6.83 it can be seen that chi-square value is significant at .05 level of confidence. Therefore there is a strong association between Life Style and Family Environment.

Table 6.83 shows that 74 respondents fall into the category of low "Domineering" Life Style, out of that 80.0% of respondents fall on high "Organization" Family Environment.

Table – 6.84: Association between Life Style – Domineering and Family Environment – Personal Growth

Life Style Domineering	FE – Personal Growth		Row Total
	Low	High	
Low	36 64.3	38 82.6	74 72.5
High	20 35.7	8 17.4	28 27.5
Respondents Total	56 54.9	46 45.1	102 100.0

Chi-Square	D.F.	Significance
3.38711	1	.0657
4.25744	1	.0391

Referring to the table 6.84 it can be seen that chi-square value is significant at .05 level of confidence. Therefore there is a strong association between Life Style and Family Environment.

Further it shows that 74 respondents fall into the category of low "Domineering" Life Style, out of that 82.6% of respondents fall on high "Personal Growth" Family Environment.

Table – 6.85

Association between Life Style – Conforming and Temperament–Active

Life Style Conforming	Temperament – Active		Row Total
	Low	High	
Low	8 88.9	39 41.9	47 46.1
High	1 11.1	54 58.1	55 53.9
Respondents Total	9 8.8	93 91.2	102 100.0

Chi-Square	D.F.	Significance
5.51400	1	.0189
7.28114	1	.0070

Referring to the table 6.85 it can be seen that chi-square value is significant at .05 level of confidence. Therefore there is a strong association between Life Style and Temperament.

It can be observed that 55 respondents fall into the category of high "Conforming" Life Style, out of that 58.1% of respondents fall on high "Active" Temperament.

Table – 6.86: Association between Life Style – Conforming and Family Environment – Expressiveness

Life Style Conforming	FE – Expressiveness		Row Total
	Low	High	
Low	37 53.6	10 30.3	47 46.1
High	32 46.4	23 69.7	55 53.9
Respondents Total	69 67.6	33 32.4	102 100.0

Chi-Square	D.F.	Significance
3.99263	1	.0457
4.88614	1	.0271

Referring to the table 6.68 it can be seen that chi-square value is significant at .05 level of confidence. Therefore there is a strong association between Life Style and Family Environment.

The data show that 69 respondents fall into the category of low "Expressiveness" Family Environment, out of that 53.6% of respondents fall on low "Conforming" Life Style.

Table – 6.87: Association between Life Style – Evasive and Temperament-Active

Life Style Evasive	Temperament – Active		Row Total
	Low	High	
Low	2 22.2	4 4.3	6 5.9
High	7 77.8	89 95.7	96 94.1
Respondents Total	9 8.8	93 91.2	102 100.0

Chi-Square	D.F.	Significance
2.07359	1	.1499
4.76030	1	.0291

Referring to the table 6.87 it can be seen that chi-square value is significant at .05 level of confidence. Therefore there is a strong association between Life Style and Temperament.

Further it can be interpreted that 96 respondents fall into the category of high "Evasive" Life Style, out of that 95.7% of respondents fall on high "Active" Temperament.

Table – 6.88: Life Style by Moral Values

Life Style	Moral Values				Total	
	Low		High			
	F	%	F	%	F	%
Individualistic						
Low	12	48.0	43	55.8	55	53.9
High	13	52.0	34	44.2	47	46.1
					102	**100.0**
Exploitive						
Low	12	48.0	29	37.7	41	40.2
High	13	52.0	48	62.3	61	59.8
					102	**100.0**
Explosive						
Low	14	56.0	38	49.4	52	51.0
High	11	44.0	39	50.6	50	49.0
					102	**100.0**
Resistive						
Low	1	4.0	4	5.2	5	4.9
High	24	96.0	73	94.8	97	95.1
					102	**100.0**
Domineering						
Low	18	72.0	56	72.7	74	72.5
High	7	28.0	21	27.3	28	27.5
					102	**100.0**
Conforming						
Low	9	36.0	38	49.4	47	46.1
High	16	64.0	39	50.6	55	53.9
					102	**100.0**
Escapist						
Low	6	24.0	9	11.7	15	14.7
High	19	76.0	68	88.3	87	85.3
					102	**100.0**
Evasive						
Low	2	8.0	4	5.2	6	5.9
High	23	92.0	73	94.8	96	94.1
Total					**102**	**100.0**

The data analysis of the Table 6.88 shows that 55 (53.9%) were having low "Individualistic" Life Style, out of which 43 (55.8%) of the women criminals were having high moral values.

Further 61 (59.8%) of them were having high "Exploitive" Life Style as well as high moral values.

It can be observed that almost equal number of respondents fall into the category of both high and low "Explosive" Life Style. Out of that 77 (75.5%) of the respondents are having high moral values.

The data revealed that majority i.e. 97 (95.1%) of the women criminals were having high "Resistive" Life Style, out of which 73 (94.8%) had high moral values. While only 1 (4.0%) had low "Resistive" Life Style and low moral values.

It was also found that 74 (72.5%) of them were falling into low "Domineering" Life Style, out of which 56 (72.7%) were having high moral values. While 7 (28.0%) were having high "Domineering" and low moral values.

The data show that low and high "Conforming" Life Style was almost equally distributed among the women criminals, and majority of them were having high moral values.

The majority of the women criminals were having high "Escapist" and "Evasive" Life Style and also high moral values.

In the present study it was found that the majority of the criminals were having high moral values. Only a quarter of them were falling into low moral values category. This may be the result of their repentance in the present after they were convicted or for some after they were detained or put into Judicial custody. Most of these women have committed the crime under social or economic stress, but on the whole may be having good moral values in practice.

Table – 6.89: Life Style by Family Environment – Relationship

Life Style	Family Environment–Relationship				Total	
	Low		High			
	F	%	F	%	F	%
Individualistic						
Low	19	46.3	36	59.0	55	53.9
High	22	53.7	25	41.0	47	46.1
					102	100.0
Exploitive						
Low	17	41.5	24	39.3	41	40.2
High	24	58.5	37	60.7	61	59.8
					102	100.0
Explosive						
Low	21	51.2	31	50.8	52	51.0
High	20	48.8	30	49.2	50	49.0
					102	100.0
Resistive						
Low	1	2.4	4	6.6	5	4.9
High	40	97.6	57	93.4	97	95.1
					102	100.0
Domineering						
Low	26	63.4	48	78.7	74	72.5
High	15	36.6	13	21.3	28	27.5
					102	100.0
Conforming						
Low	18	43.9	29	47.5	47	46.1
High	23	56.1	32	52.5	55	53.9
					102	100.0
Escapist						
Low	7	17.1	8	13.1	15	14.7
High	34	82.9	53	86.9	87	85.3
					102	100.0
Evasive						
Low	3	7.3	3	4.9	6	5.9
High	38	92.7	58	95.1	96	94.1
Total					102	100.0

Table 6.89 reveals that Family Environment – Relationship dimension has a significant effect on five of the eight life styles used for the study. It shows that 61 (59.8%) of the women criminals were having high Exploitive Life Style. Out of which 37 (60.7%) were having high and 24 (58.5%) were having low Relationship in Family Environment.

Further it shows that 97 (95.1%) of the women criminals were having high Resistive Life Style out of which 40 (97.6%) were having low Relationship in Family Environment.

The data presented in the Table show that 74 (72.5%) of them were having low Domineering Life Style and 48 (78.7%) were having high Relationship in Family Environment.

From the responses presented in the Table 6.89 it shows that 87 (85.3%) and 96 (94.1%) of the respondents were having high Escapist and Evasive Life Style respectively. Both the areas were having i.e. 86.9 per cent and 95.1 per cent of high Relationship in Family Environment.

Table 6.90 shows that 61 (59.8%) of the respondents were having high Exploitive Life Style, while 29 (51.8%) of them were having low Personal Growth in Family Environment.

It can be observed from the data that 55 (99.2%) of the respondents were having high Resistive Life Style and low Personal Growth in Family Environment, while 42 (91.3%) were having high Resistive Life Style and high Personal Growth in Family Environment.

Further it can be interpreted that 38 (82.6%) of the women criminals were having low Domineering Life Style and high Personal Growth in Family Environment.

The data show that 46 (82.1%) of the respondents were having high Escapist Life Style and low Personal Growth in Family Environment.

It can also be seen that 53 (94.6%) of them were having high Evasive Life Style and low Personal Growth in Family Environment.

Table – 6.90: Life Style by Family Environment – Personal Growth

Life Style	Family Environment – Personal Growth				Total	
	Low		High			
	F	%	F	%	F	%
Individualistic						
Low	29	51.8	26	56.5	55	53.9
High	27	48.2	20	43.5	47	46.1
					102	100.0
Exploitive						
Low	27	48.2	14	30.4	41	40.2
High	29	51.8	32	69.6	61	59.8
					102	100.0
Explosive						
Low	26	46.4	26	56.5	52	51.0
High	30	53.6	20	43.5	50	49.0
					102	100.0
Resistive						
Low	1	1.8	4	8.7	5	4.9
High	55	99.2	42	91.3	97	95.1
					102	100.0
Domineering						
Low	36	64.3	38	82.6	74	72.5
High	20	35.7	8	17.4	28	27.5
					102	100.0
Conforming						
Low	23	41.1	24	52.2	47	46.1
High	33	58.9	22	47.8	55	53.9
					102	100.0
Escapist						
Low	10	17.9	5	10.9	15	14.7
High	46	82.1	41	89.1	87	85.3
					102	100.0
Evasive						
Low	3	5.4	3	6.5	6	5.9
High	53	94.6	43	93.5	96	94.1
Total					102	100.0

Table – 6.91: Life Style by Family Environment – System Maintenance

Life Style	Family Environment– System Maintenance				Total	
	Low		High			
	F	%	F	%	F	%
Individualistic						
Low	23	54.8	32	53.3	55	53.9
High	19	45.2	28	46.7	47	46.1
					102	**100.0**
Exploitive						
Low	17	40.5	24	40.0	41	40.2
High	25	59.5	36	60.0	61	59.8
					102	**100.0**
Explosive						
Low	22	52.4	30	50.0	52	51.0
High	20	47.6	30	50.0	50	49.0
					102	**100.0**
Resistive						
Low	1	2.4	4	6.7	5	4.9
High	41	97.6	56	93.3	97	95.1
					102	**100.0**
Domineering						
Low	30	71.4	44	73.3	74	72.5
High	12	28.6	16	26.7	28	27.5
					102	**100.0**
Conforming						
Low	21	50.0	26	43.3	47	46.1
High	21	50.0	34	56.7	55	53.9
					102	**100.0**
Escapist						
Low	6	14.3	9	15.0	15	14.7
High	36	85.7	51	85.0	87	85.3
					102	**100.0**
Evasive						
Low	2	4.8	4	6.7	6	5.9
High	40	95.2	56	93.3	96	94.1
Total					102	100.0

As indicated the Table 6.91 shows that 60 (58.8%) of the respondents were having high System Maintenance in Family Environment out of this 36 (60.0%) of them were having high Exploitive Life Style and 24 (40.0%) were having low Exploitive Life Style.

The Table 6.91 also indicates that 60 (58.8%) of the women criminals fall into the category of high System Maintenance in Family Environment. Out of this 56 (93.3%) were having high Resistive Life Style.

Further, the Table shows that 60 (58.8%) of the respondents were having high System Maintenance in Family Environment, out of which 44 (73.3%) fall under the category of low Domineering Life Style.

The majority of the respondents were having high Escapist and Evasive Life Style, but at the same time they were also having high System Maintenance in their Family Environment.

The data distributed in the Table 6.92 show that 58 (56.8%) of the women prisoners were having low System Maintenance in Institutional Environment, while the majority of them i.e 61 (59.8%) were falling into the category of high Exploitive Life Style.

The majority of the respondents i.e. 97 (95.1%) though having high Resistive Life Style, yet out of this 57 (98.3%) were having low System Maintenance in Institutional Environment.

The daia also reveal that 74 (72.5%) of them were falling into the category of low Domineering Life Style; while 58 (56.8%) were having low System Maintenance in Institutional Environment.

In the last two categories of Life Style, the majority of the respondents were having high Escapist and Evasive Life Style i.e. 85.3 per cent and 94.1 per cent respectively. In both the categories 58 (56.8%) were having low System Maintenance in Institutional Environment.

Table – 6.92: Life Style by Institutional Environment – System Maintenance

Life Style	Inst. Environment – System Maintenance				Total	
	Low		High			
	F	%	F	%	F	%
Individualistic						
Low	30	51.7	25	56.8	55	53.9
High	28	48.3	19	43.2	47	46.1
					102	**100.0**
Exploitive						
Low	22	37.9	19	43.2	41	40.2
High	36	62.1	25	56.8	61	59.8
					102	**100.0**
Explosive						
Low	25	43.1	27	61.4	52	51.0
High	33	56.9	17	38.6	50	49.0
					102	**100.0**
Resistive						
Low	1	1.7	4	9.1	5	4.9
High	57	98.3	40	90.9	97	95.1
					102	**100.0**
Domineering						
Low	39	67.2	35	79.5	74	72.5
High	19	32.8	9	20.5	28	27.5
					102	**100.0**
Conforming						
Low	27	46.6	20	45.5	47	46.1
High	31	53.4	24	54.5	55	53.9
					102	**100.0**
Escapist						
Low	6	10.3	9	20.5	15	14.7
High	52	89.7	35	79.5	87	85.3
					102	**100.0**
Evasive						
Low	4	6.9	2	4.5	6	5.9
High	54	93.1	42	95.5	96	94.1
Total					**102**	**100.0**

SECTION – 8

Family Environment

The family is one of the most important sub-systems of society. It is also helpful in enriching other sub-systems like economy, polity, religion, etc., and these sub-systems too contribute to the positive functioning of the family. Individuals in the society are shaped by the family and the family shares the larger burden and own the higher accountability of them as useful members of the society. The family not only socializes to make members responsible in the society, but also regulates and controls the negative traits/characteristics/behaviour of the individuals.

In order to find out the effects of family environment on women criminality, the Family Environment Scale was used to measure the social climate of the families of the women inmates. In this three dimensions of Family Environment were studied such as :

(1) Relationship Dimensions

Cohesion, Expressiveness and Conflict

(2) Personal Growth Dimensions.

Independence, Achievement Orientation, Intellectual–Cultural Orientation, Active–Recreational Orientation and Moral Religious Orientation.

(3) System Maintenance Dimensions.

Organization and Control.

It can be interpreted from the table 6.93 that F ratio 3.3 is significant at .05 level of confidence. Therefore it can be said that there is a strong association between Conflict – Family Environment and Length of Conviction of Women Criminals.

It can further be interpreted that group 8 (Mean score – 1.8235) and group 9 (Mean score – 1.8621) differ significantly from group 7 (Mean score – 2.6829). It means that Detenus and Undertrial groups differ from Life imprisonment group with reference to Family Environment–Conflict.

Table – 6.93

Association between Family Environment – Conflict and Length of Conviction of Women Criminals

Analysis of Variance

Source	D.F	Sum of Squares	Mean Squares	F Ratio	F Prob.
Between Groups	3	17.4482	5.8161	3.3502	.0221
Within Groups	98	170.1302	1.7360		
Total	101	187.5784			

Mean	Group	Grp 8	Grp 9	Grp 6	Grp 7
1.8235	Grp 8				
1.8621	Grp 9				
2.6667	Grp 6				
2.6829	Grp 7	*	*		

Group 6 – Below 10 Years

Group 7 – 20 Years/Life Imprisonment

Group 8 – PASA / 1 Year Detention

Group 9 – Under Trial

(*) Denotes pairs of groups significantly different at the .05 level.

It can be interpreted from the table 6.94 that F ratio 5.5 is significant at :05 level of confidence. Therefore it can be said that there is a strong association between Independence – Family Environment and Nature of Crime by Women Criminals.

Table – 6.94

Association Between Family Environment – Independence and Nature of Crime by Women Criminals

Analysis of Variance

Source	D.F	Sum of Squares	Mean Squares	F Ratio	F Prob.
Between Groups	1	7.4574	7.4574	5.5122	.0211
Within Groups	90	121.7600	1.3529		
Total	91	129.2174			

Table – 6.95

Association Between FamilyEnvironment – Intellectual Cultural Orientation and Education of Women Criminals

Analysis of Variance

Source	D.F	Sum of Squares	Mean Squares	F Ratio	F Prob.
Between Groups	2	10.5250	5.2625	3.1610	.0467
Within Groups	99	164.8182	1.6648		
Total	101	175.3431			

Mean	Group	Grp 1	Grp 3	Grp 2
4.3182	Grp 1			
4.6667	Grp 3			
5.0833	Grp 2	*		

Group 1 – Illiterate

Group 2 – Primary

Group 3 – Secondary & above

(*) Denotes pairs of groups significantly different at the .05 level.

It can be interpreted from the table 6.95 that F ratio 3.1 is significant at .05 level of confidence. Therefore it can be said that there is a strong association between Intellectual Cultural Orientation – Family Environment and Education of Women Criminals.

It can further be interpreted that group 1 (Mean score – 4.3182) differs significantly from group 2 (Mean score – 5.0833). It means that Illiterate group differs from Primary education group with reference to Family Environment – Intellectual Cultural Orientation.

Table – 6.96

Association Between Family Environment – Moral Religious Orientation and Length of Conviction of Women Criminals

Analysis of Variance

Source	D.F	Sum of Squares	Mean Squares	F Ratio	F Prob.
Between Groups	3	9.4753	3.1584	3.5226	.0178
Within Groups	98	87.8678	.8966		
Total	101	97.3431			

Mean	Group	Grp 8	Grp 6	Grp 7	Grp 9
4.8235	Grp 8				
5.3333	Grp 6				
5.6341	Grp 7	*			
5.6552	Grp 9	*			

Group 6 – Below 10 Years
Group 7 – 20 Years/Life Imprisonment
Group 8 – PASA / 1 Year Detention
Group 9 – Under Trial

(*) Denotes pairs of groups significantly different at the .05 level.

It can be interpreted from the table 6.96 that F ratio 3.5 is significant at .05 level of confidence. Therefore it can be said that there is a strong association between Moral Religious Orientation – Family Environment and Length of Conviction of Women Criminals.

It can further be interpreted that group 8 (Mean score – 4.8235) differs significantly from group 7 (Mean score – 5.6341) and group 9 (Mean score – 5.6552).

It means that Detenus group differs from Life imprisonment and Undertrial groups with reference to Family Environment – Moral Religious Orientation.

Table – 6.97

Association Between Family Environment – Relationship and Education of Women Criminals

Analysis of Variance

Source	D.F	Sum of Squares	Mean Squares	F Ratio	F Prob.
Between Groups	2	20.5439	10.2719	3.6475	.0296
Within Groups	99	278.7992	2.8162		
Total	101	299.3431			

Mean	Group	Grp 1	Grp 3	Grp 2
12.5606	Grp 1			
13.0833	Grp 3			
13.6250	Grp 2	*		

Group 1 – Illiterate

Group 2 – Primary

Group 3 – Secondary & above

(*) Denotes pairs of groups significantly different at the .05 level.

It can be interpreted from the table 6.97 that F ratio 3.6 is significant at .05 level of confidence. Therefore it can be said that there is a strong association between Relationship – Family Environment and Education of Women Criminals.

It can further be interpreted that group 1 (Mean score – 12.5606) differs significantly from group 2 (Mean score – 13.6250). It means that Illiterate group differs from Primary education group with reference to Family Environment – Relationship.

Table – 6.98

Association Between Family Environment – System Maintenance and Length of Time Spent in Prison

Analysis of Variance

Source	D.F	Sum of Squares	Mean Squares	F Ratio	F Prob.
Between Groups	3	15.6192	5.2064	2.7403	. 0474
Within Groups	98	186.1945	1.8999		
Total	101	201.8137			

Mean	Group	Grp 1	Grp 2	Grp 7	Grp 5
11.2308	Grp 1				
12.0741	Grp 2	*			
12.0909	Grp 7	*			
12.2500	Grp 5	*			

Group 1 - Less than one month

Group 2 – Less than 9 months

Group 5 – Less than 2 years

Group 7 – 3 years and above

(*) Denotes pairs of groups significantly different at the .05 level.

It can be interpreted from the table 6.98 that F ratio 2.7 is significant at .05 level of confidence. Therefore it can be said that there is a strong association between System Maintenance – Family Environment and Length of Time Spent in Prison by Women Criminals.

It can further be interpreted that group 1 (Mean score – 11.2308) differs significantly from group 2 (Mean score – 12.0741), group 7 (Mean score – 12.0909) and group 5 (Mean Score – 12.2500).

It means that 'Less than one month' group differs from 'Less than 9 months', '3 years and above' and 'Less than 2 years' groups with reference to Family Environment – System Maintenance.

SECTION – 9

Correctional Institutions Environment

Prisons are considered as "total institutions", in which the prisoner's life events occur. Although the first interest of prison personnel was in controlling the criminals' behaviour during the period of custody, there has also been continuing social concern that criminals should somehow be reformed and helped in realising their own drawbacks and remolding their Life Style during the term of imprisonment.

In India, only a few studies have been conducted on prison life of criminals in relation to their socio-cultural background and prisonization, and how far the socio-cultural background influences a person to commit crime and the impact it has on prison life. In order to understand the interpersonal relations of the jail inmates with each other and with the prison personnel, emphasis was put on autonomy and practical orientation and the level of clarity and organization. The climate of a correctional institution influences many aspects of the residents' lives, such as moral, personality and behaviour including adherence to institutional rules, running away from the institution and performance during parole.

In the present study, an attempt has been made to measure the social climate of adult correctional programs in the two Central Jails of Gujarat. The nine Correctional Institutions Environment Scale (CIES) subscales assessing three dimensions were used such as :

{1} Relationship Dimensions

Involvement, Support and Expressiveness.

These dimensions assess the extent to which residents become involved in the unit, how much residents support each other and are supported by staff and the amount of spontaneity in these relationships.

{2} Personal Growth Dimensions

Autonomy, Practical Orientation and Personal Problem Orientation.

Each of these subscales taps an aspect of the unit's treatment orientation. Autonomy assesses the extent to which residents are encouraged to be independent and responsible for their own decisions. Practical and Personal Problem Orientation reflect two major treatment orientations currently used in correctional institutions like educational and vocational training programs.

{3} System Maintenance Dimensions

Order and Organization, Clarity and Staff Control

These dimensions are all related to keeping the correctional institution functioning in a well-organized, clear and coherent manner.

It can be interpreted from the table 6.99 that F ratio 3.1 is significant at .05 level of confidence. Therefore it can be said that there is a strong association between Involvement – Correctional Institutions Environment and Length of Time Spent in Prison by Women Criminals.

It can further be interpreted that group 2 (Mean score – 6.3704) differs significantly from group 5 (Mean score – 7.3125 and group 1(Mean score – 7.3462).

Table – 6.99

Association Between Correctional Institutions Environment – Involvement and Length of Time Spent in Prison by Women Criminals

Analysis of Variance

Source	D.F	Sum of Squares	Mean Squares	F Ratio	F Prob.
Between Groups	3	17.1267	5.7089	3.1617	.0280
Within Groups	98	176.9517	1.8056		
Total	101	194.0784			

Mean	Group	Grp 2	Grp 7	Grp 5	Grp 1
6.3704	Grp 2				
6.6667	Grp 7				
7.3125	Grp 5	*			
7.3462	Grp 1	*			

Group 1 - Less than one month

Group 2 – Less than 9 months

Group 5 – Less than 2 years

Group 7 – 3 years and above

(*) Denotes pairs of groups significantly different at the .05 level

It means that 'Less than 9 months' group differs from 'Less than 2 years' and 'Less than one month' groups with reference to Correctional Institutions Environment – Involvement.

Table – 6.100
Association Between Correctional Institutions Environment – Personal Problem Orientation and Length of Conviction of Women Criminals

Analysis of Variance

Source	D.F	Sum of Squares	Mean Squares	F Ratio	F Prob.
Between Groups	3	18.4339	6.1446	5.4701	.0016
Within Groups	98	110.0857	1.1233		
Total	101	128.5196			

Mean	Group	Grp 7	Grp 8	Grp 6	Grp 9
3.5610	Grp 7				
3.6471	Grp 8				
4.0667	Grp 6				
4.5517	Grp 9	*	*		

Group 6 – Below 10 Years
Group 7 – 20 Years/Life Imprisonment
Group 8 – PASA / 1 Year Detention
Group 9 – Under Trial

(*) Denotes pairs of groups significantly different at the .05 level

It can be interpreted from the table 6.100 that F ratio 3.5 is significant at .01 level of confidence. Therefore it can be said that there is a strong association between Personal Problem Orientation–Correctional Institutions Environment and Length of Conviction of Women Criminals.

It can further be interpreted that group 7 (Mean score – 3.5610) and group 8 (Mean score – 3.6471) differ significantly from group 9 (Mean score – 4.5517).

It means that 'Life imprisonment' group and 'Detenus' group differ from 'Undertrial' group with reference to Correctional Institutions Environment – Personal Problem Orientation.

Table – 6.101

Association between Correctional Institutions Environment – Personal Problem Orientation and Length of Time Spent in Prison by Women Criminals

Analysis of Variance

Source	D.F	Sum of Squares	Mean Squares	F Ratio	F Prob.
Between Groups	3	9.7225	3.2408	2.6735	.0515
Within Groups	98	118.7971	1.2122		
Total	101	128.5196			

Mean	Group	Grp 7	Grp 5	Grp 2	Grp 1
3.5758	Grp 7				
3.7500	Grp 5				
4.0741	Grp 2				
4.3462	Grp 1	*			

Group 1 - Less than one month

Group 2 – Less than 9 months

Group 5 – Less than 2 years

Group 7 – 3 years and above

(*) Denotes pairs of groups significantly different at the .05 level.

It can be interpreted from the table 6.101 that F ratio 2.6 is significant at .05 level of confidence. Therefore it can be said that there is a strong association between Personal Problem Orientation – Correctional Institutions Environment and Length of Time Spent in Prison by Women Criminals.

It can further be interpreted that group 7 (Mean score – 3.5758) differs significantly from group 1 (Mean score – 4.3462).

It means that 'three years and above' group differs from 'less than one month' group with reference to Correctional Institutions Environment – Personal Problem Orientation.

Table – 6.102

Association Between Correctional Institutions Environment – Order and Organization and Nature of Crime by Women Criminals

Analysis of Variance

Source	D.F	Sum of Squares	Mean Squares	F Ratio	F Prob.
Between Groups	1	16.2820	16.2820	16.7222	.0001
Within Groups	90	87.6310	.9737		
Total	91	103.9130			

It can be interpreted from the table 6.102 that F ratio 16.7 is significant at .01 level of confidence. Therefore it can be said that there is a strong association between Order and Organization – Correctional Institutions Environment and Nature of Crime by Women Criminals.

It can be interpreted from the table 6.103 that F ratio 4.0 is significant at .01 level of confidence. Therefore it can be said that there is a strong association between Order and Organization – Correctional Institutions Environment and Motive behind Crime Commission by Women Criminals.

Table – 6.103

Association between Correctional Institutions Environment – Order and Organization and Motive behind Crime Commission by Women Criminals

Analysis of Variance

Source	D.F	Sum of Squares	Mean Squares	F Ratio	F Prob.
Between Groups	3	11.7128	3.9043	4.0359	.0097
Within Groups	90	87.0638	.9674		
Total	93	98.7766			

Mean	Group	Grp 5	Grp 4	Grp 3	Grp 6
7.0476	Grp 5				
7.6923	Grp 4	*			
7.8000	Grp 3	*			
7.9730	Grp 6	*			

Group 3 – Accidental
Group 4 – Situational
Group 5 – To overcome Economic Stress
Group 6 – To overcome Social Stress

(*) Denotes pairs of groups significantly different at the .05 level.

It can further be interpreted that group 5 (Mean score – 7.0476) differs significantly from group 4 (Mean score – 7.6923), group 3 (Mean score – 7.8000) and group 6 (Mean score – 7.9730).

It means that 'To overcome Economic Stress' group differs from 'Situational', 'Accidental' and 'To overcome Social Stress' groups with reference to Correctional Institutions Environment – Order and Organization.

Table – 6.104

Association Between Correctional Institutions Environment – Order and Organization and Length of Conviction of Women Criminals

Analysis of Variance

Source	D.F	Sum of Squares	Mean Squares	F Ratio	F Prob.
Between Groups	3	21.1056	7.0352	7.6205	.0001
Within Groups	98	90.4728	.9232		
Total	101	111.5784			

Mean	Group	Grp 8	Grp 9	Grp 6	Grp 7
6.7059	Grp 8				
7.5862	Grp 9	*			
7.7333	Grp 6	*			
8.0244	Grp 7	*			

Group 6 – Below 10 Years

Group 7 – 20 Years/Life Imprisonment

Group 8 – PASA / 1 Year Detention

Group 9 – Under Trial

(*) Denotes pairs of groups significantly different at the .05 level.

It can be interpreted from the table 6.104 that F ratio 7.6 is significant at .01 level of confidence. Therefore it can be said that there is a strong association between Order and Organization – Correctional Institutions Environment and Length of Conviction of Women Criminals.

It can further be interpreted that group 8 (Mean score – 6.7059) differs significantly from group 9 (Mean score - 7.5862), group 6 (Mean score – 7.7333) and group 7 (Mean score – 8.0244).

It means that 'Detenus' group differs from 'Undertrials', 'below 10 years' and 'Life imprisonment' groups with reference to Correctional Institutions Environment – Order and Organization.

Table – 6.105

Association between Correctional Institutions Environment – Order and Organization and Length of Time Spent in Prison by Women Criminals

Analysis of Variance

Source	D.F	Sum of Squares	Mean Squares	F Ratio	F Prob.
Between Groups	3	10.2864	3.4288	3.3173	.0231
Within Groups	98	101.2921	1.0336		
Total	101	111.5784			

Mean	Group	Grp 2	Grp 1	Grp 5	Grp 7
7.2963	Grp 2				
7.4231	Grp 1				
7.6875	Grp 5				
8.0606	Grp 7	*	*		

Group 1 - Less than one month

Group 2 – Less than 9 months

Group 5 – Less than 2 years

Group 7 – 3 years and above

(*) Denotes pairs of groups significantly different at the .05 level

GRAPH 6.13: LENGTH OF CONVICTION C.I.E. - SYSTEM MAINTENANCE

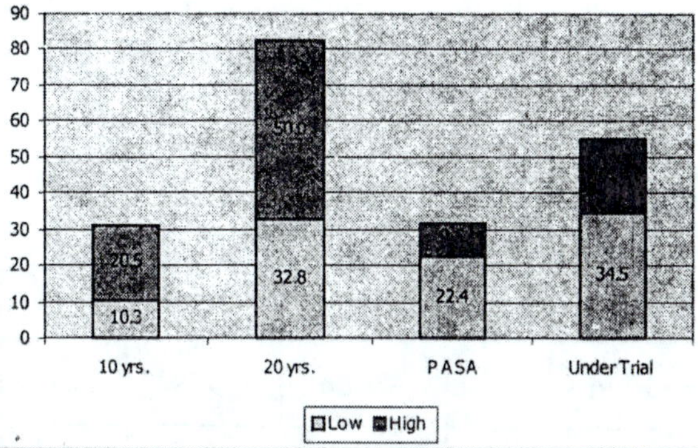

GRAPH 6.14: STYLE EXPLOSIVE AND FAMILY ENV. ACTIVE-RECREATIONAL ORGN.

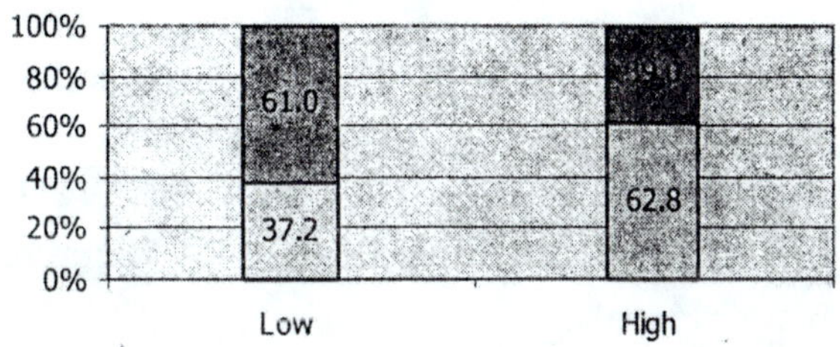

It can be interpreted from the table 6.105 that F ratio 3.3 is significant at .05 level of confidence. Therefore it can be said that there is a strong association between Order and Organization – Correctional Institutions Environment and Length of Time Spent in Prison by Women Criminals.

It can further be interpreted that group 2 (Mean score – 7.2963) and group 1 (Mean score – 7.4231) differ significantly from group 7 (Mean score – 8.0606).

It means that 'Less than 9 months' and 'Less than one month' groups differ from '3 years and above' group with reference to Correctional Institutions Environment – Order and Organization.

Table – 6.106

Association Between Correctional Institutions Environment – Clarity and Nature of Crime by Women Criminals

Analysis of Variance

Source	D.F	Sum of Squares	Mean Squares	F Ratio	F Prob.
Between Groups	1	6.9784	6.9784	4.6177	.0343
Within Groups	90	136.0107	1.5112		
Total	91	142.9891			

It can be interpreted from the table 6.106 that F ratio 4.6 is significant at .05 level of confidence. Therefore it can be said that there is a strong association between Clarity – Correctional Institutions Environment and Nature of Crime by Women Criminals.

It can be interpreted from the 6.107 table that F ratio 4.1 is significant at .01 level of confidence. Therefore it can be said that there is a strong association between Clarity – Correctional Institutions Environment and Length of Conviction of Women Criminals.

It can further be interpreted that group 8 (Mean score – 6.4118) and group 9 (Mean score – 6.6207) differ significantly from group 7 (Mean score - 7.2683) and group 6 (Mean score – 7.5333).

It means that 'Detenus' and 'Undertrial' group differ from 'Life imprisonment' and 'Below 10 years' groups with reference to Correctional Institutions Environment– Clarity.

Table – 6.107

Association Between Correctional Institutions Environment – Clarity and Length of Conviction of Women Criminals

Analysis of Variance

Source	D.F	Sum of Squares	Mean Squares	F Ratio	F Prob.
Between Groups	3	17.2334	5.7445	4.1785	.0079
Within Groups	98	134.7273	1.3748		
Total	101	151.9608			

Mean	Group	Grp 8	Grp 9	Grp 7	Grp 6
6.4118	Grp 8				
6.6207	Grp 9				
7.2683	Grp 7	*	*		
7.5333	Grp 6	*	*		

Group 6 – Below 10 Years

Group 7 – 20 Years/Life Imprisonment

Group 8 – PASA / 1 Year Detention

Group 9 – Under Trial

(*) Denotes pairs of groups significantly different at the .05 level.

It can be interpreted from the table 6.108 that F ratio 4.1 is significant at .01 level of confidence. Therefore it can be said that there is a strong association between Clarity – Correctional Institutions Environment and Length of Time Spent in Prison by Women Criminals.

Table – 6.108

Association between Correctional Institutions Environment – Clarity and Length of Time Spent in Prison by Women Criminals

Analysis of Variance

Source	D.F	Sum of Squares	Mean Squares	F Ratio	F Prob.
Between Groups	3	17.0832	5.6944	4.1375	.0083
Within Groups	98	134.8775	1.3763		
Total	101	151.9608			

Mean	Group	Grp 1	Grp 2	Grp 5	Grp 7
6.3846	Grp 1				
6.8519	Grp 2				
7.3125	Grp 5	*			
7.3939	Grp 7	*			

Group 1 - Less than one month

Group 2 – Less than 9 months

Group 5 – Less than 2 years

Group 7 – 3 years and above

(*) Denotes pairs of groups significantly different at the .05 level.

It can further be interpreted that group 1 (Mean score – 6.3846) differs significantly from group 5 (Mean score – 7.3125) and group 7 (Mean score – 7.3939).

It means that 'Less than one month' group differs from 'Less than 2 years' and '3 years and above' groups with reference to Correctional Institutions Environment – Clarity.

Table – 6.109

Association Between Correctional Institutions Environment – System Maintenance and Nature of Crime by Women Criminals.

Analysis of Variance

Source	D.F	Sum of Squares	Mean Squares	F Ratio	F Prob.
Between Groups	1	20.9087	20.9087	5.7941	.0181
Within Groups	90	324.7761	3.6086		
Total	91	345.6848			

It can be interpreted from the table 6.109 that F ratio 5.7 is significant at .05 level of confidence. Therefore it can be said that there is a strong association between System Maintenance – Correctional Institutions Environment and Nature of Crime by Women Criminals.

It can be interpreted from the table 6.110 that F ratio 5.3 is significant at .01 level of confidence. Therefore it can be said that there is a strong association between System Maintenance – Correctional Institutions Environment and Length of Conviction of Women Criminals.

It can further be interpreted that group 8 (Mean score – 18.1765) and group 9 (Mean score – 18.8621) differ significantly from group 7 (Mean score – 19.9268) and group 6 (Mean score – 20.0667).

It means that 'Detenus' and 'Undertrial' groups differ from 'Life imprisonment' and 'Below 10 years' groups with reference to Correctional Institutions Environment – System Maintenance.

Table – 6.110

Association Between Correctional Institutions Environment – System Maintenance and Length of Conviction of Women Criminals

Analysis of Variance

Source	D.F	Sum of Squares	Mean Squares	F Ratio	F Prob.
Between Groups	3	51.6614	17.2205	5.3131	.0020
Within Groups	98	317.6327	3.2411		
Total	101	369.2941			

Mean	Group	Grp 8	Grp 9	Grp 7	Grp 6
18.1765	Grp 8				
18.8621	Grp 9				
19.9268	Grp 7	*	*		
20.0667	Grp 6	*	*		

Group 6 – Below 10 Years
Group 7 – 20 Years/Life Imprisonment
Group 8 – PASA / 1 Year Detention
Group 9 – Under Trial

(*) Denotes pairs of groups significantly different at the .05 level.

It can be interpreted from the table 6.111 that F ratio 4.5 is significant at .01 level of confidence. Therefore it can be said that there is a strong association between System Maintenance – Correctional Institutions Environment and Length of Time Spent in Prison by Women Criminals.

It can further be interpreted that group 1 (Mean score – 18.4231) differs significantly from group 5 (Mean score – 19.8750) and group 7 (Mean score – 20.0606). While group 2 (Mean score – 19.0741) differs significantly from group 7 (20.0606).

Table – 6.111

Association between Correctional Institutions Environment – System Maintenance and Length of Time Spent in Prison by Women Criminals

Analysis of Variance

Source	D.F	Sum of Squares	Mean Squares	F Ratio	F Prob.
Between Groups	3	45.4673	15.1558	4.5866	.0048
Within Groups	98	323.8268	3.3044		
Total	101	369.2941			

Mean	Group	Grp 1	Grp 2	Grp 5	Grp 7
18.4231	Grp 1				
19.0741	Grp 2				
19.8750	Grp 5	*			
20.0606	Grp 7	*	*		

Group 1 - Less than one month

Group 2 – Less than 9 months

Group 5 – Less than 2 years

Group 7 – 3 years and above

(*) Denotes pairs of groups significantly different at the .05 level.

It means that 'Less than one month' group differs from 'Less than 2 yrs' and '3 yrs. and above' groups, while 'Less than 9 months' group differs from '3 yrs. and above' group with reference to Correctional Institutions Environment – System Maintenance.

7

Case Studies

In this chapter an attempt has been made in presenting qualitative information to supplement and support the data gathered through various tools and techniques like, observation, interviews, scales, etc. Young (1977) defines case study as a "comprehensive study of a social unit- be that unit a person, a group, a social institution or a community". He further explains that, "A case study seeks to determine social processes, it reveals that complexity of factors and indicates their sequences and inter-relationships. Statistical studies, on the other hand, deal with relatively few factors, but are able to provide scope by indicating extent, frequency, trends and degree of association".

Good and Hatt (1954) maintain that a case study is a "way of organizing social data so as to preserve the unitary character of the social object being studied. Expressed somewhat differently, it is an approach which views any social unit as a whole". Thus to achieve greater insights about women's criminal behaviour, qualitative data has been added for the research study.

Case-1 (Murder of Daughter-in-Law)

1. Social Background and Relationship

"P" is a Garasia woman of 65 years of age. She is illiterate and hails from a village in Surendranagar district of Gujarat. She is the eldest of the three brothers and a sister. Both her parents were illiterate and had a low economic status. She was brought up by her mother as her father died early. In her childhood, she worked with her mother in "bandhni" work on sarees and clothes. She got married at the age of 20 and had a happy married life. Her husband has a small piece of land and a house, showing low economic status. She has seven sons and one daughter. Three sons got married and the daughter who is also in prison, serving life terms is married and has two young sons. Her daughter was twelve years old when the crime was committed i.e. 12 years ago.

2. *Personality Factors*

"P" was fast in action and did not think much before any action. She was quite old when she got convicted after twelve years of committing the crime. She felt helpless and repented that because of the death of the daughter-in-law, the whole family got disturbed. But she was not feeling any guilt as she feels she has not done any offence and it was an accident.

3. *Situation of Offence/ Violation of Law*

The marriage of the son took place in 1982 and the offence was committed in 1984. The daughter-in-law spent most of the two years in her parent's place and spent only few months in her in-law's place, as she complained to her parents of the physical and mental torture by her in-laws for giving less dowry. On 14th May 1984, the daughter-in-law was burnt to death very early morning at 5.00 am and was cremated without informing her parents.

4. *Legal Responses and Criminal Reactions*

The session court on 27th Sept 84 acquitted all the accused on the ground that it was a suicidal death and not murder, as there is no written document presented in the court by the petitioner that the in-laws were asking for dowry. Thus based on the oral description, the court could not impose punishment on them and all the seventeen accused for the murder were acquitted by the session court.

Aggrieved by the decision, the petitioner filed an appeal in the High Court against the order. The High Court found that on 14th May 1984, when the daughter-in-law was being burnt in the kitchen, the five accused were standing outside on the verandah and did not make any effort to save the daughter-in-law. Before the day-break, without informing anybody, they cremated her decomposed body. They spread rumours that early in the morning at 5 o'clock while preparing tea, the stove burst and she died due to the accident. Terming the session court's decision as unjustified, the High Court division bench has said that all the five accused had murdered the daughter-in-law at late night and then the body was set on fire to make a show of accidental death and her remnants disposed of before dawn, indicating clearly they were involved. Gujarat High Court sentenced five persons of the family, i.e. father-in-law, mother-in-law, sister-in-law and 2 brothers-in-law to life imprisonment for murdering a bride, who failed to meet their dowry demands. They were sentenced to seven years of rigorous imprisonment to run concurrently with the sentence imposed on them.

When this researcher tried to understand "P"s reactions to her criminality, she told that she was sleeping and did not know anything about the incident. The neighbours informed her about the smoke coming out from the kitchen. She completely denied her role in it and repented for all that happened to the family.

5. *Analysis and Observation*

In this case it shows that the family has a very low socio-economic status, and a large number of children which are the reasons for getting more dowry from the daughter-in-laws' family. The family members are hostile and aggressive and on the spur of the moment in their anger did not think about the consequences of the murder of their daughter-in-law. The husband of the victim was not present and had gone out of the village so he was not involved in the crime.

Case–2 (Possession of Illicit Drug)

1. *Social Background and Relationship*

"U" is 35 years old, coming from Mistry community. She has primary level of education. She was born in Ahmedabad but the place of the crime was Nadiad. She was working as a labourer in building construction. According to her, she was also getting *Dakshina* from a temple in Nadiad. Her total income per month was Rs.1000. Her parents died at an early age. Her father was working in a mill and has a low socio-economic status. She has 1 brother and 3 sisters. Her husband is illiterate, repairs plastic buckets and has a very low socio-economic status. He has a bad habit of gambling and sold out his house, utensils, etc., for this purpose. "U" was having uncongenial home and often had quarrels with her husband due to poverty and his bad habit of gambling. She often left home and roamed around here and there, mostly in temples. Her in-laws were staying in Agra and she never went there to stay with them. She does not have any relation with her own family members and nobody comes to the jail to visit her. Her husband also did not keep any relation with her after she was arrested and she feels he has deceived her. She does not have any children and is now totally alone. She has not informed anybody about her arrest and conviction.

From her marital history it was found that the husband was not earning and due to bad habits was always asking for money. He was cruel towards her and sometimes both physically and verbally abused her. He had a difficult temperament and demanded more work from her. The in-laws were also indifferent towards her.

2. *Personality Factors*

"U" was active in the prison and was involved in activities like cutting vegetables, washing clothes of other inmates who could afford to pay her. She took part in singing *bhajans*. She was social and kept good relations with other fellow inmates.

She was repenting for her conviction. "U" felt that she would have a difficult time in living when she will be released. She was quite careful in talking about her personal life.

3. Situation of Offence/ Violation of Law

According to her she was sitting in the premises of a temple in Nadiad along with her husband, who is from Agra, and a few women friends from Delhi having socio-economic problems like her. So the offence was committed in a group, but as the packet of ganja was lying beside her, she was caught by the police. Her husband and others ran away from there.

4. Legal Response and Criminal Reactions

"U" was convicted for 5 years rigorous imprisonment. She has already spent 3 years in the prison. She is suffering from Asthama in the Jail. She feels the ganja did not belong to her but somebody kept it beside her and she was caught for nothing. She has adjusted well in the prison and gave suggestions for vocational training, and a job and said that education should be provided for the reformation of the female offenders.

5. Analysis and Observation

It shows that "U" comes from a broken home, having acute socio-economic problems in both the families of orientation and procreation. She was having an unhappy married life, with lots of physical and mental torture from her husband. The researcher feels that "U" was involved with a gang operating from Delhi in drug trafficking. As she was suffering from poor socio-economic condition, this must have forced her into such a company. Her husband was also involved in the same profession, which he took up, may be, to satisfy the requirements of his habit of gambling.

Case–3 (Illicit Drug Selling)

1. Social Background and Relationship

"H" is a Muslim woman from Vora community. She is 40 years old and illiterate. She has two brothers and five sisters and she is the second child of the family. Her father was having secondary education and by profession he was a truck driver earning Rs.2000 per month. Her mother was illiterate. The monthly income of the father was too little for a big family and thus has a low economic status.

She was married to a tempo driver having secondary school education and earning was between Rs.500 – Rs.700 per month. She has one son and three daughters and lived in Nadiad town.

"H" was running a tea *lari* and earning Rs.30 – 40 per day. Her husband was alcoholic and had a bad habit of gambling. She was married at an early age. Her husband started showing disinterest in home and children and started staying away from home for days. As a result, she had to shoulder all the responsibilities of the family alone. There was always quarrel with her husband. Sometimes he used to be cruel and abuse her verbally and beat her severely. Her husband was also involved in selling *Charas* and at present convicted in the jail for ten years. Though having indifferent relation with her mother-in-law, the children are now living with her, as both the parents are in jail.

2. *Personality Factors*

"H" was very bold and open. She was not at all feeling any guilt of the act. She does not bother whether people have prejudice towards her or not; she was ready to face the society after release. Before taking any action she does think over the matter. She is active and social. To attain goals, she is ready to take dangerous means. She was indifferent to religious and moral values. She is aggressive and frustrated.

3. *Situation of Offence/ Violation of Law*

When the husband was arrested and convicted for drug trafficking, she was facing serious economic pressure. The marriage of her daughter was a burden for her. Thus she took up drug trafficking to support her family. She used to bring *Charas* from Ahmedabad and sell at home in Nadiad. According to her she also got protection from the local police personnel, who were in the know of her work. But unfortunately she was caught by Kheda police.

4. *Legal Response and Criminal Reactions*

"H" was convicted for 10 years for Violating Narcotic Act. She has already served 10 months in the prison. She was not repenting for the crime as it was knowingly committed, but repents for getting arrested. She is worried for her children as both the parents are in prison. In the jail she participates in cutting, vegetable, cleaning grains, sweeping and watering the plants in the jail premises. After release she will carry on with her tea *lari*.

5. *Analysis and Observation*

In this case, it is very clear that the socio-economic condition of the family has forced her to take up this profession. She is not ashamed of her crime, because she feels she was fulfilling the needs of her family. She has lost faith in God and was indifferent about religion. She was very much frustrated as before her husband was a problem for her and now she is in Jail and the family got disrupted.

Case–4 (Murder of Husband)

1. *Social Background and Relationship*

"M" is 35 years old and belongs to the Bhil tribe and comes from a tribal area but settled in Baroda City. She is illiterate, has 2 brothers and 2 sisters. She is second in sibling order. Both father and mother were illiterate and worked as farm labourers. Both the parents died early; thus "M" was from a broken family. Her husband was a cycle rickshaw puller, illiterate and has a low economic status. They had one son and a daughter. She had uncongenial home conditions, as the husband used to beat her after drinking. She worked as a housemaid and earned monthly Rs.150 –200. Her in-laws were indifferent towards her.

She had an unhappy marital life, as daily her husband used to drink, and after coming back home used to quarrel with her and beat her everyday. Her daughter is married and at present her son is staying with her sister.

2. *Personality Factors*

"M" was not having any guilt feeling, because she said that she has not committed the crime. She was frustrated with the daily fight and socio-economic pressure. She was ready to leave her husband. She got well adjusted in prison with her fellow inmates.

3. *Situation of Offence/ Violation of Law*

According to her, as her husband daily used to drink and fight, so she left the house with her son to her sister's place. That day also he drank a lot and burnt himself. She feels that he has committed suicide and gave her name in his dying declaration. Based on this she was convicted for the crime.

4. *Legal Response & Criminal Reactions*

"M" was given life imprisonment for killing her husband. She has already spent 5 years in the prison. She was much disturbed for her son and feels that because of her husband's bad habit, the whole family got disturbed and the children are suffering for this.

5. *Analysis and Observation*

In this case, the family has migrated from their tribal village to the city in search of earning for their livelihood. The family was also undergoing sufferings due to socio-economic problems. The husband, being alcoholic, had a difficult temperament and used to physically and verbally abuse "M". It is difficult to judge whether she has left the house after burning her husband or before the crime was committed she went away to her sister's place. Frustration might have played a vital role in this case whether it is suicide or murder.

Case–5 (Illicit Drug Trafficking)

1. Social background and Relationship

"K" is 40 years old, coming from the Agarwal caste of Uttar Pradesh. She was born in Mathura, but the offence was committed in Bhavnagar, Gujarat. Her husband is staying in Benaras. She is a Commerce graduate. Her father was a school teacher and having middle class economic status. Her mother had primary education. She has two brothers and three sisters and she is the fifth child in the family. Her father died at an early age.

Her husband has a cloth shop in Benaras. He has primary education and the economic status of the husband is middle class. "K" has three sons and two daughters, and one of the sons got married while she was in prison. She could not attend the marriage. The relatives were told that she was sick and was admitted to hospital. She had a congenial home condition and there was no dispute with her husband. Both the spouse and in-laws treated her well and had cordial relationships, but reactions of her family members were indifferent, when they came to know about her arrest and conviction.

2. Personality Factors

It was found that "K" was active and dominant. She likes to work according to her own will. She is also social and an extrovert. She showed some symptoms of aggression for her present condition. Though she agreed to having high moral values yet in practice she failed to show this.

3. Situation of Offence/ Violation of Law

From Benaras she came to Bhavnagar with a male companion to a friend's house, with the purpose of starting an agency of *Kayamchurna*. Police raided the house at night and found drug in the suitcase of her companion. The man ran away from the police custody. "K" was arrested for violating the Narcotic Act. She left Benaras without informing about it to her husband. It seems she was having some kind of relationship with her neighbour who was involved with a gang in trafficking drugs.

4. *Legal Response and Criminal's Reactions*

"K" was convicted for 6 years of imprisonment. This included 2 years of fine, which she could not pay. She was arrested under NDPS i.e. Narcotic Drugs and Psychotropic Substances. She has spent 3 years in the prison. For about a year she did not inform her husband about her whereabouts. Afterwards when he was informed, he did not visit her for a year. She is ashamed of her act and feels that she as a woman got labelled, but as many people do not know about her stay in jail,.so she will have less problem to face the society when she will be released.

5. *Analysis and Observation*

The researcher found that there is a strained relationship between "K" and her husband. It seems that her husband was against her mixing with these people and thus did not come to visit her in the prison, though now he and his son come to visit her in jail. Greed for more money must have forced her to develop relations with such people. Still now she has relation with one of the gang members, who regularly comes to visit her and is also corresponding for her release. Her husband is not making any effort to release her. Though well educated and coming from a good, middle class family but the influence of bad company must have put her in such a situation, that now it is difficult for her to come out from this. She has refused to accept the crime and blamed her partner for the same, saying that she is punished because he has run away. Her attitude towards her husband shows that she was involved in wrongdoing and thus avoided informing her husband when she left for a long distant place.

Case–6 (Boot-Legging)

1. *Social background and Relationship*

"S" belongs to Chhara community, a criminal tribe in Gujarat. She is 50 years old and studied up to 1st standard.

She comes of a big family having four brothers and three sisters. Her place of residence is Ahmedabad. She is having a liquor business and earns Rs. 2000 per month. Both her parents are illiterate and work as low paid labourers. Her father died at an early age. Her husband is also illiterate and not earning as he is not keeping well. She has one son, who is handicapped and two daughters. One of the daughters is married and has a child but she along with her child is staying with her mother because her husband does not accept her. "S" is having congenial home condition.

2. *Personality Factors*

She was open and frank. She knows she is engaged in anti-social activities, but financial constraints forced her to take to liquor business to feed her families. She feels guilty about her activity but then she is helpless.

3. *Situation of Offence/ Violation of Law*

For selling liquor, one evening the police raided her house and she was arrested. To overcome economic stress, she had to do this liquor trade. She was also caught before but released on bail. This time as it is more than once, she has been warned by the Police, they did not grant her bail and detained her.

4. *Legal Response and Criminal Reactions*

"S" has been booked under the Prevention of Anti-Social Activities Act for bootlegging. She has been detained for one year in judicial custody and has, so far, spent 2 months in the prison. She is trying to adjust in the prison with other inmates. As a PASA detainee, she does not have to do any work in the prison and passes her time by gossiping and seeing T.V. All the women criminals detained under PASA, know each other, so they sit together in the jail premises and gossip. She also gets food from an outside hotel and does not take jail food. Her son comes to visit her. She also openly said that as there is no other way to earn or alternate source of income, she will have to continue with the same trade.

5. *Analysis and Observation*

The socio-economic condition of "S" has forced her to sell liquor, because it had a ready market and promised high returns with little effort. Moreover in Chhara community, this profession and life style is well accepted as a sub-culture. She does not bother about the label. She has learned boot-legging from her neighbours, who are also in the boot-legging business.

Thus poverty, a sick and jobless husband, a handicapped son and a daughter with a small child thrown out by her husband, all these social problems created a situation for her, where she needs to feed her children and this was the most easiest way of earning for an uneducated, unskilled woman. This also is not going to be easy now as the police is going to keep a watch on her, once she gets released from the prison.

Case–7 (Murder of Husband)

1. *Social Background and Relationship*

"S" is 60 years old, illiterate and belongs to the Rajput community. She is the eldest daughter of the family, having 2 more brothers and one sister. She is from Nadiad district. She has her own land which she herself takes care and earns her livelihood. She is having 1 son and 2 daughters. All of them are married and settled in their own house. Her husband is illiterate and prepares liquor as his business having a middle class economic status. Both her parents were illiterate and having poor economic condition. Her father was not working and has been drinking all the time.

She had uncongenial home conditions after marriage as the husband was an alcoholic. He had a difficult temperament and used to verbally abuse her. Even her in-laws were indifferent towards her.

2. *Personality Factors*

She is active in the prison and seems to be dominant and having leadership qualities. She is liked by her co-inmates and jail staff, because she is quite social; she is an extrovert and possesses high moral values.

3. *Situation of Offence/ Violation of Law*

The elder brother of her husband filed a case against her for killing her husband. After killing, the body was hidden and it was not traceable. She did not accept the crime committed by her, saying she did not see his body after he was murdered. The offence was committed with her neighbour accomplice.

4. *Legal Response and Criminal Reactions*

"S" has been given life imprisonment, of which she has spent 10 years in the jail. Her neighbours and daughter were also arrested but released on bail, later on they were acquitted. She feels due to the death of her husband, family got affected. Her son's wife stopped all the relations and went back to her parents. After spending 10 years in Jail, she got involved in the Jail activities, where she is doing the duty of a watchman and supervising the work of others. She got adjusted in the routine work and has cordial relationship with everybody in the Jail.

5. *Analysis and Observation*

"S" seems to have poor socio-economic condition during her childhood. Later on, after her marriage, she had marital conflict with her husband. May be daily conflict with her husband and maltreatment by him provoked her in killing her husband. Her sufferings from childhood till late age must have created strain, causing frustration, which must have been the cause of her crime. Her father was also a chronic alcoholic and the same situation she found after her marriage. So to overcome the social stress, she might have committed the crime.

Case–8 (Murder of Daughter-in-law)

1. *Social Background and Relationship*

"K" belongs to the Koli community. She is 60 years old, illiterate and 2nd child of the family. She has one brother and 3 sisters and comes from Bhavnagar, a city in Saurashtra. She was working as a housemaid and earning Rs. 150 per month.

Her parents were illiterate, her father working as a mill worker, having a low economic status. The father died at an early age. Her husband is also an illiterate, mill worker, having a low economic status. She has 4 sons. Only the first son is married. She had a congenial home condition, cordial and affectionate relations with both spouse and her in-laws.

2. *Personality Factors*

"K" seems to be dominant and likes things to be done as per her wish. She realised and feels guilty as tears were in her eyes when she talked about her criminal act. She is an extrovert, emotional and likes to work alone. The crime was committed alone by her which means she is a very strong-headed person.

3. *Situation of Offence/ Violation of Law*

The marriage of her son took place 3 – 4 months ago. On the previous night of the murder, the daughter-in-law came from her father's place. The daughter-in-law was making preparations for a separate kitchen by collecting all the cooking ingredients. This might have enraged her. The next morning the bride got burnt and died. Kerosene was used for burning the bride.

4. *Legal Response and Criminal Reactions*

"K" has been convicted for life imprisonment for 5 years she was on bail and then after conviction she has spent 5 years in the jail. She keeps herself busy by cleaning grains and cutting vegetables. She uses her leisure time by singing *Bhajans* and praying to God. The husband is not keeping well so her son and her *Jethani* come to see her in jail. Son got remarried as ten years passed since the offence was committed. She has also got adjusted to her co-inmates and counting days to go back to her family and take care of her grand children.

5. *Analysis and Observation*

The family was quite happy before the marriage took place. Everything went wrong after the marriage of the son.

It seems both the mother-in-law and daughter-in-law were not getting along well. The daughter-in-law visited her parent's house where she must have been guided to separate the kitchen. So after coming back, immediately she started separating the kitchen, which "K" could not tolerate. One thing to be noted here is that all these years "K" was the only female in the house, taking care of all the household activities. When another female member came to the family, it became difficult for her to share with each other, and especially "K" thought that her son had been taken away from her by separating him from the family. This must have led to regular quarrels with the new bride. To avoid all these, the new bride must have thought to separate the kitchen and get rid of all the problems. This went beyond the tolerance limit of "K" and thus it provoked her to commit the offence.

Case–9 (Murder of Neighbour)

1. *Social Background and Relationship*

"B" belongs to the Vasava tribal community. She is illiterate, 38 years old and the eldest of 5 children. She was a construction labourer, getting Rs. 20/25 per day and residing in Bharuch. The parents were also illiterate; the father was selling kerosene, having a very low socio-economic condition. Both her parents died early and she had to take the responsibility of her younger brothers and sister. Her husband was working as a mason and earned Rs.20/25 per day. He was also illiterate and had a poor socio-economic condition. She has 2 sons and 1 daughter, who is married. Her husband used to leave home and run away with another woman at night. He was not helping her with any monetary assistance too. Her husband deserted her 5 years ago.

2. *Personality Factors*

"B" was undergoing a lot of stress and strain. She had a big family of eight members to look after. The burden of her brothers and sister and her own 3 children and the spouse's involvement with another woman made her feel neglected and depressed. She is God-fearing and feels guilty about what has happened. When under pressure, she is unable to control herself. She gets tense and nervous.

3. *Situation of Offence/ Violation of Law*

Before committing the offence, she had a severe fight with her neighbour, for their children. In the evening the neighbour, who is a female, got burnt at her home. "B" and her brother were suspected of killing her and got arrested.

4. *Legal Response and Criminal Reaction*

"B" and her brother both got life imprisonment and are serving rigorous imprisonment in the jail. She has spent 3 years in the jail. She is facing difficulties in adjusting with the jail routine and food. She helps in cutting vegetables and cleaning grains. She feels because of the fight the woman killed herself in her own home. She prays to god for forgiveness. She is worried for her 2 small sons. Just for a fight, her whole family got disturbed.. Her sons and son-in-law come to the jail to visit her. After she will be released, she will work as before and take care of the family.

5. *Analysis and Observation*

The case shows that she has undergone a lot of stress and frustration in her life, due to social and economic pressure. Rejection by her husband was a shame for her. The marital conflict gave her unhappiness in her life. Thus her fight with the neighbour, due to their children, might have led to a loss of mental balance and the heated exchange between them caused the crime.

Case–10 (Murder of Maternal Aunt)

1. *Social Background and Relationship*

"M" is 28 years old, coming from a Maratha family and settled in Ahmedabad. She has studied till 6th Std and is the second child of the family. She has one brother and four sisters. Her mother is illiterate and father has primary education. The father is a mill worker and earns well, to have a middle class economic condition. Her husband has secondary school education but is jobless. He is alcoholic and physically and verbally abuses her. He overdemands work from her. She is also having strained relations with her in-laws and regularly has clashes with the in-laws and her husband. The cruelty of the husband and in-laws forced her to leave the husband's house and stay with her parents. She does not have any children.

2. *Personality Factors*

"M" is very young, especially when the crime was committed, she was about 18 years old. She is active, and dominant, she is strongly built. She is having good leadership qualities, as she is working as a Jail Watchman and supervises the work of others. Though she is young she is able to control others. Her feelings of insecurity and low self-esteem led to an aggressive behaviour.

3. *Situation of Offence/ Violation of Law*

"M" was living with her parents due to marital conflict with her husband and in-laws. Her maternal uncle (mama), who is the younger brother of her mother and his wife were also staying with them in the next room to their house. It seems the aunt and her mother were not getting along and having quarrel everyday. At night her maternal aunt got burnt and died. "M" and her mother got arrested for the crime as their names were given by her aunt in her dying declaration.

4. *Legal Response and Criminal Reactions*

Both mother and the daughter have been convicted for life imprisonment. "M" has already served 8 years of rigorous imprisonment. She says she was sleeping at the time of the incident, and has been trapped into it. The in-laws will not accept her anymore and she will have to stay with her parents. She is well adjusted in the prison and has cordial relations with co-inmates. She is also working in the prison with responsibility.

5. *Analysis and Observation*

"M" was passing through social stress, because of her husband who was not working but having the habit of drinking. At the same time he was cruel to his wife and used to physically and mentally torture her. When she came to her parent's house to live, there must have been some problem between her mother and her maternal aunt. It is not clear how much she supported her mother in this, whether she took part in burning her aunt along with her mother or not. As she denied having any involvement and was sleeping at the time when the incident took place. She is undergoing the Jail term because the victim took her name in the dying declaration. She was already having a lot of strain and stress and this has added more to her mental stress.

The following cases give an insight to understand as how stressful situations in the family cause maladjustments and result into deviant behaviour. Another thing, which can be noted from these case studies, is that a woman has been committing a crime to overcome social or economic pressure which is the result of loss of self control or acting impulsively. She must have been under constant strain, which made her either to murder her near ones or get into illicit liquor or drug business.

8

Discussion and Suggestions

Social work with offenders has a long history, as long as that of social work itself. The status and purpose of social work with offenders have been the subject of political and professional debate, often organised around such polar opposites as welfare and justice, care and control, or help and surveillance. According to Stewart et al. (1994), the possibilities of working for change within the criminal justice system and the implications for practice of poverty, unemployment and housing and health problems, all wearyingly familiar to practitioners as common features of the lives of offenders. Social work with offenders might be conceived more broadly to include social change as well as individual change among its aim as effective practice.

In recent academic and professional discussions of the aims and purposes of work with offenders, it has become usual to find at least some reference to victims, actual or potential, and to the responsibilities of social work towards them and towards the communities in which they and the offender – clients of social work live. Social work as a developing profession needs to understand the complexity of the human situation and other factors, which will be possible through social work research in identifying the problems or the outcomes of the specific programmes.

The present research has focused on the life style of women criminals, in which socio-cultural, economic and psychological aspects have been studied. The outcome of the study of criminal behaviour will be useful for social work intervention and for curative, preventive and rehabilitative programming.

SECTION - A

Major Findings

1. Socio-Economic Background

- Majority (60%) of the women criminals were in the category of mid - age group , 31 – 50 years.
- Majority (64.7%) of them were illiterate.
- A large majority of (87.3%) of women criminals were from Hindu families and 55 per cent of women were from ST, SC or SEBC background.
- Majority (66.7%) were married.
- Majority (60%) engaged in different types of economic activities, with very little income.
- About 55.9 per cent of the respondents belong to broken families and 25.5 per cent had uncongenial home conditions.
- Majority of the husbands of the respondents were occupationally of low economic level and 37.3 per cent of them were illiterate.
- Reasons for marital conflicts were alcoholism, poverty or financial constraints, and respondents suffered physical and verbal abuse.

2. Causes of Crime

- About 33.3 per cent had aspirations to reach their goals, through unfair means.
- Only 10.8 per cent had criminal association.
- Majority (66.7%) had social stress/pressure and (28.4%) had economic pressure for which they had committed the crime.

3. *Nature & Pattern of Crime*

- Majority (67.6%) were convicted for murder.
- About 36.3 per cent of the respondents had social stress in the families like domestic quarrels, strain, intra-personal relationships as a motive behind the crime.
- 42.2 per cent of the respondents burnt their victims. Most of the victims were daughters-in-law.
- Majority (61.8%) of the crime was performed in company of family members or non-family members.
- Most of the crime (67.7%) were committed in urban areas during day time.

4. *Imprisonment*

- Majority (54.9%) were convicted, serving rigorous imprisonment.
- 42.2 per cent could adjust jail routine. While 22.5 per cent were having difficulties to adjust.
- Majority of the respondents were satisfied with the attitudes of their co-inmates, Jail officers, Guarding staff and Superintendent. They were cordial and sympathetic towards them.
- Almost half of the respondents (47.1%) suggested for education and employment after release, so that they could be on their own.
- 27.5 per cent of respondents felt vocational training and guidance could help them after release.
- 25.5 per cent were keen to go back to their families and felt their problems and insecurity would be over if their family members accepted them.

5. *Guilt Feelings*

- Majority of the respondents (66.7%) were repenting for their crime and pray to god for forgiveness.
- More than half of the respondents (55.8%) were confused as to what would be society's reactions towards them.
- Majority (75.4%) were confident that if not society, at least their family would accept them.

6. Moral Values

- Illiterate (66.2%) respondents have higher moral values.

7. Temperament

- Illiterate group differs significantly from secondary and above education group with reference to *Active* -Temperament.
- There is a strong association between *Impulsive* Temperament and Nature of crime.
- The longer the stay in prison, the more prisoners were likely to have *Dominant*-Temperament.
- Illiterate majority (77.3%) fall on low *Impulsive*-Temperament.
- Respondents from Nuclear families are of more *Active, Reflective and Aggressive* - Temperament.
- Respondents with murder of daughter-in-law as Reasons for Arrest have low *Reflective* – Temperament.
- A strong association has been found between Reasons for Arrest and *Emotional, Reflective and Sociable* – Temperament.
- A strong association between Motive behind Crime Commission by women criminals and *Reflective*-Temperament.
- A strong association between Length of Time spent in prison and *Reflective*- Temperament.
- A strong association between Motive behind Crime Commission by women criminals and *Nervous*–Temperament.
- A strong association between Reasons for Arrest of women criminals and *Introvert/ Extrovert* – Temperament.

8. Life Style

- *Individualistic* Life style was found more among 31 – 40 age group.
- Strong association between *Individualistic*-Life Style and Education.
- Respondents from Nuclear families fall on high *Exploitive*-Life Style i.e. they were more *Exploitive* than Respondents from joint families.

- Respondents from Urban places were having more *Conforming* – Life Style than Respondents from Rural places.
- Majority of the Respondents (85.3 per cent) were having high *Escapist* – Life Style.
- Longer stay in prison leads to low *Explosive* Life Style, lesser stay in prison leads to high *Explosive*-Life Style.
- Respondents with murder of daughter-in-law as Reasons for Arrest had low *Individualistic*-Life Style.
- Majority (more than 80.0%) of the Respondents in the category of murder fall on the low *Individualistic*-Life Style and low *Explosive*-Life Style.
- Majority (54.9%) of the Respondents in the category of Need to Overcome Social Stress fall on low *Individualistic* – Life Style.
- More than half (56.3%) of Respondents falling on Need to Overcome Social Stress fall on low *Explosive*-Life Style.
- 50.3 per cent of Respondents with high Active Temperament fall on low *Individualistic*-Life Style.
- Majority (62.9%) of the Respondents with high *Individualistic*-Life Style fall on high Dominant Temperament.
- Majority (67.6%) of the Respondents with high *Introvert/Extrovert*-Temperament fall on low *Individualistic*-Life Style.
- Majority (64.8%) of the Respondents with low *Individualistic*-Life Style fall on low Aggression – Temperament.
- Majority (63.8%) of the Respondents with low *Individualistic*-Life Style fall on high Order and Organization – Correctional Institutions Environment.
- Majority (63.4%) of the Respondents with high Active Temperament fall on high *Exploitive*-Life Style.
- A large majority (82.5%) of the Respondents with high *Exploitive*-Life Style fall on high Reflective – Temperament.
- Majority (79.4%) of the Respondents with high *Exploitive*-Life Style fall on low Nervous-Temperament.
- Majority (70.8%) of the Respondents with high *Exploitive*-Life Style fall on high Aggression-Temperament.

- Majority (67.7%) of the Respondents with high *Exploitive*-Life Style fall on high Achievement Orientation-Family Environment.
- There is a strong association between *Explosive*-Life Style and Income of Women Criminals.
- 52.7 per cent of the Respondents with high Active-Temperament fall on high *Explosive*-Life Style.
- More than half (59.7%) of the Respondents with low Dominant – Temperament fall on low *Explosive*-Life Style.
- Majority (64.5%) of the Respondents with low Reflective – Temperament fall on low *Explosive* – Life Style.
- More than half (58.8%) of the Respondents with high Nervous - Temperament fall on low *Explosive*-Life Style.
- Majority (61%) of the Respondents with low Reflective-Temperament fall on low *Explosive* -Life Style.
- A large majority (70.5%) of the Respondents with high *Explosive*-Life Style fall on low Order and Organization - Correctional Institutions Environment.
- A majority of the Respondents with low Intellectual Cultural Orientation-Family Environment fall on high *Resistive* - Life Style.
- A large majority (91.7%) of the Respondents with high Organization Family Environment fall on high *Resistive* - Life Style.
- There is a strong association between *Domineering*-Life style and Length of time spent prison by women Criminals.
- Majority (80.9%) of the Respondents with high Nervous – Temperament fall on low *Domineering*-Life Style.
- Majority (83.1%) of the Respondents with high Introvert/ Extrovert-Temperament fall on low *Domineering*-Life Style.
- Majority (83.3%) of the Respondents with low Aggression-Temperament fall on low *Domineering*-Life Style.
- Majority (83.1%) of the Respondents with high Active-Recreational Orientation Family Environment fall on low *Domineering*-Life Style.

- Majority (80%) of the Respondents with high Organization–Family Environment fall on low *Domineering*-Life Style.
- More than half i.e. (58.1%) of the Respondents with high Active-Temperament fall on high *Conforming*-Life Style.
- About (53.6%) of the Respondents with low Expressiveness-Family Environment fall on low *Conforming*-Life Style.
- A large majority (95.7%) of the Respondents with high Active–Temperament fall on high *Evasive*-Life Style.
- More than half i.e. (55.8%) of the Respondents with low *Individualistic* – Life Style have high Moral Values.
- A large majority (94.8%) of the Respondents with high *Resistive* – Life Style have high Moral Values.
- Majority (72.7%) of the Respondents with low *Domineering* – Life Style have high Moral Values.
- A large majority (97.6%) of the Respondents having low Relationship in Family Environment were falling on high *Resistive* – Life Style.
- Majority (78.7%) of the Respondents with low *Domineering* – Life Style fall on high Relationship Family Environment.
- About half (51.8%) of the Respondents with high *Exploitive* – Life Style fall on low Personal Growth in Family Environment.
- A high majority (91.3%) were having high *Resistive* – Life Style and high Personal Growth in Family Environment.
- A large majority (82.6%) of the Respondents were having low *Domineering* – Life Style and high Personal Growth in Family Environment.
- A large majority (82.1%) of the Respondents having high *Escapist* – Life Style, fall on low Personal Growth in Family Environment.
- A large majority (94.6%) of the Respondents were having high *Evasive* – Life Style and low Personal Growth in Family Environment.
- Majority (73.3%) of the Respondents falling on high System Maintenance in Family Environment have low *Domineering* – Life Style.

- A large majority (97.6%) of the Respondents with high *Resistive* – Life Style fall on low System Maintenance in Family Environment.
- 62.1 per cent of Respondents with high *Exploitive* – Life Style fall on low System Maintenance in Correctional Institutions Environment.
- A large majority (98.3%) of the Respondents with high *Resistive* – Life Style fall on low System Maintenance in Correctional Institutions Environment.

9. *Family Environment*

- Majority i.e. more than 70 per cent of the illiterate Respondents fall on low *Expressive* and *Personal Growth*–Family Environment.
- 68 per cent of the Respondents from Rural background fall on low *Expressiveness* – Family Environment.
- Respondents from Urban background were more *Independent* in Family Environment than those from Rural background.
- 69.2 per cent of the Respondents from Rural & Tribal background fall on low *Intellectual–Cultural Orientation* – Family Environment.
- Urban Respondents were more *Organized* in Family Environment.
- 37.3 per cent of the Respondents with Murder as Reason for Arrest fall on low *Cohesion* Family Environment.
- There is a strong association between *Conflict* – Family Environment and Length of conviction of women criminals.
- A large majority (82%) of the Respondents with low *Independence*– Family Environment fall on Murder as Nature of Crime.
- There is a strong association between *Intellectual Cultural Orientation* in Family Environment and Education of women criminals.
- 49.1 per cent of the Respondents serving Life Imprisonment fall on high *Moral – Religions Orientation* in Family Environment.
- There is a strong association between *Relationship* in Family Environment and Education of women Criminals.

- There is a strong association between *System Maintenance–* Family Environment and Length of Time spent in prison by women Criminals.

10. Correctional Institution Environment

- Majority of the Respondents from Joint family are more *Expressive* and *Autonomous* in Correctional Institutions Environment than those from Nuclear families.
- About half (50.9%) of the Respondents having motive of Need to Overcome Social Stress fall on high *Order and Organization* in Correctional Institutions Environment.
- There is a strong association between length of time spent in prison by women criminals and *Involvement* in Correctional Institutions Environment.
- More than half (56.7%) of the respondents falling on low *Personal Problem Orientation* in Correctional Institutions Environment are serving Life Time in the prison.
- A large majority (88.5%) of the Respondents with high *Order and Organization* Correctional Institutions Environment fall into the category of Murder.
- Half of the (51.7%) Respondents with high *Order and Organization* Correctional Institutions Environment are serving Life Term imprisonment in the prison.
- 43.1 per cent of the Respondents with less than 14 years stay in the prison, fall on high *Order and Organization* Correctional Institutions Environment.
- There is a strong association between *Clarity* in Correctional Institutions Environment and Nature of Crime by women criminals.
- Majority (64.7%) of the Respondents fall into the category of high *Clarity* Correctional Institutions Environment of which 33.3 per cent were in the prison for less than 14 years.
- About half (50%) of the Respondents serving Life Imprisonment fall on high *System Maintenance* Correctional Institutions Environment.
- There is s strong association between System Maintenance in Correctional Institutions Environment and Length of Time Spent in prison by women criminals.

- 38.5 per cent of respondents in the age group of 31-50 years fall on low *"Staff Control"* Correctional Institutions Environment.

The entire research work is divided into various areas for the purpose of discussion viz. socioe-conomic background, causes of crime, nature and patterns of crime, imprisonment, guilt feelings, moral values, temperament, life style, family environment and correctional institutions environment.

SECTION – B

1. Socio-Economic Background

It was found from the study that the majority i.e. 60 per cent of the women criminals fall into the category of middle age group i.e. 31 to 50 years. The same trend has been observed by other researchers also like Nagla (1991), Sohoni (1989), Ghosh (1986), Ahuja (1969), Rani (1983) and Saxena (1994). May be in the traditional protective Indian Society, there is perhaps lesser likelihood or risk of a female resorting to criminality during their early youth. In Indian culture girls are more protected and controlled by their parents because they are considered as the prestige of the family. So their interaction with outside home is less, when they are young and unmarried. On the other hand beyond age 50, they are more stable and settled with their family and thus can be less provoking of criminality among the older age group. It is during the mid-age 31 to 50 years when both temptation and provocation lead to criminality.

The study found illiteracy is more (64.7%) common in women criminals. Similar findings have been revealed from the study of Ahuja (1969) and Misra and Gautam (1982). In India, a majority of the population live below the subsistence level and thus poverty became a predominant factor leading to illiteracy among women. As most of the women were illiterate, they fail to supplement the family income and were not in a position to solve the economic problems facing the family. These economic and social pressures due to illiteracy and low standard of education have led to frustrations, economic insecurity and emotional stresses, which have played a dominant role in leading these women to criminality.

A large majority (87.3%) of women criminals were from Hindu families and 55 per cent of the women were from ST, SC or SEBC background. This is because the Hindus are in majority in general population. Rani (1981) and Mathew (1992) also found a high proportion of women criminals belonged to the Hindu backward community. In Hindu religion, there are a number of regulations and restrictions imposed on women. These constraints may have created an impact on the personality patterns of Indian women. With the changing social patterns and the liberation movement, such women may find it difficult to adjust. In Indian society caste plays an important role in deciding a person's social and economic status. Crime is traditionally associated with poverty and low social and economic status. As the lower caste women in India are illiterate, superstitions due to ignorance and under religious and caste sentiments they become victims of exploitation. These women facing several problems both socially and economically, sometimes confront them by getting themselves involved in crime. Thus the majority of the women criminals belonged to the lower castes.

A majority (66.7%) of these women criminals were married. Numerous researchers like Ahuja (1969), Sohoni (1989), Ghosh (1986), Nagla (1991), Sharma (1993) and Saxena (1994) observed the same in their studies too. A high rate of married women involved in crime commission may be due to the adjustment problems with in-laws and husbands. As coming from lower socio-economic and illiterate families, their marriages at an early age were arranged by parents without taking into consideration of these women. Thus they lack maturity, responsibility and information regarding sexual activities. Many of these women are serving life term for killing their daughters–in-law or sisters-in-law, which again shows a great deal of environmental pressure on these women for taking the drastic step. Widowed women living either with older sons or may be having to shoulder the responsibility of raising the children, suffered from social or financial stress of a different nature, which may have compelled them to get involved in offences.

Economic status is an important factor in determining a person's well-being. Therefore in the present study the respondent's earning and employment status were studied. It was found that 60 per cent i.e. majority of them were engaged in different types of economic activities, with very little income. It may be due to the low economic level, forcing a sense of despair and frustration and compelling respondents to resort to deviance. Many of them were aware of their economic situation as poor and helpless. It can be concluded that due to lower occupations and insufficient income, these women were economically frustrated and distressed and may be, to meet their needs, they have involved themselves in criminal activities. Thus it can be maintained that socio-economic conditions appeared to be some of the factors responsible for creating inhibitions and urges, which lead these women to crime and deviant behavior. The low economic status among female criminals was also found by Ahuja (1969), Kawale (1982), Rani (1983), Prasad (1982) Misra, Gautam (1982) etc.

The majority of the parents were illiterate or poorly educated, 35.3 per cent of the fathers were labourers and the majority i.e. 63.7 per cent had low economic status. More than half of the respondents, i.e. 55.9 per cent belonged to broken families. The above findings show that the respondents in their childhood also passed through poor socio-economic conditions. As parents were less educated, with limited income, they might have been overburdened with liabilities to support the family. This type of economic stress and strains give a picture of their life style during the childhood of the respondents. More than 50 per cent of the respondents struggled in their up-bringing as they came from broken homes, where both the parents or father expired in their early age. They had to be contented with whatever they had, postponing their desires and personal needs. Thus it can be concluded that economic status of a family may prone to anti-social behaviour among the family members.

The study reveled that 37.3 per cent of the husbands of the respondents were illiterate and the majority of them were occupationally of low economic level. Besides, 39.2 per cent of them had large sized families. This shows that many of the respondents even after marriage continued living in a low economic status. It can be concluded that poor economic conditions play a significant role in contributing towards criminal behaviour.

Sociologists like Ram Ahuja agree that unsatisfied economic needs may lead persons to the feelings of economically deprived, leading to emotional insecurity, thus creating a conducive climate for the individual to take to criminality.

Marital tensions are often assumed to be the root cause of deviance. In the present study 24.5 per cent were having unhappy marital life. The reasons for marital conflict were alcoholism, poverty and financial constraints. About 22.5 per cent suffered physical abuse from their husbands. These findings tend to show that unhappy and strained marital life result in instability and tensions between husband and wife. The study also reveals that many respondents had conflicting relationships with their daughters-in-law and majority of the respondents were convicted on the charge of bride-burning. From the above discussion it can be concluded that many of the women criminals resort to various forms of deviant behaviour, as they failed to adjust themselves to these stressful situations. Thus conflicting intra-familial patterns produce maladjustment among inter-personal relations of the family. Marital maladjustments have been found in the research studies of Nagla (1991), Ahuja (1996), Mathew (1992) and Saxena (1994). They have also observed that the majority of the women convicted were poorly adjusted in the family settings.

2. Causes of Crime

Based on the responses received, it was observed that the majority (66.7%) had social stress and (28.4%) had economic stress as the root cause of the criminality of the women and was the most prominent factor leading respondents to crime. Besides poverty, social and family circumstances as contributing factors to crime, 33.3 per cent had aspirations in their life to have better socio-economic conditions. It was because of their poor economic condition in their childhood that they aspired for a better life style in their family of procreation. Only 10.8 per cent had criminal association. In order to overcome the crisis of economic condition, these women got involved with friends and neighbours who already indulged in the crimes and learned the illegal ways of earning money by getting into illicit liquor and drug trafficking. Whereas marital and family life situations were most prevalent in the cases of murder, where severely strained marital relations or daughters-in-law and mothers-in-law family quarrels provoked them either to kill their husbands or daughters-in-law. Economic crisis as a cause of female criminality was observed by Mathew (1992), Nagla (1991) and Saxena (1994).

3. Nature and Patterns of Crime

The majority of the offenders (67.6%) were convicted for murder. It was found that 36.3% of the respondents have social stress in the families like domestic quarrels, strained intra-personal relationships as a motive behind the crime. This strain relationship caused the murder of near ones in a very emotional situation. About 42.2 per cent of the criminals burnt their victims. Most of these victims were daughters-in-law. Most of the crime (67.7%) were committed in urban areas during day time. The majority (61.8%) of the crimes were performed in company of family members or non-family members.

All these observations lead to the inference that these women could not tolerate certain situations and due to jealousy and frustration committed the offence, which was beyond their control. These women committed the act on the spur of the moment and many of them in their mid-age repent for what they have lost. Unlike male convicts, who are mostly hardcore recidivists, these women are first-time, situational offenders.

4. Imprisonment

Imprisonment creates stress and strain to the women criminals. Being locked away in a prison deprives a woman of many of the normal day-to-day activities and joys of free living. In the present study a significant number of respondents (54.9%) were convicted for long terms and serving rigorous imprisonment. Some of them have already spent some time in the prison and have experienced the process of prisonization. Almost all of them have contacts with family members, either through letters or visitors. Thus the contact with their relations help them to overcome to some extent the feelings of isolation in prison from the family members.

It was observed that 42.2 per cent could adjust to Jail routine, while 22.5 per cent were having difficulties to adjust in the prison system and culture. Life-timers had less problem to adjust with the Jail routine as they could prepare themselves mentally that they have to spend many years of their life in the prison. Those prisoners who have spent some time in the prison were also influenced by the process of prisonization. The majority of the respondents were satisfied with the attitudes of their co–inmates, Jail officers, Guarding staff and superintendent. The findings revealed that the convicts have expressed favqurable opinion about them. The authorities had sympathetic attitude towards the prisoners. About 47 per cent suggested for education and employment after release, which might help them to be on their own. As expressed by 27.5 per cent of the inmates, vocational training and guidance could help them to become independent after release from the prison, if they will not be accepted by the family members. Though 25.5 per cent were keen to go back to their families and felt that their problems and insecurity would be over if their family members accepted them.

Imprisonment of women causes pain, sufferings, emotional shock, deprivation of liberty, security and anxiety for children and other family members. Without any proper vocation to fill their time, the respondents had a feeling of isolation and boredom. Not only this, but even the absence of a woman from her home due to her imprisonment creates a situation of crisis for her family.

5. Guilt Feelings

The majority of the respondents (66.7%) were repenting for their crime and pray to God for forgiveness. The majority (75.4%) of the women criminals were confident that if not society, at least their family would accept them, because 55.8 per cent of them were confused as what would be society's reactions towards them.

Sometimes a crime may be committed as a revolt against injustice or a particular situation, which the offender had to face. These offenders justify their actions and get relief from the feeling of guilt which may be in their unconscious mind. Criminals also try to relieve themselves of their guilt by making another person responsible for the offence. In the present study, it has been observed that, in the bride burning cases, mothers-in-law blamed their daughters-in-law for the situation and causing disturbances to the whole family. When the women criminals were interviewed, they tried to express their innocence to the researcher.

6. Moral Values

The study observed that those respondents that were illiterate (66.2%) had higher moral values. The illiterates were traditional and religious oriented; moreover, the data were collected after they have spent sometime in the prison. During this period, they have gone through the process of prisonization, in which religious and spiritual activities were conducted by the prison authorities. This may have raised their moral values while in the process of reformation and thus showing high moral values among the women criminals.

7. Temperament

7.1 *Active* – The study reveals that the illiterate group differs significantly from secondary and above group with reference to Active Temperament. It was also observed that the respondents from nuclear families were of more Active Temperament than those from joint families. This may be because the respondents left their rural homes and migrated to the urban areas, where they are self–dependent and take care of their family members without the support of in-laws or other family members.

7.2 ***Impulsive*** – There is a strong association between Impulsive– Temperament and Nature of Crime. As it has been seen, the crime committed by women is mostly on the spur of the moment or in a quick impulse. In the present study also this was experienced by the researcher. The majority (77.3%) of the respondents were illiterate and fall on low Impulsive – Temperament. Thus it may be low education among these women which creates low impulsive temperament and makes them take to crime.

7.3 ***Dominant*** – The present study shows that the longer the stay in prison, the more prisoners are likely to have Dominant– Temperament. For those prisoners who have been staying for a long time, prison becomes their home as they spend some precious years of their life in the prison. In Gujarat, Baroda prison is the only place for the life term convicts. So these life-termers try to create dominance on the new and short-term prisoners.

7.4 ***Emotional*** – A strong association has been found between reasons for arrest and Emotional–Temperament. The women criminals get motivated to deviate due to the emotional situations which are caused by intra-familial conflicting role patterns which produce maladjustments in inter–personal relation creating conflicts in the family.

7.5 ***Sociable*** – A strong association has been also found in the present study between reasons for arrest and Sociable–Temperament.

7.6 ***Reflective*** – The respondents from nuclear families are more Reflective in Temperament than those who are from joint families. It was also noted that the respondents with murder of daughter-in-law as reasons for arrest have a low Reflective – Temperament, which shows there is a strong association between the two. Further, it was observed that there is a strong association between motive behind crime commission by women criminals and Reflective – Temperament. A strong association was also found between the length of time spent in prison and Reflective– Temperament. The above findings revealed that Reflective–Temperament plays a significant role in the personality of the women criminals.

7.7 *Nervous* – In this component it was noted that there is a strong association between motive behind crime commission by women criminals and Nervous – Temperament. As the crime is usually committed due to certain circumstances, it was seen that after the commission of the act, they become nervous and helpless. This creates stresses and strains among the offenders.

7.8 *Introvert/ Extrovert* – A strong association has been found between reasons for arrest of women offenders and Introvert/Extrovert – Temperament.

7.9 *Aggression* – The respondents from nuclear families were found to be more Aggressive in Temperament than those coming from joint families. This may be because of the migration from a rural to an urban set-up, shouldering responsibilities alone and tension of economic constraints. Sometime she has to face bad ill-treatment from husband, and all these causes lead to frustration and aggression among women criminals.

8. Life Style

8.1. *Individualistic* – This life style was found more among the age group of 31–40 years. There was also a strong association between Individualistic – Life style and Education. Further the study has revealed that respondents with murder of daughters-in-law as reasons for arrest have low Individualistic–Life Style. This shows clearly that those women who are Individualistic have difficult relationship with others which leads to strain and conflict in the family. This was very much proved in the present study as the majority (82.4%) of the respondents fall in the category of murder have low Individualistic – Life Style. More than half i.e 54.9 per cent of the respondents, who committed the crime to overcome the social stress fall on low Individualistic – Life style, which means there is a strong association between crime in women and Individualistic – Life Style. An important finding of the study shows the strong relation between Temperament and Individualistic–Life style. The study concludes that respondents with low Individualistic–Life Style have high Active and Extrovert – Temperament. Offenders having high Individualistic–Life Style fall on high Dominant–Temperament. Thus, a highly active, extrovert and dominant personality matches very well with a deviant or criminal type of behavior. Moreover it was found that 64.8 per cent of the respondents with low Individualistic–Life style fall on low Aggression-- Temperament which means they are also aggressive.

Moral Values were high among 55.8 per cent of respondents with low Individualistic–Life Style. In Correctional Institutions Environment 63.8 per cent with low Individualistic–Life Style had high Order and Organization in Institutional Environment.

8.2. *Exploitive* – Respondents from nuclear families fall on high Exploitive Life Style. Living in an urban set-up in a nuclear family may have forced to have this type of life style. The results in Temperament shows that 63.4 per cent respondents with high Active Temperament fall on high Exploitive Life Style. A large majority of the women Criminals with high Exploitive life style fall on high Reflective, low Nervous and high Aggression Temperament. It shows there is a significant relationship between various components of Temperament and Exploitive Life Style.

The majority (67.7%) of the Respondents with high Exploitive Life Style fall on high Achievement Orientation Family Environment, while 51.8 per cent of them with high Exploitive life style fall on low Personal Growth in Family Environment. With high Exploitive Life Style 62.1 per cent of the prisoners fall on low System Maintenance in Correctional Institutions Environment. May be, because of the Exploitive nature these women offenders do not adjust well and have difficulties to maintain and observe rules and regulations in the prison.

8.3. *Explosive* – The present study shows that a longer stay in prison leads to low Explosive life style and a lesser stay in prison leads to high Explosive life style. This may be the effect of the strict discipline and routine of the jail which every inmate has to go through.

To overcome the social stress as motive 56.3 per cent of the respondents falling on low Explosive life style have committed the crime. There is also a strong association between Explosive life style and income of women Criminals, nature of crime and motive behind Crime commission.

While relating this life style with Temperament, it was found that more than 50 per cent of the respondents with high Active Temperament fall on high explosive life style. Again this type of combination does show a strong significant effect on criminal behaviour, because of the extreme personality and life style. Further, a majority of the respondents with low Explosive Life Style have low Dominant and Reflective Temperament and high Nervous Temperament. Thus it shows that persons with low Explosive - Life Style are less dominant and reflective in their personality.

The majority (70.5%) of the prisoners with high Explosive life style fall on low Order and Organization Correctional Institutional Environment, while 61 per cent of the respondents with low Explosive life style fall on high

Active Recreational Orientation Family Environment. Again high explosive life style makes a person difficult to follow the law and order of an institution and at the same time if the family offers high active recreational Orientation then it may reduce the explosive life style.

8.4. ***Resistive*** – A large majority of the respondents who fall on high Resistive life style have low Intellectual Cultural Orientation and high Organization Family Environment. It was also found that a large majority, 91.3 per cent of respondents with high Resistive life style have high Personal Growth in Family Environment and 97.6 per cent of them with high Resistive life style fall on low Relationship and System Maintenance in Family Environment. The same result was also seen in Institutional Environment, where 98.3 per cent of the respondents with high Resistive life style fall on low System Maintenance in Correctional Institutions Environment. While many of these respondents i.e. 94.8 per cent of them with high Resistive Life Style had high Moral values. From the above findings, it can be concluded that there is a strong association between Resistive life style and Family Environment.

8.5. ***Domineering*** – There is a strong association between length of time spent in prison by women Criminals and Domineering life style. More than 80 per cent i.e. a large majority of the women Criminals with low Domineering life style have high Nervous and Introvert/Extrovert Temperament, while 83.3 per cent of them with low Aggression Temperament fall on low Domineering life style. This concludes that the women Criminals are not having domineering life style but may be the circumstances have forced them to take law into their hands. The majority of these women with low Domineering life style also have high Moral Values.

The study reveals that 83.1 per cent of the respondents with high Active Recreational Orientation Family Environment fall on low Domineering life style. It was also noted that a large majority of the offenders with low Domineering life style have high Organization, Relationship, Personal Growth and System Maintenance in Family Environment. This concludes that there is a strong relation between Domineering life style and Family Environment, because family plays an important role in developing an individual's life style.

8.6. *Conforming* – The present study revealed that respondents from urban places are having more Conforming life style than those coming form rural places. Further, 58.1 per cent of the women Criminals with high Active Temperament fall on high conforming life style. While 53.6 per cent of the respondents with low Expressiveness Family Environment fall on low Conforming life style.

8.7. *Escapist* – It was found that the majority of the respondents (85.3%) were having high Escapist life style. In Family Environment, the respondents (82.1%) with low Personal Growth were having high Escapist life style. This shows that these women Criminals usually tried to avoid certain unpleasant situations, which they did not want to get involved in.

8.8 *Evasive* – A large number of respondents (95.7%) with high Active Temperament were falling on high Evasive life style. Further, 94.6 per cent of them with high Evasive life style were having low personal growth in Family Environment. Here also, it can be concluded that Personal Growth plays a significant role in Producing Evasive life style. Most of these women Criminals were trying to evade themselves from any unpleasant communication.

9. Family Environment

9.1 *Relationship Dimensions* – The present study reveals that 37.3 per cent of the respondents with murder as reason for arrest fall on low *Cohesion* Family Environment. This concludes that poor cohesion among the family members creates conflict and stressful situations in the family, which plays an Important role in pushing the respondents towards criminal acts.

The majority i.e. more than 70 per cent of illiterate respondents fall on low *Expressive* Family Environment, while 68 per cent of the respondents from rural background fall on low Expressive Family Environment. Thus a person with illiteracy and is from a rural background finds difficulties in expressing his/her feelings.

There is a strong association between the length of conviction of women criminals and *Conflict* Family Environment. There is also a strong association between *Relationship* in Family Environment and Education of women criminals. So education plays an important role to develop understanding among each other and have a harmonious life in the family.

9.2. ***Personal Growth Dimensions*** – It was found that the respondents from the urban background were more *Independent* in Family Environment than those who came from the rural background. This again is because of the urban life style which makes a person to act independently, so women criminals from urban areas were assertive and took their own decisions. A large majority (82%) of these respondents with low Independence in Family Environment fall on murder as nature of crime. It may be the frustration for less independence as the cause of murder.

The respondents (69.2%) from the rural background fall on low *Intellectual Cultural Orientation* in Family Environment. Since in Indian Villages women get very rare opportunities for their intellectual growth and cultural activities, this was also found in the women criminals coming from such a background. There was also a strong association between education of women criminals and Intellectual Cultural Orientation.

Those prisoners (49.1%) serving life imprisonment fall on high *Moral Religions Orientation* in Family

Environment. This has been discussed before also that, due to situational crime and committed on the heat of the moment, the women criminals usually have high moral religions orientation from their families. Another thing which can be concluded here is that education plays an important role in the *Personal Growth* of a person.

9.3. ***System Maintenance Dimensions*** – The study observed that urban respondents were more *Organized* in Family Environment. Here also the urban life style may have made these women more organized in their family activities. There was also a strong association between the length of time spent in prison by women criminals and System Maintenance in Family Environment.

10. Correctional Institutions Environment

10.1 ***Relationship Dimensions*** - There was a strong association between length of time spent in prison by women criminals and *Involvement* in Correctional Institutions Environment. Those inmates staying for a longer period were more active and more involved in the day-to-day functioning of their routine work in the prison. These women were more adjusted and accepted their stay in the prison.

The majority of the respondents from joint families are more *Expressive* in Correctional Institutions Environment than those inmates, who were from nuclear families. May be as they were staying in joint families they were more open and frank with other co-inmates and staff. While those from nuclear families stay within small families and find difficulties to adjust themselves with a large number of people.

Personal Growth Dimensions - In this dimension also it was found that the majority of the respondents from joint families were more *Autonomous* in Correctional Institutions Environment than those from nuclear families.

The life-time convicts (56.7%) fall on low *Personal Problem Orientation* in Correctional Institutions Environment. Thus, it can be concluded here that criminals in the prison have less Personal Growth especially for women criminals for whom reformation and rehabilitation programmes are few.

10.3 ***System Maintenance Dimensions*** – It was found that 50.9 per cent of the women criminals had high *Order and Organization* in Correctional Institutions Environment and these women committed the crime with a motive to overcome social stress. A large majority (88.5%) of the respondents with high Order and Organization in Correctional Institutions Environment fall into the category of murder as crime. The respondents (51.7%) serving life term imprisonment in the prison were with high Order and Organization. Those respondents, who stayed in the prison for less than 14 years, fall on high Order and Organization in Correctional Institutions Environment. The above finding shows that the inmates were under strict discipline and thus were having high Order and Organization.

The majority 64.7 per cent respondents fall into the category of high *Clarity* in Correctional Institutions Environment, of which 33.3 per cent are in the prison for less than 14 years. There is also a strong association between Clarity in Correctional Institutions Environment and Nature of Crime by women criminals.

It was observed that 38.5 per cent of respondents in the age group of 31–50 years fall on low *Staff Control* in Correctional Institutions Environment. Further, it was found that 50 per cent inmates serving Life Imprisonment fall on high System Maintenance in Correctional Institutions Environment. Thus it can be concluded that there is a strong association between System Maintenance in Correctional Institutions Environment and the length of time spent in prison by women criminals.

SECTION – C

Suggested Therapeutic Approaches

In this part a brief account of the various correctional therapies have been discussed, which could be useful in deciding on the treatment and rehabilitative programmes for the female offenders. Rehabilitation means "restoring to a previous state of wholeness". In corrections, this means restoring to some previous state of non-criminal behaviour. The term rehabilitation is commonly applied to many forms of correctional intervention. In fact, all available programmes in prison like education, vocational training, religion, volunteer services, etc., all fall under the rehabilitative services. More specific definitions of rehabilitation include the following : "a programmed effort to alter attitudes and behaviours, of inmates which is focused on the elimination of their future criminal behaviours," (Senese and Kalinich, 1992). Those programmes that have specific goals, a specific structure and method, a history of success, are based on a clear concept or theory, are intense and require time, run by trained counsellors and offered to inmates who can benefit from them can be defined as treatment programmes.

1. Behaviour Modification Therapy

Behaviour is learnt and, therefore, can be corrected. All programmes using this model operate under the assumption that all behaviour is affected by environmental rewards; thus to affect behaviour, one must structure the environment to reward desirable behaviour and not reward discouraged behaviour. Programmes have used aversive conditioning and positive conditioning to achieve these goals. Taking away privileges or less desirable assignment can be used in aversive conditioning. Rewards include greater privileges, more freedom of movement and "tokens" that can be exchanged for desired goods or activities. Behaviour modification may be combined with other approaches, such as the cognitive – based programmes.

2. Cognitive Approach or Therapy

Cognitive therapy assumes that underlying beliefs affect the way individuals respond to external stimuli. It contrasts with behavioural therapy by placing a greater emphasis on the client's internal experiences, such as thoughts, feelings, wishes, day dreams and attitudes. The goals of cognitive therapy for the client are to be able to (a) identify and monitor negative thoughts, (b) recognize the connections between cognitions and behaviour, (c) examine the evidence for and against distorted thoughts, (d) substitute more reality – oriented interpretations for biased cognitions, (e) learn to identify and alter the dysfunctional beliefs that predispose one to distort experiences. During cognitive therapy, the individuals may be asked to monitor their activities, schedule activities, conduct behavioural rehearsals of goal behaviour and model behaviour, practise relaxation techniques and perform tasks, such as role-playing, reliving childhood experiences and using imagery.

A Cognitive Therapy Model adapted from Beck and Freeman (1990) has been presented here.

Cognitive Therapy Model

(1) Conceptualization of case (Identify history and core beliefs)

(2) Collaboration and guided discovery

(3) Therapeutic relationship (Provide role models, guidance, transference, reaction)

(4) Identify automatic thoughts and rational responses

(5) Role playing (Also other forms of skill development)

(6) Imagery

(7) Identify and test basic beliefs

(8) Build new "Schemas"

(9) Set goals

(10) Use homework (keep a diary, identify automatic thoughts, label errors)

3. Moral Development Approaches

Lawrence Kohlberg added moral development to the contributions of Jean Piaget. The basic assumption of their work was that moral development and cognitive development were positively correlated. According to Kohlberg, all people go through the following stages of moral development :-

Stage-1 : Obedience to authority and avoidance of punishment are the elements of moral reasoning. There is little independent thought regarding right and wrong, and an egoistic view of the world prevails.

Stage-2 : There is still a strong egoistic element to morality. What is right is what feels good to self. There is, however, awareness of relativism, that is, what feels good may be different to different people. There is some commitment to exchange and reciprocity.

Stage-3 : This is the good boy – good girl orientation. Role modeling is a major mechanism for shaping values and behaviour. Actions are judged by intent as well as consequences.

Stage-4 : Morality is associated with doing one's duty and showing respect for authority. Maintaining the social order is seen as the sum result of moral rules.

Stage-5 : There is recognition of legalistic agreement in the social order which may be an arbitrary creation at any particular point in time. Majority rules is a rule of morality.

Stage-6 : This is the conscience or principles-based orientation. Social universality and consistency are the themes that are used to determine moral decisions.

Offenders, compared to non-offenders with similar background, tend to cluster in Stage 1 and 2, whereas most adult non-offenders tend to cluster in Stage 3 and 4. Few people reach stages 5 and 6. The possibility that women and men approach moral reasoning differently might be used in treatment approaches. Stage sequence may be less important than helping the individual practise moral reasoning skills. For women, it may be more effective to help them learn to emphasize with others rather than emphasize the efficacy of universal rules of behaviour. Women already may have an "edge" on an ability to empathize with a victim and perhaps be more likely to develop altruistic values that will prevent further lawbreaking. Further, spiritual and religious activities should be conducted in the prison to raise their moral values.

4. Group Therapy

Group therapy is an approach that can be used with treatment modalities. Groups have special powers that individual-client relationships do not have. Group process has many advantages :

(1) The group is able to present more information than a single counsellor. Several individuals give advice, guidance and suggest solutions, rather than just one.

(2) Group members instil hope by exposing members to others who are further along in treatment.

(3) Members see that others share their problems and they realize they are not alone in their troubles.

(4) Members help and support one another, can concentrate on someone else for a change and stop being self – absorbed.

(5) The group provides a partial family system in which the members can transfer their feeling regarding family members to group members and resolve long-standing interpersonal problems with the counsellor's guidance.

(6) The group experience provides a laboratory for practising social skills.

(7) Social learning is also facilitated by role modeling. Members may use each other as role models and imitate pro-social behaviour.

(8) Each member grows and learns from the group process through feedback and other communication dynamics.

(9) The group is a setting for emotional catharsis.

Members develop social cohesion and a feeling of belongingness in the group.

These are specific advantages of the group process for prisoner populations.

Masters (1994) identified the following :

It is more economical than individual treatment; it can provide immediate peer pressure, feedback and information; challenges from peers are harder for offenders to deny or rationalize; it helps to relieve everyday tension from the prison environment and provides a better way to deal with conflicts; it can help to address the prisoner's subculture; it can help communication between staff and offenders; it is helpful to use for problem-solving; it provides reinforcement for positive values; lay group leaders do not need extensive training; many different treatment modalities can be adapted to the group process.

Two major factors contribute to the use of group counselling for offender populations. The first is economic, in which counsellors can interact with several inmates during the same time period rather than conduct many individual sessions. The second factor that contributes to the popularity of the group approach is that offenders are notoriously manipulative and resistant to change. Many different techniques are used in the group approach, depending on the particular treatment modality in use. Women tend to be more disclosing and cooperative in the group process. Although female inmates are just as prone to game playing as male inmates, they develop closer relationships more quickly than do the males. Women usually tend to develop groups that are focused on relationships, feelings and emotional support.

5. Life Skills

"Life Skills" as the term is used in prison, includes classes in balancing a checkbook, self-esteem parenting and many other practical skills or personal development components. A skill is useless unless there is some degree of self-confidence to go along with it. Learning healthy leisure activities can replace less healthy ones, such as drug use and drinking. Learning to understand one's emotions and how to express them and control them is essential for health parenting, keeping a job and having healthy, loving relationships with partners and family members. Although group therapy and one-to-one counselling may help the woman understand her past, the only way she will be able to affect her own future is through action . Any successful intervention must involve activity designed to learn a skill, develop self-confidence, gain an education, and improve the skills necessary for a positive life- style. They can be taught personal issues like value systems, decision-making, recognizing emotions, how to deal with anger, communication styles of individuals, study skills, goal setting, etc. The tools used may be vocational interest surveys, value exercises, visiting experts in the areas of women's health issues, parenting, etc. Practice sessions on interviewing, role playing on how to deal with difficult people and self-studies are some of the activities practised in these life skill classes. The methods of teaching range from straight lecture or classroom to something that approaches group therapy. Many of the female prisoners never learned some of the relatively simple lessons of life. Communication, health education, nutrition, relaxation, identifying emotions, handling stress – all these issues may be dealt with in a life skills course. Besides, dealing with depression, anger management and self-esteem development are few specific classes on programme offered to prison population.

6. Counselling in Prison

Correctional clients are described as irresponsible, impulsive, and manipulative, with a tendency to shift blame. They have a history of poor interpersonal relationships, an inability to deal with authority, and seem unable to learn from experience. Females are described as more openly emotional than male prisoners, with a tendency to act out. Women in prison are frustrated and angry. They will express these emotions in whatever way they can; sometimes women in prison will "act out" to those who they trust, will not hurt them for their outburst. A woman may test such an individual with her worst behaviour, daring the person to turn his or her back and reject her, so she can justify her own lack of trust in authority figures and validate her feeling or worthlessness.

The mechanism of any change effort lies in the counselling relationship. This relationship may take many forms. The counsellor may interact with inmates in a continuing group-therapy setting or with those living in a therapeutic community. He or she may be a single counsellor in a programme using individual therapy or be engaged in a more general case worker relationship with correctional clients. Whatever the relationship, communication is the key to the identification and implementation of change efforts. The stages of change, which occur through some steps, are as the following : establishing the relationship, identifying the change, undertaking change efforts and using feedback and termination. Okum (1987) identified the following : the first stage is the relationship that includes initiation or entry, identification and clarification of problems, the structure or contract of helping, intensive exploration of problems and identification of goals. Then the second stage is the working place, which includes acceptance of the defined goals, planning strategies, the use of strategies, evaluation, termination and follow-up.

In the prison, there are special problems that exist in establishing the relationship and trying to effect strategies of change. The difficulties of the relationship include agreeing on mutual goals, counter transference, resistant clients, barriers in communication and the implementing of the second stage of change includes all the problems of working in a bureaucracy and especially, the inability to "try out" change.

Social Work Interventions

Social work, as a profession, emphasizes on interaction between individuals and system in the social situation. Social work principles based upon an understanding of the dynamics of the helping process, hold great promise for useful service in correctional settings. Social work seeks to enhance the social functioning of individuals, by activities focused upon their social relationships which constitute the interaction between man and his environment. The activities can be grouped into the three functions of social work.

(1) Restoration of impaired capacity, which can be curative and rehabilitative. Its curative aspects are to eliminate factors, which have caused breakdown of functioning and its rehabilitative aspects to organize and rebuild interactional patterns.

(2) Provision of individual and social resources can be developmental and educational.

(3) Prevention of social dysfunction involves early discovery, control and elimination of conditions and situations which potentially could hamper effective social functioning.

Social Case Work in Corrections

In correctional settings, social case work is the process of dealing with the individual case. It enables the client to express facts and feelings with a sense of security. The worker facilitates verbal and non-verbal communication, so that the client is helped to adjust better in his environment. Two types of case work treatment used in correctional settings are the supportive and curative treatment methods. The former requires the use of techniques that help the client to improve his functioning within established mechanisms of defence and the latter requires the use of techniques that help the client to improve his functioning through modification of selected mechanisms of defence.

In correction the social case worker attempts to establish a relationship, which frees the individual to express his feelings, change his antisocial values and become a law-abiding citizen. Thus relationship is the core of the social case worker's contribution along with the use of community resources. The caseworker accepts the client, understands and respects him/her. The client develops feelings towards the case worker and shares his ideas, emotions and worries. Then through a bond of warmth and support, changes are effected. The case worker assists the offender to understand his needs and helps him to develop his own social programme through the use of available resources. In correctional settings casework has been in use especially in relation to probation.

Social Group Work in Corrections

This has been discussed in detail in the chapter already as a therapy. Group work with criminals is seen as a powerful technique for modifying behaviour. Social group work is a method of rendering service to persons, which provides experience to people and helps them develop potential, improves relationships and their social functioning. The group members must allow for outlet of hostility and take up a programme for real achievement, enjoyment and aesthetic satisfaction.

Social Group work can offer a source of power for members, mutual support, an exchange of information, motivation and hope, opportunities to learn and test interpersonal and other social skills, a sense of belonging, role models, feedback on behaviour and coping attempts and a chance to help as well as be helped. Group work brings people together with common needs and problems to work together on their own behalf and represents the possibility of empowerment of these women.

Community-Based Programmes

Community work has been associated with holistic, collective and preventive approaches in meeting social needs, based on value commitments to participation and empowerment. Community work is concerned with enabling people to improve the quality of their lives and gain greater influence over the processes that affect them. Some implications for social workers have been suggested here. Social workers can develop school-based programmes that encourage affiliation and membership that would substitute for gang membership. Such programs can include sports, art and educational groups and peer interest groups. By belonging to these alternative groups, teenage girls can establish their identity, gratify social needs, and increase their sense of acceptance and recognition by their peers. School systems can create a safe environment in which students can learn. Social workers along with the teachers can identify and treat the students. while they are at school and report the serious cases to low enforcement agencies. Social workers need to focus prevention and intervention efforts on younger children.

Social workers need to direct interventions towards the family. They can develop community-based parent-training classes and outreach programmes. Helping parents acquire new skills can increase positive communication between them and their children and eliminate the need for the children to seek for an alternative. The family environment and economic factors have a vital role to play in the phenomenon of women crime. Thus it may be suggested that as an ameliorative step, there is a need to strengthen the family and marriage bonds, especially among the lower economic strata. These institutions can control the behaviour of its members by internalizing in them values like loyalty, security, protection, love and affection. Community-based organizations can take care of this great need for suitable family welfare interventions. Due to the rapid changes in our society, neglect in this area may raise the incidence of women crime. Through mass media, systematic campaigning, women's organisations can counsel and become effective instruments and strategies in combating. the problem. Various patterns of social education and continuing education programme intended for the prevention of criminal behaviour especially among village women can be implemented. Education, job opportunities, social security, guaranteed income, awareness of laws and other welfare programmes should be introduced by the government or local NGO's in both urban and rural set-up, particularly among the lower and middle class women. Lastly, there is a need to counsel women to deal with the stresses of poor family relationships and with their dependencies on others.

Advocacy and Mediation

Advocacy and mediation can also be seen as parts of the social worker's job in working with criminal women. Social workers may act as an advocate or mediate on behalf of a client or group of clients. Social workers have traditionally self – identified and set themselves apart from other professionals as being promoters of the interaction between individuals and their environment for the betterment of both. This traditional identification fits the jail or prison setting well. Social workers are advocates for the people in this society who are powerless. In the detention corrections system, advocacy for the inmate population is a key role. The inmate, on an individual level must be assisted in coming to believe that he or she has the ability to change his or her own present and future position in life. Social workers have a duty to act as advocates for the institution and its staff by assisting with policy and procedure decisions, helping the institution more in positive and progressive direction. Social worker requires to perform a balancing act while providing social work services to the inmate and the institution concurrently.

Mediating conflict between crime victims and offenders represents an emerging area of international social work practice. Victim-offender mediation and dialogue is a process which provides interested victims the opportunity to meet the offenders, in a safe and structured setting, with the goal of holding the offender directly accountable for their behavior while providing important assistance and compensation to the victim. With the assistance of a trained mediator who facilitates a dialogue between the involved parties, the victim is able to let the offender know how the crime affected him/

her and to be directly involved in developing a restitution plan so that the offender is accountable for the losses incurred. The offender is able to take direct responsibility for their behaviour, to learn of the impact of their action, and to develop a plan for making amends to the person violated.

Social workers in communities can become involved in victim-offender mediation programmes as community organizers, programme developers and mediators. Mediation is now recognized as a method of social work practice. Social workers can serve as mediators in a number of conflict situations such as marital conflict, strained interpersonal relations between husband and in-laws which lead to bride-burning, husband's adultery and immoral behaviour, which motivates women to resort to crimes of murderous violence, etc. Victim offender mediation is primarily dialogue-driven, emphasizing victim healing, offender accountability and restoration of losses.

Rehabilitation

Facilities for education and vocational training for earning wages are not provided to women in most of the prisons. They are given unproductive assignments. Thus, there is a need to introduce such work programmes for female offenders to earn extra remission, to introduce wage system, providing them facilities for education, giving them training in crafts which will enable them to become self-reliant and empowered. To understand the offender's needs and her reformation, and to reorganise staff-inmate relations, social workers can inspire a sense of responsibility, discipline, co-operation and better mutual understanding between the officials and the inmates. Social workers can help them to regain the confidence they need to face the future. They can also motivate them to lead a law-abiding and socially purposeful life after release. Thus all these programmes restore an individual to the society and will not make the individual to repeat the crime.

FIGURE : 8.1

SOCIAL WORK ACTION PLAN

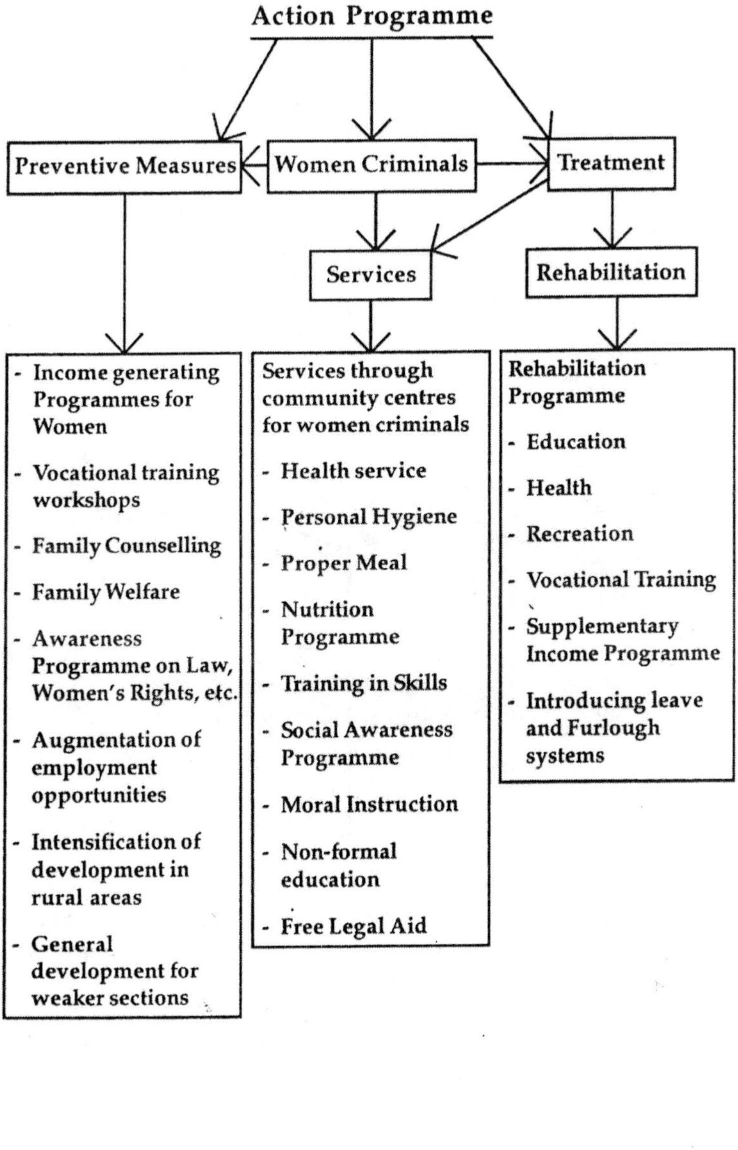

FIGURE : 8.2

INTERVENTION STRATEGIES FOR REHABILITATION

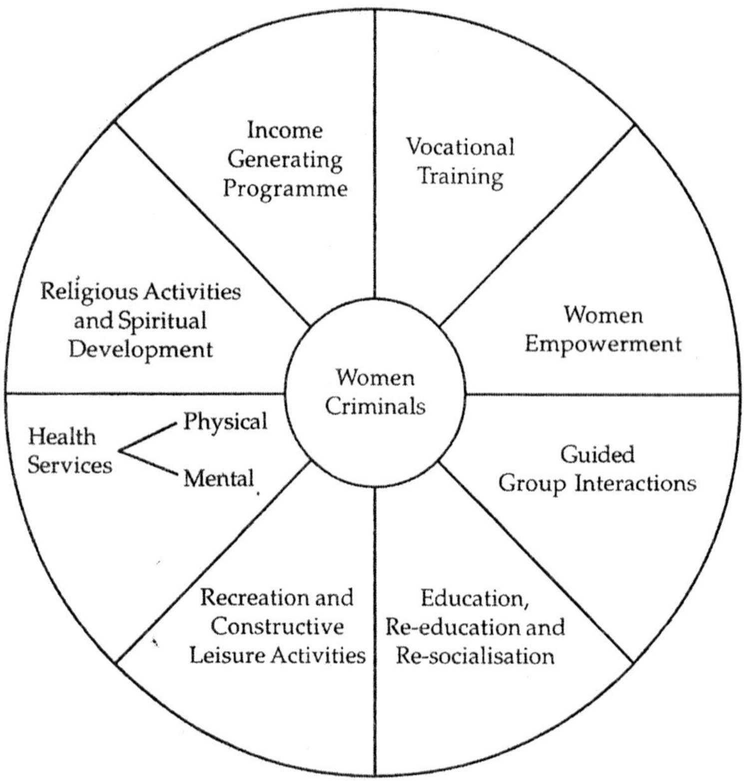

These two figures can be used as guidelines in planning curative, preventive, rehabilitative and developmental programmes for the women criminals.

BIBLIOGRAPHY

Abrahamsen, David. (1960), *The Psychology of Crime*, New York, John Wiley and Sons.

Adams, R, Dominelli, L. and Payne, M. eds. (1998), *Social Work : Themes, Issues and Critical Detates*, London, Macmillan Press Ltd.

Adler, A. (1929), *The Science of Living*, New York, Greenberg.

Adler, A. (1931), *What Life Should Mean to You*, Boston, Little Brown.

Adler, Freda. (1975), *Sisters in Crime*, New York, McGraw Hill.

Adler, Freda and R.J. Simon. (1979), *The Criminality of Deviant Women*, Boston, Houghton Mifflin Company.

Adwani, Nirmala. H. (1978), *Perspectives on Adult Crime and Correction : A Comparative Study of Adult Prisoners and Probationers*, New Delhi, Abhinav Publications.

Ahuja, Ram. (1969), *Female Offenders in India*, Meerut, Meenakshi Prakashan.

Ahuja, Ram. (1970), *Female Murderers in India : A Sociological Study*, Indian Journal of Social Work, 31(3) : 272 – 84.

Ahuja, Ram. (1996), *Sociological Criminology*, New Delhi, New Age International (P) Ltd.

Allport, G.W. (1961), *Pattern of Growth in Personality*, New York, John Willey.

American Correctional Association. (1990), *The Female Offender : What Does the Future Hold* ? Washington, D.C. St. Mary's.

Austin, Roy L. (1982), *Liberation and Female Criminality in England and Wales*, British Journal of Criminology, 21,371-374.

Balkan, Shiela and Ronald Berger. (1979), *The Changing Nature of Female Delinquency*, in Claire B. Koop and M. Kirkpatrick ed.

Becoming Female : Perspectives on Development, New York, Plenum Press.

Bandura, A. and R.H. Walters. (1959), *Adolescent Aggression*, New York, Ronald Press.

Bandura, A. (1973), *Aggression : A Social Learning Analysis*, New York, Prentice Hall.

Barnes, H.E. and N.K. Teeters. (1966), *New Horizons in Criminology*, New York, Prentice Hall, Inc.

Bartol, C.R. (1980), *Criminal Behavior : A Psycho-Social Approach*, New Jersey, Prentice Hall, Inc.

Baunach, P.J. (1977), *Women Offenders : A Commentary on Current Conceptions of Women in Crime*, Quarterly Journal of Corrections, Vol. 1, No.4, Fall.

Baunach, Phyllis. Jo. (1985), *Mothers in Prison*, New Brunswick, N. J. Transaction.

Beane, J.C. (1931), *A Study of Three Hundred Delinquent Girls*, Juvenile Research, 15.

Beck, A. and Freeman, A. (1990) *Cognitive Therapy of Personality Disorders*, New York, Guilford.

Belle, O.S. and Akran, A.M. (1970), *A Pilot Study of Anti-Social and Pro-Social Offenders*, Canadian Journal of Correction, 11, 2.

Bertrand, Marie-Andree. (1969), *Self-image and Delinquency : A Contribution to the Study of Female Criminality and Women's Image*, Acta Criminologica, Jan.

Bhanot, M.L. and Mishra, S. (1978), *Criminality Amongst Women*. Bureau of Police Research and Development, New Delhi, Government of India.

Bhatnagar, R.R. (1990), *Crimes in India : Problems and Policy*, New Delhi, Ashish Publishing House.

Bingham, T.A. (1923), *Determinants of Sex Delinquency in Adolescent Girls based on Intensive study of 500 cases*, Journal of Criminal law and Criminology.

Bishop, C. (1931), *Women and Crime*, London, From Information Received.

Blagg, H. and Wilson, C. (1912), *Women and Prisons*, London, Fabian Society.

Boehm, W.W. (1959), *Objectives of Social Curriculum of the Future, Social Work Curriculum Study*, New York, Council of Social Work Education.

Boritch, Helen. (1997), *Fallen Women : Female Crime and Criminal Justice in Canada*, Scarborough, CAN : ITP Nelson, pp. 288.

Bowker, L. (1978), *A Scream in the Night : Women as Victims*, Bowker L. ed. *Women, Crime and the Criminal Justice System*, Lexington, D.C. Heath and Co.

Bowker, Lee (1980), *Women, Crime and the Criminal Justice System*, Lexington. D. C. Heath and Company.

Bowersox, M. (1981), *Women in Corrections : Competence, Competing the Social Responsibility Norm, Criminal Justice and Behaviour*, 8, 491.

Box, S. and Hale, C. (1983), *Liberation and Female Criminality in England and Wales*, British Journal of Criminology, 23,35.

Brodsky, A..M. and M. Rosenzweig. (1974), *Research on the Female Offender*, Center for Correctional Psychology, University of Alabania.

Brodsky, Annette. (1975), *The Female Offender*, London, Sage Publication.

Brodsky, Annette M. (1981), *Planning for the Female Offender* M. Q. Warren ed., *Comparing Female and Male Offenders*, American Society of Criminology, Beverly Hills, Sage Publications.

Burkhardt, W.K. (1973), *Women in Prison*, New York, Double Day.

Burt, Cyril. (1925), *The Young Delinquent*, New York, Appleton Century Crofts. I.N.C.

Caldwell, C.Robert. (1956), *Criminology*, New York, The Ronald Press Company.

Carlen, Pat. (1983), *Women's Imprisonment : A Study in Social Control*, London, Routledge and Kegan Paul

Carlen, P. ed. (1985), *Criminal Women*, Cambridge, Polity Press.

Carlen, Pat and Anne Worrall, eds. (1987), *Gender, Crime and Justice*, Philadelphia, Open University.

Carney, Louis. P. (1974), *Introduction to Correctional Science*, New York, Mcgraw Hill Book Company.

Challinger, D. (1982), *Crime, Females and Statistics*, Australian and New Zealand Journal of Criminology 15, 123, 128.

Chang, H. Dae. (1976) *Criminology : A Cross – Cultural Perspective*, vol I, New Delhi, Vikas Publishing House Pvt. Ltd.,

Chesney – Lind, M. (1982), *Guilty by Reason of Sex : Young Women and the Juvenile Justice System*, in B. Price and N. Sokoloff, The Criminal Justice System and Women, New York, Clark Boardman.

Chesney – Lind, Meda and Noelie Rodriquez. (1983), *Women Under Lock and Key : A View from the Inside*, The Prison Journal, 63 (2) : 47 – 65.

Chesney-Lind, Meda. (1997), *The Female Offender : Girls, Women and Crime*, Thousands Oaks, CA, Sage, pp. 220.

Clemmer, Donald. (1958), *Prison Community*, New York, Holt, Rinehart and Winston.

Clinard, M.B. (1957/1974), *Sociology of Deviant Behaviour*, New York, Holt, Rinehart and Winston.

Cloward, R. A and Ohlin, L.E. (1960), *Delinquency and Opportunity: A Theory of Delinquent Gangs*, Glencoe, Free Press.

Cloward, R.A. and Ohlin, L.E. (1961), *Delinquency and Opportunity*, London, Routledge and Keyan Paul.

Cohen, Albert. K. (1955), *Delinquent Boys Culture of the Gang*, London, Free Press.

Cohen, A. K. (1970), *Deviance and Control*, New Dehli, Prentice Hall of India Pvt. Ltd.

Copper, H. (1979), *Women as Terrorist*, in F. Adler and R. Simon. eds., *The Criminology of Deviant Women*, Boston, Houghton Mifflin Co.

Cowie, J. V. and Elliot, Slater et. al. (1968), *Delinquency in Girls*, London, Heinemann Publishers.

Crime in India, (1993, 1995,1997), Government of India, New Delhi, National Crime Record Bureau

Crime Prevention and Criminal Justice. (1984), Newsletter, United Nations.

Crites, Laura ed., (1976), *The Female Offender*, Lexington, D. C. Heath and Company.

Dalton, K. (1969), *The Menstruation Cycle*, England, Peguin Books.

Dalton, K. (1961), *Menstruation and Crime*, British Medical Journal, II.

Dalton, K. (1979), *The Premenstrual Syndrome*, Proc. Roy. Mod. 48, 5, 337.

Datesman, S.K. and Scarpitti, F.R. (1975), *Female Delinquency and Broken Homes : A Reassessment*, Criminology, 13, May.

Datir, R.N. (1978), *Prison as a Social System*, Bombay, Popular Prakashan.

Davis, K. (1961), *Prostitution : Contemporary Social Problems*, ed. by R.K. Merton and R. A. Nisbet, New York : Harcourt Brace and Jovanovich. Originally Published as "The Sociology of Prostitution", American Sociological Review, 2(5), October, 1937.

Desai, Morarji. (1977), Los Angeles, March, 28.

Devasia, V.V. and Devasia, L. (1982), *Prison as a Treatment Institution*, Nagpur Times, Nov. 9th.

Devasia V.V. & Devasia L. (1984), *Socio-cultural Background on Homicide and Prison Life : A Study of Life Term Prisoners*, Ind. Jr. of Criminology and Criminalisms, Vol. 4, Jan-Apr, No. 1 and 2, PP. 5-8.

Devasia, V.V. and Devasia L. (1989), *Prison as a Social System and Prisonization in Relation to Prison Administration*, Indian Journal of Public Administration, Vol. 34, No. 1, 144 -151.

Devasia, V.V. and Devasia, L. (1992), *Criminology , Victimology and Corrections*, New Delhi, Ashish Publishing House.

Devi, P. and Rao, V.A. (1972), *The Premenstrual Phase and Suicide Attempts*, Indian Journal of Psychiatry, 14, 359 – 79.

Dobash, R. and S. Gutteridge. (1986), *The Imprisonment of Women*, Oxford, Basil Blackwell.

Dollard, J. et. al. (1939), *Frustration and Aggression*, New Haven, Yale University Press.

Durkheim, Emile. (1951), *Suicide*, Trans. J.A. Spaulding and G. Sympsons, New York, Free Press.

Editorial. (1975), *'Female Criminality'*, Social Defence, Vol. 11, No. 42, October.

Edwards, S. (1984), *Women on Trial*, Manchester, Manchester University Press.

Elliott, Mabel. A. (1952), *Crime in Modern Society*, New York , Harper and Bros.

Elliott, M.A. and Merrill, E. Francis. (1961) *Social Disorganization*, New York, Harper and Row Publishers.

Elliot and Voss. (1974), in Daniel Glaser *'Crime in Our Changing Society*, New York, Holt, Rinehart and Winston.

Eswari, T. Shariff, I.A. and Sekar, K.K. (1982), *Hysterical Personality Traits Among Female Offenders*, Indian Journal of Criminology, Vol. 10, No. 2 July, pp. 124 –128.

Eysenck, S.B.G. and Eysenck.(1973), *The Personality of Female Prisoners*, British Journal of Psychiatry, 122, 693-698

Ferguson, Thomas. (1952), *The Young Delinquent in his Social Setting*, London, Oxford University Press

Fernald, M.R., M.H.S. Hayes and A. Dawley. (1920), *A Study of Women Delinquents in New York State*, New York, Century.

Fox, G. L. (1977), *Female Delinquency*, in O. Wilson ed., Delinquency in Australia: A Critical Appraisal, Queensland, University Press.

Fox, Vernon. (1972), *Introduction to Corrections*, New Jersey, Prentice Hall, I.N.C.

Freud, Sigmond. (1931), *Female Sexuality*, London, Hogarth.

Freud, S. (1933), *The Psychology of Women : New Introductory Lectures on Psychoanalysis*, New York, W.W. Norton & Co.

Gelsthorpe, L. and Allison Morris, eds. (1990), *Feminist Perspectives in Criminology*, England, Open University.

Ghosh, S. (1986), *Female Criminals in India*, New Delhi, Uppal Publishing House.

Giallombardo, Rose. (1966), *Social Roles in a Prison for Women*, Social Problems, Vol. 13.

Gibbens, T.C.N. (1971), *Female Offender*, British Journal of Hospital Medicine, Vo. 6, Sept.

Gibbons, Don. C. (1970), *Delinquent Behavior*, New York, Prentice Hall.

Gibbsons, Don. (1978), *Society, Crime and Criminal Careers*, 3rd ed., Englewood Cliffs : New Jersey, Prentice-Hall.

Gibson, Helen. E. (1976), *Women's Prisons : Laboratories for Penal Reform*, in Laura Crites, The Female Offender, Lexington, D. C. Heath and Co.

Glueck, E. and S. Glueck. (1934), *Five Hundred Delinquent Women*, New York, Alfred A. Knopf.

Glueck, Sheldon and Eleanor T. Glueck. (1965), *Five Hundred Delinquent Women*, New York, Kraus Reprint Corporation.

Goode, W.J. and Hatt, P. R (1952), *Methods in Social Research*, New York, Mcgraw Hill.

Goodman, N. and Price, J. (1967), *Studies of Female Offenders*, Home Office Research Unit, Report No. 11, HMSO.

Government of India. (1986), *Report of National Expert Committee on Women Prisoners*, Vol. 1 and 2, New Delhi, Ministry of Human Resource Development.

Government of India. (1986-87), *Report of National Expert Committee on Women Prisoners*, New Delhi, Human Resource Development, Department of Women and Child Development.

Greenwood, V. (1981), *The Myth of Female Crime*, Morris. A. and Gelsthorpe, L. eds., Women and Crime, Cambridge, Institute of Criminology.

Grosser, G. H. (1951), *Juvenile Delinquency and Contemporary American Sex Roles*, Harvard, Unpublished Ph. D. thesis.

Harland, A.T. (1996), *Choosing Correctional Options that Work*, London, Sage Publications.

Haskell, M. R. and L. Yablonsky. (1974), *Crime and Delinquency*, Chicago, Rand McNally College Pub. Company. 254-262.

Heidensohn, F. (1968), *The Deviance of Women : A Critique and an Enquiry*, British Journal of Sociology, 19, 2, 160-175.

Heidensohn, F. (1985), *Women and Crime*, Basingstoke, Macmillan.

Hillgard, (1962), *Introduction to Psychology*, New York, Harcourt and World.

Hill, Reuben. (1949), *Families under Stress*, New York, Harper Bros.

Hindalang, M.J. (1973), *Causes of Delinquency: A Partial Replication and Extension*, Social Problems, 20, 4, PP.471.

Hirsch, Miriam, F. (1981), *Women and Violence*, New York, Van Nostrand Reinhold Company.

Hirsch, Travis. (1969), *Causes of Delinquency*, Berkeley, University of California Press.

Hoffman Bustamante, Dale. (1973), *The Nature of Female Criminality, Issues in Criminology*, 8, (Fall), 117-136.

Johnson, L.C. (1998), *Social Work Practice*, Boston, Allyn and Bacon.

Kawale, K.G. (1982), *Nature of Crimes Committed by Women in Nanded, Readings in Criminology*, News Bulletin, ISC, Calcutta.

Kellor, Frances. (1900), *Psychological and Environmental Study of Women Criminals*, American Journal of Sociology, Vol.5.

Klein, Dorie. (1973), *The Etiology of Female Crime : A review of literature*, Issues in Criminology, Vol. 8, Fall.

Klein, D. and J. Kress. (1976), *Any Woman's Blues : A Critical Overview of Women Crime and the Criminal Justice System*, Crime and Social Justice, 5, 34.

Konopka, Geisla. (1966), *The Adolescent Girl in Conflict*, New Jersey, Princeton Englewood Cliffs.

Krohn, M., J. Curry and S. Nelson-Kilger. (1983), *Is Chivalry Dead ?* Criminology, 21, 3, 417.

Lekkerkerker, E. C. (1931), *Reformatories for Women in the United States*, Holland, J. B. Wolters.

Leonard, Eileen. (1982), *Women, Crime and Society : A Critique of Theoretical Criminology*, New York, Longman.

Lombroso, Caesar and Ferrero William (1920, 1899), *The Female Offender*, New York, Appleton, 288, 85.

Lombroso, Caesar and Ferrero William (1958), *The Female Offender*, New York, Philosophical Library.

Lumpkin, K.Du.P. (1931), *Factors in the Commitment of Correctional School Girls in Wisconsin*, American Journal of Sociology , 37.

Mann, C. (1984), *Female Crime and Delinquency*, Birmingham, University of Alabama Press.

Mannheim, H. (1965), *Comparative Criminology*, London, Routledge and Kegan Paul, 47.

Masters, R. (1994), *Counselling Criminal Justice Offenders*, Thousands Oaks, CA : Sage.

Matthews, J. (1981), *Women in the Penal System*, London, NACRO Briefing.

Mathew, A. (1992), *Fair Sex in Unfair Society: Women and Crime*, New Delhi, Ashish Publishing House.

Mawby, R. (1980), *Sex and Crime : The Results of a Self-Report Study*, British Journal of Sociology, 31, 525.

McClellan, D. S. (1994), *Disparity in the Discipline of Male and Female Inmates in Texas Prisons*, Women and Criminal Justice, 5 (2), 71 – 97.

Merton, R . K. (1938), *Social Structure and Anomie*, American Sociological Review, 3, Oct.

Merton, R.K. (1949), *Social Theory and Social Structure*, New York, Free Press.

Merton, R. K. (1957), *Social Theory and Social Structure*, New York, The Free Press.

Messerschmidt, J.W. (1986), *Capitalism, Patriarchy and Crime : Towards a Socialist Feminist Criminology*, Totowa, N..J. Rowman and Littlefield.

Misra, L.S. and Gautam, B.D.S. (1982), *Female Criminality–Causes and Consequences*, Readings in Criminology, Souvenir, Vol.1 Calcutta.

Mohammad, Noor. (1984), *Battered Wives : A Study of Sócially and Economically Backward People of Slum Areas*, Indian Journal of Criminology, Vol. 12, No. 2, July, 102-107.

Mohan, Vidhu and Arvinder Singh. (1980), *Sex Differences in the Adjustment of Murderers*, Indian Journal of Criminology, Vol. 10, No. 1, Jan, 53-55.

Mohanty, A. and Hazary, N.(1990), *Indian Prison System*, New Delhi, Ashish Publishing House.

Moos, R.H. (1974), *Family Environment Scale and Correctional Institution Scale*, California, Press Inc.

Morris, Allison. (1987), *Women, Crime and Criminal Justice*, New York, Basil Blackwell.

Morris, A, and L. Gelsthorpe. (1981), *False Clues and Female Crime*, in A. Morris and L. Gelsthorpe eds., Women and Crime, Cambridge, Institute of Criminology.

Morris, R. (1964), *Female Delinquency and Relational Problems*, Social Forces, Vol. 43, October, pp. 82-89.

Moss, H..A. (1972), *Age, Sex and State as Determinants of Mother-Infant Interaction*, Judith H. Barduick ed., *Readings on the Psychology of Women*, New York, Harper and Row.

Mukherjee, R.K. and J.A. Scutt eds., (1981), *Women and Crime*, Australia, George Allen and Unwin.

Naffine Ngaire (1987), *Female Crime : The Construction of Women in Criminology*, London, Allen & Unwin.

Nagla, B.K. (1982), *The Criminality of Women in India*, Indian Journal of Social Work, Vol. 63, No. 3, Oct.

Nagla, B.K. (1991), *Women, Crime and Law*, Jaipur, Rawat Publications.

Newman, B.M. and Newman, P.R. (1980), *Personality Development through the Life Span*, California, Book/Cole, Monterey.

Nirmal, H.L. (1977), *A Study of Personality and Adjustment of Juvenile Delinquents*, Chandigarh, Unpublished M.Ed. Thesis, Punjab University .

Norland, S. and N. Shover. (1977), *Gender Roles and Female Criminality : Some Critical Comments*, Criminology, 15, pp. 87-104.

Nye, F. Ivan. (1958), *Family Relationships and Delinquent Behaviour*, New York, John Wiley.

Okum, B. (1987/1997), *Effective Helping : Interviewing and Counselling Techniques*, Pacific Grove, C.A. : Brooks/Cole.

Omodei, R. (1981), *The Myth Interpretation of Female Crime*, Mukherjee S.K. ed., *Women and Crime*, Australia, George Allen and Unwin.

Pantazis, Christina and Gordon, David. (1997), *Television Licence Evasion and the Criminalization of Female Poverty*, Howard Journal, 36, (2), pp. 170-186.

Paramguru, Pon. (1984), *Women and Crime*, Indian Journal of Criminology, Vol. 12, No. 2, July.

Parsons, Talcott. (1949), *Essays in Sociological Theory*, Glencoe, The Free Press.

Parsons, Talcott. (1954), *Family Structure and the Socialization of the Child*, in T. Parsons and R.F. Bales eds., *Family, Socialization and Interaction Process*, Glencoe. The Free Press.

Payak, Bertha. (1963), *Understanding the Female Offender*, Federal Probation 27, pp. 13-21.

Peckham, A. (1985), *A Woman in Custody*, Glasgow, Fontana.

Pollak, Otto. (1950), *The Criminality of Women*, Philadelphia, The University of Pennsylvania Press.

Pollak, Otto. (1951), *The Criminality of Women*, Philadelphia, The University of Pennsylvania Press, 80.

Pollak, Otto. (1959), *The Criminality of Women*, New York, A.S. Barnes.

Pollak, O. (1961), *The Criminality of Women*, New York, A.S. Barnes.

Pollock-Byrne, J.M. (1990), *Women, Prison and Crime*, California, Broks/Cole Publishing Company.

Pollack, J.M. (1998), *Counselling Women in Prison*, London, Sage Publications.

Pollak, Otto. (1961), *The Criminality of Women*, New York, A. S. Barnes Company.

Prasad, S.K.K. (1982), *A Study of Women Murderers in Tamil Nadu*, Readings in Criminology, Souvenir Volume, Indian Society of Criminology.

Price, Ray. R. (1977), *The Forgotten Female Offender, Crime and Delinquency*, 23 (2); pp. 101-108.

Prison Statistics, (1996), National Crime Records Bureau, Govt. of India, New Delhi.

Punekar, S.D. and Rao, K. (1967), *A Study of Prostitution in Bombay*, Bombay, Lalvani Publishing House.

Quinney, Richard. (1977), *The Social Reality of Crime*, Boston, Little Brown.

Ramadevi, B.N. (1982), *A Study of Women Murders in Tamil Nadu*, Readings in Criminology, Souvenir Volume, Calcutta.

Rani, Bilmoria. M. (1980), *Female Criminality in Andhra Pradesh*, unpublished, Ph.D Thesis.

Rani Bilmoria, M. (1981), *The Pattern and Nature of Female Criminality in Andhra Pradesh*, Indian Journal of Social Work, Vol. 61, No. 4, pp. 393-401.

Rani Bilmoria, M. (1983), *Homicides by Females*, Indian Journal of Criminology, Vol. 2, No. 1, pp. 8-17.

Rao, S. Venugopal. (1981), *Female Criminality*, Paper presented at the Tenth Annual Conference of the Indian Society of Criminology, Aurangabad.

Rao, S. Venugopal. (1982), *Female Criminality*, Readings in Criminology, Souvenir volume, Calcutta.

Rao, S. Venugopal. (1967), *Dynamics of Crime in India*, Bombay, Allied Publishers Pvt. Ltd.

Rasche, Christine. E. (1974), *The Female Offender as an Object of Criminological Research*, Criminal Justice and Behaviour.

Reckless, Walter C. (1957), *Female Criminality*, National Probation and Parole Association Journal, 3rd January, pp. 1-5.

Reckless, W. (1961), *The Crime Problem*, New York, Appleton Century Croffs.

Reckless, W. and B. Kay. (1967), *The Female Offender* (Consultants' paper), President's Commission on Law Enforcement, Washington DC, Mimeo.

Reckless, Walter C. (1971), *The Crime Problem*, Bombay, Vakils, Feffer and Simons Pvt. Ltd.

Reckless, Walter. C. (1973), *The Crime Problem*, Appleton, Century Croffs.

Report of National Expert Committee on Women (1990), Prisoners, Vol. 1 & 2, Government of India, New Delhi.

Sagarin, Edward and et al. (1973), *Corrections : Problems of Punishment and Rehabilitation*, New York, Praeger Publishers.

Sandhu, Harjit. S. (1983), *Female Criminality*, International Handbook of Contemporary Developments in Criminology eds., London, Greenwood Press.

Sanyal, S. (1974), *An Empirical Study of Certain Personality Characteristics and Attitudes of 25 Female Convicts of Nari Bandi Niketan*, Lucknow, Journal of Correctional Works, No. 20, 70-82.

Sanyal, S. and Agarwal, V. (1982), *Self Esteem of Female Convicts*, Readings in Criminology Souvenir Volume, Calcutta.

Saxena, Rekha and S. Sanyal. (1989), *Rehabilitational Problems of Women Prisoners*, Indian Police Journal, Vol. 36, No. 1, Jan.-March., PP. 33-39.

Saxena, R. (1994), *Women and Crime in India : A Study in Socio-cultural Dynamics*, New Delhi, Inter-India Publications.

Schur, Edwin. M. (1984), *Labelling Women Deviant : Gender, Stigma and Social Control*, New York, Random House.

Scutt, Jocelynne A. (1974), *A Factor in Female Crime*, The Criminologist, Vol. 9, No. 34, pp. 56-71.

Senese, J. & Kalinich, D. B. (1992), *Activities and Rehabilitation Programs for Offenders*, in Stojkovic and R. Lovell eds., *Correction : An Introduction*, pp. 213 – 244, Cincinatti, OH : Anderson.

Sharma, B.A.V. et al. (1983), *Research Methods in Social Sciences*, New Delhi, Sterling Publishers Pvt. Ltd.

Sharma, Madhu. (1987), *Crime and Women : A Psychological Perspective*, Indian Journal of Criminology, 15 (2) July, 126-30.

Sharma, R.K. (1965), *Women Offenders of U.P. : A Psychological Social Study of Women Convicts and Undertrial Prisoners in U.P. Jails*, Lucknow, Unpublished Ph.D, Thesis.

Sharma, Shridhar. (1985), *Mass Murder by Women*, Indian Journal of Criminology, Vol. 13. No. 1, January, 11-15.

Shastri, Tara. (1981/1975), *Women Prisoners in Maharashtra State: A Socio-economic Survey*, Social Defence, 17, 66, October.

Shover, N. et. al. (1980), *Gender Roles and Delinquency*, Social Forces, 58, 1, pp. 162-175.

Shukla, K.S. and Rekha Saxena. (1984), *Women and Crime : An Emerging Issue for Social Enquiry in India*, Indian Journal of Criminology and Criminalistics, Vol. 14, No. 3-4, Sept-Dec.

Shukla, K.S. and Rekha Sexena. (1987), *Women and Crime : A Perspective* ed., The Other Side of Development : Socio-Psychological Implications, New Delhi, Sage Publications India Ltd.

Sikka, K.D. (1980), *Professional Social Work in Correctional Institutions*, Indian Journal of Criminology, 8,1, January, pp. 55 – 61.

Simon, Rita James. (1975), *Women and Crime*, Lexington, D.C. Heath and company.

Simpson, Sally. (1989), *Feminist Theory, Crime and Justice*, 27 (4), 605 – 631.

Singh, Hira. (1973), *Welfare in Prisons*, Paper presented at the All India Seminar on Probation and other Allied Measures, Deptt. of Social Welfare, Govt. of Rajasthan, Jaipur, Dec. 29-31, 3.

Singh, Inder. J. (1978), *Indian Prison : A Sociological Enquiry*, Delhi. Concept.

Singh, M. (1980), *A Study of Personality of Murderers and the Psycho–Social Factors related to Murder*, Indian Journal of Criminology, 8, 1, 15 – 20.

Singh, M. K. (1981), *Women and Crime Phenomenon*, Indian Journal of Social Work, Vol. 62, No. 3, October, pp. 281-292.

Singh, S. and Singh, A. (1979), *The Relationship between Premenstrual Tension and Murder*, Indian Journal of Criminology.

Singh, S. (1982), *The Relationship between Menstruation and Crime*, Indian Journal of Criminology, Vol. 10, No.2, pp. 129-131.

Singh, et. al. (1998), *Values Among Females Convicted for Different Types of Crimes : A Comparative Analysis*, Journal of Community Guidance and Research, Vol. 15, No. 3.

Sivanandam, C. (1974), *A Comparative Study of the Intelligence of the Normal Delinquent and Criminal Female Subjects*, Indian Journal of Criminology.

Smart, C. (1976), *Women Crime and Criminology*, London. Routledge and Kegan Paul.

Smith, Ann. D. (1962), *Women in Prison : A Study in Penal Methods*, London, Stevens and Sons.

Smith, David. (1995), *Criminology for Social Work*, London, Macmillan.

Sohoni, N.K. (1974), *Women Prisoners*, Indian Journal of Social Work, Vol. 35, No. 2, July, pp. 137-148.

Sohoni, N.K. (1975), *Women Prisoners in India*, International Social Work, 18.

Sohoni, N.K. (1989), *Women Behind Bars*, New Delhi, Vikas Publishing House.

Sparrow, Gerald. (1970), *Women Who Murder*, London, Arthur Barder Limited.

Spaulding, E.R. (1923), *An Experimental Study of Psychopathic Delinquent Women*, New York, Rand McNally.

Srivastava, S.P. (1984), *Women Crime and Criminal Justice System in India*, Indian Journal of Criminology and Criminalistics, Vol. 4, No. 3 and 4, Sept-Dec, 92-105.

Srivastava, S.P. (1989), *Juvenile Justice in India : Policy Programme and Perspective*, New Delhi, Ajanta Publications.

Steffensmeier, D. (1978), *Crime and the Contemporary Woman : An Analysis of Changing Levels of Female Property Crime*, 1960-75, Social Forces, 57, 2, 566.

Steffensmeier, D. (1980), *Assessing the Impact of the Women's Movement on Sex-based Differences in the Handling of Adult Defendants, Crime and Delinquency*, 26, 3, 344.

Steffensmeier, D. (1980), *Sex Differences in Pattern of Adult Crime : A Review and Assessment*, Social Forces, Vol. 58, No. 4, pp. 1080-1108.

Steffensmeier, D. and R. Steffensmeier and A. Rosenthal. (1979), *Trends in Female Violence*, 1960-77, Sociological Focus, 12,3, 217.

Stewart, J. Smith and Stewart, G. (1994), *Understanding Offending Behaviour*, Harlow, Longman.

Studt, E. (1959), *Education for Social Workers in Correctional Field*, New York, Council for Social Work Education.

Sutherland, E.H. (1960), *Principles of Criminology*, Philadelphia, J.B. Lippincott.

Thomas, W.I. (1907/1923/1967), *The Unadjusted Girl*, New York, Harper and Row.

Trivedi, V.B. and K.P. Krishna. (1983), *Murderer and Her Victim*, Indian Journal of Criminology, Vol. 2, No. 2, July, 115-118.

Umbreit, Mark.S. (1992), *Victim – Offender Mediation in Canada – The Impact of an Emerging Social Work Intervention*, International Social Work, Vol 42, No. 2.

Varma, Paripurnanand. (1972), *Pathology of Crime and Delinquency*, Sahitya Bhawan.

Vedder, Clyde B. and Dora, B. Somerville. (1970), *The Delinquent Girl*, Illinois, Charles, C. Thomas, Springfield.

Visher, C. (1983), *Gender, Police Arrest Decisions and Notions of Chivalry*, Criminology, 21,5.

Warren, Marquerite Q. (1975), *Gender Comparisons in Crime and Delinquency*, A.M. Brodsky, ed., The Female Offender, Boverly Hills, Ca : Sage,.

Waterberg, W. and Saunders, F. (1954), *Sex Differences among Juvenile Offenders*, Sociology and Social Research, XXXIX, Sept. - Oct.

Weidensall, J. (1916), *The Mentality of the Criminal Women*, Baltimore, Warwick and York.

Weinberg, K.S. (1973), *Female Delinquency in Ghana, West Africa* : A Comparative Analysis, International Review of Modern Sociology, 3.

West, D. J. (1965), *Murder followed by Suicide*, London, Heinemann.

Wheeler, Santon. (1961), *Socialization in Correctional Communities*, American Sociological Review, 26.

Wilkinson, Karen. (1974), *The Broken Family and Juvenile Delinquency : Scientific Exploration of Ideology*, Social Problems, 21, 35-55

Windschuttle, E. (1981) in *Women and Crime*, S.K Mukherjee and Jocelynne, A. Scutt, London, George Allen & Unwin.

Wolfgang, Marvin. E. (1958), *Patterns in Criminal Homicide*, Philadelphia, University of Pennsylvania.

Wolfgang, N. F. and Femante, F. (1967), *The Sub-Culture Violence*, London, Chaucer Press.

Worth, J. (1981), *Characteristics of Female Lifers*, Prison Medical Journal, No. 22,16.

Yelaja, S.A. (1979), *Some Recent Studies in Social Work Practice: Implications for Social Work Education*, Indian Journal of Social Work, 60, 2, July, pp. 153-164.

Young, P.V. (1977), *Scientific Social Surveys and Research*, New Delhi, Prentice – Hall of India Pvt. Ltd.

Young, V. (1980), *Women, Race and Crime*, Criminology, 18, 26.

Younghusband, E. (1978), *Social Work in Britain: A Follow up Study*, Vol. 1 and 2, London, George Allen and Unwin.

Zingroff, M.T. (1975), *Prisonization as an Inhibitor of Effective Resocialization*, Criminology, 13/3, 366-388.

INDEX

❑❑❑